MAKING THE CASE

PAUL W. KAHN

Making the Case

The Art of the Judicial Opinion

Yale UNIVERSITY PRESS
NEW HAVEN AND LONDON

Published with assistance from the foundation established in memory of Calvin Chapin of the Class of 1788, Yale College.

Copyright © 2016 by Paul W. Kahn.
All rights reserved.
This book may not be reproduced, in whole or in part, including illustrations, in any form (beyond that copying permitted by Sections 107 and 108 of the U.S. Copyright Law and except by reviewers for the public press), without written permission from the publishers.

Yale University Press books may be purchased in quantity for educational, business, or promotional use. For information, please e-mail sales.press@yale.edu (U.S. office) or sales@yaleup.co.uk (U.K. office).

Set in Janson type by Westchester Publishing Services, Danbury, Connecticut.
Printed in the United States of America.

Library of Congress Control Number: 2015948637
ISBN 978-0-300-21208-2 (cloth : alk. paper)

A catalogue record for this book is available from the British Library.

This paper meets the requirements of ANSI/NISO Z39.48–1992 (Permanence of Paper).

10 9 8 7 6 5 4 3 2 1

To my students

CONTENTS

A Preface for Students, with a Note to Everyone Else   ix

Acknowledgments   xvii

one   Why Read the Opinions?   1

two   The Opinion and Narrative   18

three   Unity: The Judicial Voice   46

four   Legal Doctrine: Between Erudition and Fundamentalism   88

five   Facts: Stating the Case   135

Conclusion: Making the Case for a Humanist Study of the Law   173

Notes   181

Index   231

A PREFACE FOR STUDENTS, WITH A NOTE TO EVERYONE ELSE

Most law students venture outside of their assigned casebooks only to find something that will make their lives easier: a study guide, an outline, a nutshell. In this book, I will ask you to take exactly the opposite course. The casebooks that are used in most courses today hide much of the life of the law. They focus on brief excerpts from appellate opinions, as if you will find in such highly edited passages the legal significance of the cases. The excerpts are reduced to propositions of law that students outline and try to remember. Students are often left puzzling about this form of presentation. Why bother with presenting even a part of the opinion, if the substantive point can be reduced to a proposition? Why hide the ball behind the bits and pieces of judicial opinions? If the task is to discern the kernel of law within the chaff of the opinion, the endless proliferation of outlines, case notes, study guides, and hornbooks is hardly surprising.

The original promise of the casebook method was to immerse students in the richness of the law in action, the law as it actually works in the details of human interactions. That promise has long gone unfulfilled as the casebook has grown in size (and cost), while shifting its focus to doctrinal comprehensiveness. Instead of heading for an outline, I will urge you to head to the opinions themselves. The casebook will teach you a lot of law, but it will not teach you how to read an opinion. The casebook edits opinions down to manageable excerpts, arranged to make a series of discrete points filling in an outline of a substantive area of law. The law, however, does not come this way in ordinary life. In the actual practice of law, no one tells you which parts of the opinion are the important ones. No one even tells you which are the important opinions. You won't find the answers in a casebook or a course outline. Nor are you likely to find it through a word search on Lexis or Westlaw.

PREFACE

No one can do this work for you because legal problems do not appear with labels already attached. Someone walks into your office with a complaint about an employer, a neighbor, or a government official. Your job will be to translate that complaint into a legal problem. Until you know what kind of a problem it is, you will not be able to figure out what sort of legal solutions may be available. You accomplish this translation by reconstructing the facts in light of the available law. This means emphasizing certain facts and relationships while de-emphasizing others. Law and facts have to inform each other not just at the point of judgment, but before you can take even your first step toward a resolution of the problem. Your client may be more worried about the offense to his dignity than the violation of his property, but offenses to dignity may not be legally cognizable. He may be brokenhearted, but the law offers no cure for that injury.

Law school is not just about learning legal doctrine. More importantly, it is about learning how to move back and forth between facts and law such that each informs the other. The effect of this movement is to make both sides of the equation more complex. Because law does not work as abstract doctrine, it does not come with distinct borders. There is always more law that can be brought to bear. There are more opinions that can be read, more arguments that can be made. A lawyer needs to learn when to stop reading and start arguing. You stop when you have learned enough to make a persuasive case. Similarly, there are always multiple ways to give an account of the facts. Legal argument, for the most part, works through analogy and distinction. We figure out what to do in one case by understanding how its facts stand with respect to those of past cases (precedents) and future possible cases (hypotheticals). Competing analogies rely on different ways of presenting the facts; these differences in turn lead us to understand the law differently. There is no right or wrong way to do this. The right way is that which persuades others to see the case as you do.

You cannot learn how to deal with the superabundance of law or how to build persuasive analogies by reading only excerpts in a case-

PREFACE

book. Those excerpts have been stripped of most of the factual details; they have been artificially isolated from the multiple connections by which they are tied to other opinions. Opinions are great pedagogical resources because from them one can learn how facts and law must be woven into a single narrative. One learns from them that law is a practice of persuasion. The opinion is written to persuade a community that must see the reasons for the law and, more importantly, must accept the law as its own. Opinions can teach none of this if they are read only for the doctrinal positions they set forth.

Accordingly, one of the skills that a lawyer must develop is that of knowing how to read opinions—even long ones. The lawyer is not reading in order to find that single proposition of law for which the case stands. If that were all there were to it, judges would not bother to write opinions that were more than formal statements of the relevant law. Indeed, traditionally judges on the European continent wrote short opinions that listed propositions in a strictly formal manner. Law was applied to facts, as if it were a matter of logical deduction or syllogistic reasoning. Writers of opinions did not reason by analogy, which appeared too open-ended and contestable for continental ideas of the limits of judicial authority. Nor was there a practice of public disagreement on the bench. Dissents would have suggested the contestable character of the law. Instead, judges wrote in a manner that looked a good deal like the outlines that you probably generate for yourselves or buy in preparation for an exam.

What those judges were doing out of ideological conviction, we are doing in law school for the sake of pedagogical convenience. Of course, some of this is necessary since there is a lot of law to learn and students cannot possibly read every opinion of every case they study. At some point, however, you must turn to the opinions themselves. Learning the law is most like learning a new language: both require engagement with the actual practice.[1] You don't learn a language by outlining formal rules and memorizing words. You learn the language by putting it to use; you learn how to describe a situation or to work your way through a transaction by actually using the language. The same is true of the law: you must learn by doing.

PREFACE

This approach to legal education has largely motivated the development of clinical education. But the line between clinical and classroom education is a false line. The pedagogic techniques may be different, but there simply is no law in the abstract. All law is embedded in facts; all law is contextual. For every principle, there are exceptions; for every formal statement of law, there are available other statements that point in different directions. You read opinions not just because they are a source from which you are to derive abstract norms but because they show us what the law is—a practice of persuasion in which norms and facts work together. If you want to learn how to think creatively within the law, or if you believe that law has something to do with the practice of persuasion in a democratic community, then you must turn to the opinions. This book is meant to help you understand what it is you will find there. My aim is to analyze and explain where and how the persuasive quality of the opinion does its work.

Most of my examples are drawn from one particular category of judicial opinions: those that involve constitutional law. Some decades ago, Karl Llewellyn took up a similar pedagogical task but turned mostly to commercial law and contract cases.[2] He drew upon these examples because they were the cases he knew best. I turn to opinions dealing with constitutional law because they are the cases I know best. They are also the opinions of which Americans today are likely to think when they consider the power and role of the courts, and of the Supreme Court in particular. These opinions have come to set the pattern of expectations of a court, both for judges and for the wider community.

This is not, however, a book about constitutional law. I offer no view of the field and make no effort to be comprehensive. My concern is with the opinion as the work product of the courts and as a resource for legal argument. What I have to say about the skills necessary to read these particular opinions is no less true of other opinions that deal with the problems of interpreting legal texts, whether statutes, regulations, or judicial precedents. The canons of interpretation and the practices of deference to other decision makers may

PREFACE

not always be the same, but the problems of narrative and voice, of building a persuasive argument by negotiating between authoritative texts and precedents interpreting those texts, and of setting the context within which one sees the facts remain the same. The stakes may not be as high as in constitutional cases, but the opinion as a literary genre demands of us the same sort of reading skills wherever it appears.[3]

I like to think of a successful reading as getting the opinion to sing. There is music in the law. Its players are the judges, and its audience is the well-trained lawyer. Unless you have a trained ear, you will not hear the melody. No single book can teach you how to hear the music of the courts, but it can make a start. I try to point you in the right direction by sharing a reading of some prominent and some not so prominent opinions. If you want to make the best use of this book, I suggest that you read the entire opinion along with my discussion.

Now a word for everyone else. There is a genre of academic, legal writing in which an introductory work is no less a serious work on law. The most famous text in this tradition is Karl Llewellyn's *The Bramble Bush*, but there are also Edward Levi's *Introduction to Legal Reasoning*, Oliver Wendell Holmes's *The Path of the Law*, Benjamin Cardozo's *The Nature of the Judicial Process*, and H. L. A. Hart's *The Concept of Law*. More broadly, one might include Ronald Dworkin's *Law's Empire* and Roberto Unger's *What Should Legal Analysis Become?* Law shares this character with philosophy. One begins to study philosophy by reading Plato's dialogues. The philosopher could happily spend a career with those same texts. The law student begins with *Marbury* or *Palsgraf*. The law professor is still reading those same opinions.

One wants to explain to the student what the law is, how it comes to be, maintains itself, and changes in a complex world that is itself in constant flux. These are questions for a lifetime of study. In law school, the simplest issues are also the deepest: questions of the nature of law, judicial role, precedent, and authority. These are not just the starting points of an inquiry into law; rather, they define the field.

PREFACE

In neither philosophy nor law is there a step-by-step, incremental approach to the subject by which we move from the simple to the more complex. The pedagogical task in these disciplines is entirely different from that in the sciences, where one builds up a body of knowledge. Some contemporary academics are bringing the tools of the social sciences—particularly economics—to the study of law. Whatever the success of that endeavor in the academy, it does not go to the heart of our legal practice, which remains a text-based process of persuasion through interpretation. Economists may have lots to say about what laws and administrative regulations should be, but they have little to say to the practicing lawyer or judge.

If law is a practice of interpretation, then teaching the law shares a good deal with teaching other humanistic disciplines.[4] There is no way to teach an interpretive discipline except by treating one's students as if they are already partners in the inquiry. The Socratic method may look hierarchical from the outside, but ideally it is a reciprocity of discourse in pursuit of a common inquiry. Its model is answer and response; it requires that each side listen to the other. Listening, each is capable of persuading and being persuaded by the other. Together, professor and student are pursuing an interpretation of fact and law.

My effort has, accordingly, been to write a book that is accessible to students and simultaneously of interest to scholars. Some of what I have to say covers familiar ground; surely most of the opinions I discuss are well known. The organization and approach are likely to be unfamiliar. I approach the opinion as a form of rhetorical address performing the broadly political task of maintaining belief in self-government through law.[5] An opinion announces a judgment, but the content of that judgment is the least interesting aspect of the opinion from the perspective of this work. Here, dicta are as important as holding.

In chapters 2 and 3, I take up issues of narrative and voice. Every opinion relies on narrative; every narrative constructs a voice. Reading the opinion, whom do we hear? These are critical elements for understanding the way in which an opinion claims a kind of democratic legitimacy. In chapters 4 and 5, I turn to issues of the development of doctrine, that is, to assertions of law and fact. An opinion is always situated with respect to some body of doctrine, which it can create, maintain, or destroy. I explore the work of the opinion in each of these three dimensions. Similarly, an opinion must situate itself with respect to some set of facts. The most important facts of an opinion are not the evidentiary findings of the trial court. Rather, they are those that set the context or what I call the "horizon." Without this common horizon, analogical argument would be impossible, for in the abstract everything is both alike and different. One important consequence of the situated character of an opinion is that law can never be more than relatively autonomous with respect to other forms of knowledge and belief. This is just another way of saying that law is not a science but a practice of living together.

No doubt, law students today must learn a good deal more than how to read an opinion. Law schools must teach fluency in policy construction, administrative proceedings, and regulatory process; they must teach specific subject matters—from health care to environmental protection. Students must know how to read a statute as well as an opinion; they must know what to argue to a regulatory body as well as to a judge. To those who teach in these fields, my approach may seem overly jurocentric—a bit old-fashioned, as if we still lived in the age of the common law. They need have no fears that the approach I set forth here will take legal pedagogy backward. The casebook is not about to disappear, particularly in those fields where the very point of the course is to offer a broad survey of the law. I am proposing to teach a practice of interpretation, not an entire curriculum. I am trying to recover and hold on to a disciplinary approach that is in danger of disappearing.

The need for such an act of recovery is pressing. As I write this, the Supreme Court has handed down *McCutcheon v. Federal Election Commission*, declaring unconstitutional limits on overall campaign contributions by individuals.[6] The various opinions in the case run to about a hundred pages. While the popular press asks which interest groups won, collectively we—all of us—are very much in need of a way to evaluate these opinions apart from the competition of political parties. What are the Justices doing in these opinions? What should they be doing, and are they succeeding or failing in that task? If we are to understand our own practices of self-government under law, these are necessary questions. In this book, I try to answer them.

At stake in this book, therefore, is not just how we should teach law, but how we should understand law. Law students today are likely to think that law is either a matter of doctrine to be memorized or of politics to be disputed. I aim to open a space in between, where interpretation and persuasion have their own standards. If I am successful, this approach should feel to most lawyers less like something new than like a recovery of something familiar. It should be recognizable and persuasive to others as well, for the rule of law is something we have been doing together for a very long time.

ACKNOWLEDGMENTS

In my experience, the idea of a book rarely appears in a single moment. This book, however, did have a clear and exact moment of birth: when, after a vigorous walk during which I had been going on for some time about recent opinions of the Supreme Court, my friend Douglas Maclean said to me, "You ought to write something about cases." He planted an idea that stayed with me over the next several years. The birth of the idea of the book, however, was hardly the start of the process. I have been working on the material in this book for at least thirty years. The site of much of that work was my annual first-term class in constitutional law—a class known at Yale Law School as a "small group." I owe a huge debt to all my small group students over the years; they helped me to see what it was that I was up to. I hope that some of them recognize themselves in these pages.

A book of this sort is a project requiring the direct involvement of many people. I was lucky to have a number of excellent research assistants. I want to thank, in particular, Arthur Kau, Noah Kazis, Christina Koningisor, Jacob Miller, and Caitlin Tully. I had as well important help from Kiel Brenan-Marquez and my assistant Barbara Mianzo. My colleagues Owen Fiss and Bruce Ackerman read the whole of the manuscript and made many useful suggestions.

Finally, I want to thank my family: Catherine, Suzanne, and Hannah. For longer than they probably care to remember, they have been listening to me talk about cases.

one
WHY READ THE OPINIONS?

While there are many different kinds of legal texts—statutes, regulations, contracts, treaties—the judicial opinion occupies a special place. Only here does law link command to explanation. A statute is not trying to persuade; it commands. It need not explain itself, for the authority of a legislature to make law is not contested. An opinion, on the other hand, is an exercise in persuasion. A court that writes an opinion believes that it labors under an obligation to persuade.[1] Since it is in the nature of judicial controversy that one party loses, we can think of the opinion as addressed, at least in part, to the losing party. The opinion explains the result to a party likely to approach the text with a fair degree of skepticism.[2] It is not just the losing party that is owed an explanation; we all are, for the opinion is a public act setting forth the meaning of law for everyone.

An opinion accompanies a judgment, but the two are not the same. The judgment can be as simple as "affirm" or "reverse." We often see a judge joining in the judgment but declining to join the opinion. In that case, she agrees with the court's order but not with its reasons. The judgment is what philosophers call a "performative speech act": speaking these words, the court accomplishes a result in the world.[3] Rights and responsibilities have been established such that people may be differently situated than they were before the judgment. By contrast, nothing follows from the opinion until and unless it is interpreted by someone as an element of a deliberative process leading to a decision.

The judgment is an exercise of a court's authority, just as a statute is an exercise of legislative authority. Both determine legal rights and responsibilities and threaten sanctions for failing to respect those rights. We don't have to agree with the judgment for it to be effective. The point of the judgment is that it is effective regardless of what anyone thinks. The opinion does not work this way. It is, instead, a rhetorical act that works more or less well as it persuades or fails to persuade. The opinion is a resource for future argument that remains well after the judgment with respect to particular parties has become irrelevant. When we shift our focus from the judgment to the opinion, we move from issues of compliance to those of persuasion; we move from vote to voice.

Voice or Vote?

We can imagine a state in which courts issued judgments without explanation. The need to settle disputes requires some form of adjudicatory mechanism; it does not necessarily require explanation of the decisions.[4] When there is explanation, the form of presentation has varied over time. The American practice of issuing "an opinion for the Court" began early, but it was not there from the start. British practice had been for the multiple judges collectively hearing a case to each issue an oral opinion. This "seriatim practice" was followed by our Supreme Court in its early years.[5] A Justice would speak in his own voice, expressing his views on the right disposition of the case. And why not? Each Justice is, after all, equal to the others; each is appointed on the same terms and exercises the same authority. Some might tend to vote together, but factions can form in any political body. Thomas Jefferson famously defended the seriatim practice on the ground that every Justice has an obligation to defend his own decision; none should seek to "hide" behind the Court's opinion.[6]

This view of the individual character of the judge's authority is hardly dead. Justice Clarence Thomas, for example, insists on expressing what he personally thinks the law means, even after that view has been rejected by a majority of the Court.[7] He does not consider the Court to be an institution that authoritatively sets forth the meaning of the law to which he, like everyone else, is bound. He thinks that *his* authority flows from *his* appointment. He can, therefore, continue to insist that everyone else is wrong. Like the traditional British judge, Justice Thomas thinks that the law is fixed in place and time, independently of the courts: each judge's role is to discern its content and announce what it is that he sees.[8]

There is a certain irony here: the more objective a judge thinks the law, the more likely he is to believe that judicial authority runs to the individual. A claim of legal objectivity is likely, therefore, to lead to dissensus, not unity, among judges. That dissensus is not limited to disagreement on the Supreme Court but can extend all the way down the judicial hierarchy. After all, every judge derives her authority from her appointment, not from higher courts. This idea of individual authority is entirely familiar in the sciences: the scientist does not acquiesce to a dominant view when she believes it to be wrong. If the law is a fact to be discovered, authority must be based on truth, not on obtaining a majority on the court. On this view, the work of the opinion is not persuasion but demonstration. Justice Thomas believes he has hold of the truth. For him, those who have been persuaded otherwise cannot determine the content of the law—even when they are a majority—any more than scientists can establish the truth simply by agreeing with each other.

Whenever we think there is a legal truth of the matter, we will move toward the personalization of judicial power. Interestingly, a similar view of judicial power gains support from those who take quite the opposite position on the objective character of the law.[9] Those who deny the distinction between law and politics, who think that a judgment is based on nothing but the values of the judges, also view judges as individuals not bound by others. This view is particularly strong among popular commentators on legal affairs. They assess the judgments of the Supreme Court along the same liberal/conservative spectrum by which they measure other political actors. They count judicial votes just as they count votes in the legislature. They want to know whether the liberals or the conservatives are winning. Viewing the courts this way, they want to know how individual judges will exercise their power. There is no place in this calculus for consideration of the opinion as a collective exercise in persuasion. The opinion is meaningful only as an indicator of which faction's views are dominant at any given time.[10]

There is no denying that judicial factions exist. Nor is there any doubt that such a factional analysis is important if you want to predict how a case might come out. Nevertheless, the analogy between legislators and judges quickly becomes quite strained. Legislators do not generally issue opinions.[11] The point at which they try to persuade a citizen audience is in the political campaign that precedes legislative action. Those campaigns tend to focus on the future: a candidate ordinarily spends her time promising, not justifying, past behavior. A candidate who spends too much time on the latter is already in deep trouble. The judicial opinion has just the opposite character.

Every public authority performs in two dimensions: vote and voice. The weights of voice and vote stand in an inverse relationship when we compare legislators and judges. Legislation can, and usually does, reflect the relative weight of different interest groups: a weight measured in the ability to gather votes. There is no expectation, let alone requirement, that legislative policy be consistent across broad areas of regulation. Subsidies for corn, but not for soybeans, is not a problem, even if there is no good, economic reason for the distinction. It is not a problem even if it would be better policy to subsidize soybeans instead of corn. Moving from a policy focused on economic stimulus to one focused on deficit reduction may not make sense under a single theory of economic growth. A legislature, however, need not explain itself; it need not give voice to reasons that stand apart from the vote. Compromise can be a legislative virtue—so much so that we might appreciate a practice of horse-trading among legislators.[12]

Of course, this does not mean that there are never substantively good reasons for legislation or that there are no limits on the arbitrariness of outcomes. Policy justifications for legislation are expressed in committee reports and floor remarks—as well as in public speeches and regulatory studies. Other reasons—political reasons—are rarely expressed in those reports. Because we know both sorts of reasons are operating, we may distrust the explicit rationales. Some theories of the judicial practice of legislative interpretation are so distrustful that they would forbid the courts from considering the explanations expressed in the legislative history.[13] Expecting legislators to act for political reasons, we are likely to assess a legislator by plotting her votes on various partisan, legislative rankings.

Judges, too, decide cases by voting. It is not written anywhere that a court must issue an opinion; there are no rules requiring the opinion to take a certain form. Commercial arbitrators settle cases and rarely publicize an opinion; juries usually issue verdicts without explanation. The appellate courts' role, however, is not just to vote but to speak. Indeed, voice is far more important than vote. The outcome of the vote—the judgment—may affect only the parties; the expression of voice—the opinion—will affect countless individuals and groups, some of whom may not yet even exist. An appellate court opinion explains the law to those who are to live under it.

A court's decision is to follow from its explanation—not the other way around. The opinion must first persuade the members of the court—or at least a majority of them. When a draft opinion is not persuasive, members change their minds about how to vote.[14] When the Supreme Court decides a substantial case without issuing an opinion for the court—meaning no opinion has majority support—we know who won, but we do not know what the law is. Were the Court regularly to fall into this position, we would confront a crisis of legality, even though we would continue to know the outcomes of individual cases.[15]

The courts are always telling us to listen, not just to count. About a judgment, we are always entitled—and expected—to ask "why?" The court owes us an explanation. It cannot simply point to voter interests or constituency groups; it cannot point to the last election. It must give reasons grounded in law, not politics. This has led some to argue that the Supreme Court's role is to conduct a "national seminar" on the meaning of the Constitution.[16] Similarly, others have said that voice points to a "discursive democracy" in which reasonable argument, not naked power, is our manner of self-government.[17] Of course, some scholars and commentators are not persuaded that the judicial voice is more than window dressing; they insist that we keep our eye on the vote. Whatever one might think, the courts themselves surely takes this exercise of voice seriously. The Supreme Court actually votes on the merits of very few cases. Of the thousands of petitions for review it receives each year, it accepts and issues opinions in fewer than one hundred.[18] With so few cases being decided, the actual winners and losers matter much less to us—and to the Court—than what it is that the opinions say.[19] When the Court agrees to take a case, it takes upon itself the task of speaking to an issue of law.

Appellate judges—federal and state—spend most of their time writing, not voting. If the judicial role is to speak, then the lawyer's first task must be to learn how to listen. If we focus only on the individual judge's vote, we are likely to treat her the same way we treat any other person exercising political authority. We will ask whether that authority is exercised in ways that are to our advantage. If we don't see the advantage, we will wonder why we should defer to this exercise of authority. We have an easy answer with respect to elected authorities: we defer precisely because they were elected. If we disagree with their votes, we can work for the election of the political opposition. What plays this role when we disagree with the position of a judge who has been appointed for life or at least a lengthy term? The need for finality in the individual case will take us only part of the distance. Resolution of the individual case may ground the work of the trial-court judge, just as it grounds the work of an arbitrator. As we ascend the judicial hierarchy, however, the interest in resolving the individual case becomes less important.[20]

The puzzle has always been why we should defer to appellate courts that exercise authority over our political choices. This is a particularly acute question in a democracy: why should the fifth member of a political faction on the Supreme Court assert such power over us? Indeed, focusing on the vote of the individual Justice, the academic discipline of constitutional law has been obsessed with this question for the last two generations. This is the famous "counter-majoritarian difficulty."[21] My aim is not to offer yet another answer to this problem. Rather, it is to put you in a position from which you can assess the problem from inside our legal practice of writing and reading opinions. Thinking about the question from inside the practice is quite a different matter from theorizing about judicial authority in the abstract. Lawyers are not political philosophers dealing in abstractions. The lawyer's role is embedded in practices that are part of the exercise of the power and authority of the state. Surely it will help to know your way around.

Reading and Professional Responsibility

It is possible to imagine a political situation in which offering an opinion—an explanation for the exercise of power—might look like weakness. It tells us something about the strength of our own judicial practices that we are likely to think the opposite: a court that failed to explain itself would appear to be one that does not have good reasons for what it is doing. If a court does not try to persuade us, we are suspicious with respect to what actually persuaded it.

Presenting an opinion, a court acknowledges that it has an obligation to persuade: it must present reasons for its conclusion. Opinions serve a legitimating function for the courts parallel to, or in place of, elections of representatives. We are convinced that a legislature should have authority when its members are selected through regular, free, and fair elections. We are convinced that judges should have authority when they have persuaded us that they are applying the law, not exercising arbitrary power. Elections and opinions are both mechanisms for holding political authorities accountable. If we no longer thought that opinions could persuade us, then we might very well find ourselves arguing that judges too should be elected.[22]

While the idea of opinion writing points us toward a view of democratic accountability, contemporary practices are in some tension with this view. The judicial opinion, after all, is not exactly accessible to the ordinary citizen.[23] When the Supreme Court effectively ruled that George W. Bush was the president, after the troubled election of 2000, who could read its opinion?[24] It was impenetrable even to the reporters, who struggled to explain the outcome to the nation.

Of course, that was an opinion produced under extraordinary circumstances, without the ordinary luxury of time for writing and deliberating. Yet, when the Court recently ruled on the major health care initiative of the Obama administration, the Affordable Care Act, it produced hundreds of pages of opinions so complex that few professionals, let alone ordinary citizens, could comprehend them.[25] These complex opinions, we might think, could have little, if any, effect on the political controversy surrounding the law. This time, however, the Court had scheduled an exceptional amount of oral argument and took months to deliberate and write. Opinion-writing practices seem to have shifted dramatically since the 1950s when the Court produced the unanimous opinion in *Brown v. Board of Education*—a short, direct text that was immediately accessible to the public.

If the courts are addressing anyone directly, it is lawyers. That puts a special burden of democratic responsibility on the legal community. If we stop reading, there may be no one left. Power, in that case, would become unhinged from persuasion. Without that, to whom, or in what manner, would the courts be accountable? Lawyers bring the courts to the people and the people to the courts. They do this not just for their clients and those who might become their clients. Their professional role is inseparable from their role as citizens, for they represent the democratic audience that the Court must persuade if it is to have legitimacy as well as authority.

Despite this democratic responsibility, of all the skills that a law student must learn, the most difficult is that of learning how to read an opinion. As I suggested in the preface, this is difficult in the same way that learning a foreign language is difficult. The language seems, at the start, wholly impenetrable—a complete mystery. We cannot imagine that these sounds will come to make sense. But if we keep at it, we eventually find ourselves on the other side of the mystery. Learning to read the judicial opinion is no different. One moves from mystery to proficiency through practice. Most important, just as learning how to read French is inseparable from learning how to speak and write French, so learning how to read opinions is inseparable from learning how to speak and write like a lawyer. Learning to read the opinion, one becomes a lawyer.

The judicial opinion models what it is to make a legal argument. The opinion tells us what counts and, therefore, what works in constructing an argument. Reading opinions—including concurrences and dissents—one enters into conversation with the courts. The lawyer usually aims to write in the same voice as that with which the courts speak. Often, an excellent brief sounds to the judge like something that she might say. She can imagine speaking these words, and frequently will do just that, if the lawyer is successful.[26]

Lawyers with such fluency will converge in their thinking about a problem regardless of which side they are on. They will situate the problem in the same legal frame, even as they disagree about the outcome. Each knows what the other side is saying and why. They understand their disagreement, and they know what resources can be brought to bear to resolve the controversy. Without that common understanding, argument would drop aside as each side sought to compel the assent of the decision maker. Arguments about the law would give way to something that looked and worked like lobbying before the legislature.

Many lawyers are not particularly persuasive because they have never learned to speak this language. They are like tourists visiting a foreign country. Bound to their phrase book, they fail to understand much of what is going on around them. They may still be experts in a particular area of practice. They know the rules; they know the local actors; they know the procedures necessary to achieve their clients' ends. They are effectively extensions of the administrative necessities of the modern state. They can take a client through the regulatory labyrinth of the state, whether that means filing taxes, applying for a permit, or resolving a local dispute. There is nothing "wrong" with being this sort of a lawyer.

There is, however, another sort of lawyer. This lawyer doesn't just understand how to get some things done, she understands what it is that our nation is trying to accomplish when we speak of the rule of law. She understands law as a living culture, with its own way of speaking, its own internal values, its own way of seeing the world. She understands that the rule of law is the project of a democratic community that has a particular past and that aspires to maintain that identity into the future. She is not looking for the phrase book but has become a native speaker. She knows how to be creative within this common language. This is what makes her particularly valuable to her client. To be this lawyer, you must look beyond the judgment to the opinion, for only then can you come to understand how courts construct an entire world of meaning.

Lawyers may have a bad reputation, but America remains a country that defines itself by the rule of law. We cannot think of ourselves apart from this commitment to law. Americans are bound together not by a common ethnicity or religion but by the rule of law that begins, but hardly ends, with the Constitution. Lincoln spoke of a civil religion of reverence for law.[27] This idea still resonates. Judicial appointments may be contested politically, but judges remain figures of immense respect.[28] Maintaining the belief that law is not just politics by other means is exactly what is at stake in learning to read the judicial opinion.

The promise held out to the law student is to live as part of this democratic polity in which authority rests on persuasion. This is the promise to which legal pedagogy should be held accountable. Law students may, at times, forget this aspiration as they face the pressures of exams and finding jobs. Nevertheless, law school does them a disservice if it does not cultivate this aspiration. Short of that, law schools risk becoming technical schools. This risk is very real even at our leading law schools, for there too law students are rarely taught how to read the judicial opinion.

Law professors certainly know how to read opinions. What they lack is a way to think of this know-how as central to their pedagogy. For some, this is because they believe that judges vote their own political preferences and this practice will not be changed by persuasion. For others, it is because they think of their own expertise as lying in a different direction: that of setting forth what the law is.

Teaching from a casebook, one can feel a sense of mastery of a body of knowledge. The professor places the content of law over the discourse of law. It may well be that this is necessary for much of the law school curriculum. Yet, at some point, student and professor should turn to the judicial opinion itself, in order to take up the task of learning to think and argue as a lawyer. Learning the substance of the law is important, but no less important is learning the life of the law as a practice of persuading and being persuaded.

Do Judges Still Know How to Write?

If students are no longer taught how to read, is it so clear that judges still know how to write? There is reason to worry about this, especially if the opinions are increasingly written by the law clerks.[29] After all, the clerks are recent graduates. Has their education prepared them to write persuasive opinions? There are certainly reasons for concern.

Some have noted, for example, the way in which opinions are increasingly taking on the appearance of law journal articles. They are getting (much) longer and they include more footnotes.[30] There often seems to be a reluctance to speak directly. Opinions are largely composed by stringing together quotations from prior opinions. It is as if writing an opinion has become a task of cutting and pasting.[31] The aim is to suppress the identity of the author. This form of writing suggests a mistaken idea of the sources of judicial authority. A court's authority does not come from mining previous opinions, as if they were little more than dictionaries. The text of such opinions is, more than likely, the work of recent law school graduates.

Why, however, would the judges permit this? I suspect a more disturbing reason for this degradation of the opinion. As I will explore in chapter 3, the judicial opinion has a complex relationship to the issue of voice: in whose voice does the opinion speak? A Justice "delivers" the opinion for the Court; he does not author it. On the Supreme Court, authorship is a quality of dissents and concurrences. Unable to claim authorship, the judge who delivers has no special claim upon the text. The practice of cutting and pasting is a kind of confused rendering of this tradition of suppression of individual voice. The practice is more than likely a sign of judges who can no longer confidently respond to the accusation that their work is just politics in another form.

This suspicion that judges are themselves uncertain of the distinction of law from politics gains support from what we find when we look to what judges say when they do speak in their own voices—for example, in concurring and dissenting opinions. They accuse each other of acting for political reasons, of disregarding law, of imposing their own values. No doubt they believe this about each other. Why else make such personal charges? No one can trade in such charges without worrying that the same is true of themselves. If this is what they believe, however, then they are unlikely to persuade or be persuaded by legal arguments offered in the opinions.

One might argue that there is a sort of hard-headed realism in all of this. Judges should be aware of what they are doing; they should not take their own rhetoric too seriously. What matters is how they vote. Academics should take the same advice and study acts, not mere rhetoric. We should analyze what it is that particular judges or collections of judges do when a case is before them. Many academics do indeed support this turn to "the facts," thinking it offers a firm point for analysis. Interpretation threatens to introduce personal bias and subjective judgment into academic work. Why trust opinions when we can count votes? Why interpret when you can run regressions?

In this book, I will argue that the function of the opinion is not merely rhetorical. Or, rather, there is nothing "merely" about the role of rhetoric. The need for persuasion is not a weakness of the law but its strength. Law is not simply another site for the exercise of political power. Rather, the rule of law is a way of seeing and maintaining our common social world. That world is at stake in the judicial opinion, for the task of the opinion is simultaneously to draw upon that world and to sustain it. If judges no longer know how to write, this common world is threatened.

WHY READ THE OPINIONS?

While judges may no longer exist in an easy relationship to the imaginative constructions that long sustained the courts as an institution within a democratic political order, individual judges can, no doubt, rise to the occasion. The problem may be that many judges no longer believe there is much of a reason to do so. Why should they, if lawyers look to the courts asking only who won and who lost? Whatever the political persuasiveness of this point of view, law schools should certainly resist it. If not here, where?

These problems of the relationship of politics to law are most evident in the appointments process, which has produced today a federal judiciary deeply divided along ideological lines. Each side in our politically polarized nation views the courts through the prism of vote, not voice. Neither side believes they will be persuaded by the judicial voice. Each side has, accordingly, a huge interest in who is appointed—not because of what they will say but because of how they will vote. Inevitably, every appellate judge knows that he or she has been appointed for political reasons, regardless of what has been said during the process. The rest of us know this as well. It is not surprising that this mix of politics and power, which is the reality never spoken during the appointments process itself, lingers on in a personal skepticism about the judge's own capacity authentically to speak in the voice of the law.

We have no reason, however, to believe that our current political conflicts, and their effects on the courts, will continue forever. We are the bearers of a rich tradition of living within the rule of law. This tradition has survived worse situations than our current politics. If law students are to help to carry forward this grand project of the rule of law, they have first to become a part of it. They must learn to read, to speak, and to imagine the law. They must hear again the music of the opinion. Some will go on to become law clerks to various judges and help to produce opinions; some will become judges. All will speak to officials—including judges—and to other lawyers. The professional responsibility of the lawyer is to learn the language and maintain the aspirations that constitute the rule of law.

WHY READ THE OPINIONS?

Approaching the Judicial Opinion

Coming to law school, you probably had an idea of the judicial opinion that goes something like this. First, the court states the facts. Next, it states the law. Finally, it applies the law to the facts and announces a conclusion. Stating the facts, the opinion borrows from the genre of journalism. Stating the law, it borrows from the genre of legal code. Reaching its conclusion, it borrows from the logic of syllogism: the statement of law serves as the major premise, and the account of facts serves as the minor premise. This is just the form of law enforcement that we see on the street all the time: your vehicle was traveling at seventy-five miles per hour (journalism); no vehicle is allowed to travel at more than sixty-five miles per hour (code); therefore, you violated the law (deduction). If you think this is the form of the judicial opinion, you will often be disappointed when you open a court reporter.

When the rules and facts are this clear, there is no dispute. When there is no dispute, there is little for the courts to do beyond stating the penalty. There is not likely to be an appellate opinion in such a case. You pay your fine and hopefully you drive more cautiously in the future. When there is a real dispute, this entire structure of reasoning will get us precisely nowhere. We don't know what the law is; we don't know what the relevant facts are; and we don't know how the law applies to these facts. Everything is at issue at the same time, and everything is related to everything else. I cannot determine the relevant facts until I know the law, but I cannot know the law until I know which facts are relevant.[32] The task of the opinion is to bring order to this jumble of contesting views about the substance of the law, the proper characterization of the facts, and the meaning of the law in this situation.

A court must determine law and facts at once. We cannot know which are the relevant facts, or what is the relevant characterization of the facts, until we know the law. But the reverse is also true, for different characterizations of the facts bring to bear different understandings of the law. Casting the facts one way, we get a case about labor law; casting them another way, we get a case about national security. Do we see a government mandate to obtain health insurance as a regulation of commerce or as a tax? The answer depends upon how we describe the facts, but that in turn depends upon how we understand the meaning of commerce and of taxes. That meaning always arises from an intersection of fact and law—neither exists abstracted from the other. Thus, we don't know which is the "right way" to describe the facts independently of our understanding of the law, but our understanding of the law changes as we see it from the perspective of new situations of fact. We reason our way forward by making analogies and drawing distinctions. But this kind of reasoning can never be done in the abstract. It is only possible from within a context. That context too must be established in the opinion.

The cynic may seize on this and say that courts first decide and then rationalize, for they cannot know what to say until they know where they are going. This view rests on the same simple model of legal reasoning as the application of law to facts that informs popular opinion. It takes only a moment, however, to see that in our own lives we are constantly bringing together facts with norms without knowing the outcome in advance. We find ourselves moving back and forth, from facts to norms, and norms to facts. We are trying to persuade ourselves to see our situation one way rather than another. Norms only become clear in context, and the context can only be clarified by norms.

There are, for example, no abstract rules that tell me how to deal with my children; every interaction includes contingent facts embedded in multiple norms. I come to understand good parenting only as I seek to become a good parent. To bring order to this kind of complexity in which facts and values cannot be separated is to tell a story. Our lives are organized by and around these stories that we tell and that we hear. We are constantly offering narratives that explain what we have done, why we have done it, and where we are going. We resolve difficult situations not by applying an abstract rule but by writing or rewriting a narrative. We don't know our destination in advance. We figure it out only as we move forward.

We seek to give an account of what we are doing; we too want to persuade. In the first instance, we want to persuade ourselves, but that task is inseparable from persuading others. Think about how you argue with your parents or friends when you confront a significant choice. You don't state a rule and then apply it to the facts. Your understanding of the facts emerges only from within the normative context, but the normative context takes shape in light of the facts. What we should want from a court is just what we want of ourselves: a persuasive account of the way forward.

Like each of us, a court has to deploy a kind of situation sense.[33] It must make sense of the whole, which combines the normative and the descriptive. That combination of fact and law is presented in the opinion, which might be better analogized to a short story than to either journalism or deduction. It is, like other forms of persuasion, a work of the imagination: an effort to persuade us that a particular way of seeing the situation makes sense. If it succeeds, we come away with a sense of the way forward.

A case formally begins because someone believes she has suffered an injury. That controversy becomes a matter of concern to the courts when it is placed in a context constituted by a whole series of controversies that have already been resolved judicially. Law does not deal with the singular event as such. A political body might work out a compromise; an arbitrator might split the difference between the parties. A court can decide only by seeing through the facts to the law. In the opinion, accordingly, the particular controversy comes to stand for broader interests, controversies, norms, and points of view. If we remain embedded in the particular, we treat the courts as if they were arbitrators concerned only with reaching a resolution acceptable to the parties. The point of the opinion, however, is to embed the particular controversy not just in the history of the parties but in the history of the law.

The court is not only looking backwards; it is also looking ahead. It knows that it will have to live with whatever it says. A court is writing our common future by constructing the narrative of our past. The law always demands this double movement toward the past and future at once. Interpreting past sources, including judicial precedents, the court takes responsibility for what legal texts mean to us not just in this case but in the future as well.

The court's task is not to construct a deduction but to write a persuasive account of fact and law. There is, however, rarely just one account available. We read the dissenting opinion and may find it equally convincing. We have, then, to judge between two accounts. At that point, it is important that we trust the courts as an institution. If we do, the fact that one account is "the opinion of the Court" is not irrelevant to its persuasiveness. An argument becomes more persuasive as we trust the speaker. Trust, of course, builds up over time as we see how the courts have done. Indeed, someone who read the opinions from only a single case would be lost confronting these contending accounts. He would have no basis apart from his personal interests for judging among them. The courts as an institution must earn our confidence. This is the professional ethos of lawyering: respect for the law and trust in those institutions that are responsible for its operations. These are the stakes in learning to read opinions.

two
THE OPINION AND NARRATIVE

Common sense suggests that there are three tasks an opinion must accomplish. It must set forth the facts of the controversy; it must set out the relevant law; it must apply the law to these facts. In the abstract, the three steps suggest a sort of practical syllogism: set out a legal rule, specify the facts, apply the rule. The rule serves as the major premise; the statement of facts provides the minor premise. The holding is the conclusion of the syllogism. Formally, the argument applies law to facts, even though facts are usually presented first in the opinion. While I will have much to say about whether these functions can be separated and how they actually work, the threefold division does point to the multiple literary genres that play a role in the opinion.

An opinion must set out the facts of the case. Someone allegedly suffered an injury from the actions of others. We want to know who did what to whom and under what circumstances. In this respect, we might think of the opinion as borrowing from the genre of reporting. Often the facts that are relevant are not limited to the alleged injury. To reach a decision about the meaning of the law, the opinion may investigate practices, traditions, expectations, and the development of policy. It may inquire into the origins of legislation and the reasons for its creation. It may investigate failed intentions as well as inadvertent consequences. In some of these cases, the relevant genre from which the opinion borrows may look less like reporting and more like history.

The opinions with which I am primarily concerned are readings of authoritative texts: the Constitution, statutes, regulations, and canonical precedents.[1] To set forth the law, however, requires more than writing down the positive text alone. After all, the case arises because of some controversy over the meaning of the law under these circumstances. Interpreting the law more often than not leads a court to consider other past interpretations of the same authoritative text. These past interpretations are the relevant precedents. The opinion situates the present case against these prior opinions, which were themselves interpretations. In this respect, we might think of an opinion as drawing on genres of literary criticism or even biblical hermeneutics, since there too the interpreter is dealing with authoritative texts and a developing body of erudite commentary on those texts. The judge, like the scholar, moves back and forth between an authoritative text and commentaries on that text.[2]

Finally, the opinion must establish the relationship between fact and law. Sometimes that relationship seems as straightforward as the application of the traffic laws to a speeding vehicle. The opinion looks in that case as if it belongs to the genre of deductive proof. More often, the connection between law and fact will be built through the use of analogies and the drawing of distinctions, in which case the genre looks like rhetorical persuasion. For example, the Constitution establishes a norm of "equal protection of the law." To determine whether an affirmative action program violates that norm, we must ask how such a program is alike or different from other programs that we know—or think we know—satisfy or violate that norm. Likeness and difference are not qualities subject to demonstrable proof but rather are characteristics about which we must be persuaded. In these situations, our inquiry is neither into law alone nor fact alone. We are trying to understand the norm in light of the facts at the same time that we are trying to understand the facts in light of the norm.

Reporting, history, interpretation, deduction, and persuasion are all at issue in the opinion. A court's task is to draw all of these elements into a single whole, which is the opinion. Drawing on all of these different forms, it makes sense to speak of the opinion as a unique literary genre. A successful opinion provides a coherent, single account, which persuades us to see the outcome of the case as if it were the sensible, or at least an appropriate, resolution of a problem. It will appear that way if the opinion persuades us to see the situation in light of one of the broad narrative accounts by which we regularly give order to our social and political life. These narratives to which judges appeal are not detached or free floating inventions. Rather, they are familiar themes of American history and contemporary life.

The opinion weaves fact and law into a single pattern that connects to an easily accessible normative perspective on ourselves, our community, our history, and even our destiny. Sometimes the account reaches back to the founding act of constitutional creation; sometimes the relevant history extends no further than to an act of Congress responding to a contemporary problem; sometimes the account refers to past decisions of the courts, which must themselves be fit within a coherent account of an effort to accomplish some end or ends. In each case, the opinion situates the present controversy in a history of the rule of law. Regardless of the time frame, the opinion responds to an expectation that it will provide a general sense of how this case fits into the larger whole. A persuasive account does not allow for arbitrary action; it does not leave loose ends.

Offering a complete account of facts and law, the literary genre of the opinion can be compared to a short story. We are introduced to actors confronting a problem. In the course of the opinion, that problem must be resolved in a way that leaves us with a sense of order, a sense that the problem has been resolved fairly. The opinion allows us to see through the particular facts to a larger theme that is broadly representative of our understanding of ourselves as a people engaged in a project of self-government under law. This is no less true of private law cases—torts, contracts, and property—than of public law cases. Private law too works with the authority of the state. When the state enforces this law, we are collectively imposing an order upon ourselves. For that reason, courts will not enforce contracts that are unconscionable or property transfers that violate our public values.[3]

The opinion, then, is neither an abstract exercise in legal formalism nor a descriptive account of facts. It is not a demonstration following the rules of logical deduction, and it is not a discovery of a truth or truths that exist apart from the opinion. Perhaps the worst description ever given of an appellate decision—at least in constitutional cases—was that offered by Justice Owen Roberts, who said that

THE OPINION AND NARRATIVE

"the judicial branch of the Government has only one duty—to lay the article of the Constitution which is invoked beside the statute which is challenged and to decide whether the latter squares with the former."[4] If we could "just see" the difference, we would not need opinions at all. We might not even need courts.

Often what undermines a clear understanding of the character of judicial opinions is a fear of politics. Judges and academics fear that unless they can describe an opinion in terms that suggest an "objective" activity, they are left with nothing more than a political act— that is, an *undemocratic* political act. That felt need for objectivity sets different scholars and judges searching in different directions: for example, history, text, or professional practices.[5] The problem with each of these sources of objectivity is not only that actual opinions never meet the standards suggested, but that no opinion could possibly meet those standards. Judges are not historians, linguists, philosophers, or logicians. Nor do we want them to be, for they would inevitably be not very good practitioners of those disciplines. The courthouse is not, and should not be, a university.[6]

Judges are lawyers and their work product is inevitably a lawerly product. Every lawyer speaking to a decision maker, but particularly to a court, needs to tell the client's story. The lawyer needs to convey a sense of the client's world to the judge; he needs to persuade the judge to see the world in such a way that his client's actions or interests make sense. They must appear to have been the right thing to have done or the appropriate claims to have made under the circumstances. An opinion is doing the same thing, but now the court is speaking rather than listening.

The opinion tries to present the particular case as an instance of a more general narrative that is already familiar to readers. These narratives are the imaginative structures to which we constantly appeal in making sense of our experience. These are stories of family, of community, of care and responsibility, of success, but also of failure and dereliction. They are ready-to-hand not in the sense that they perpetuate biases or prejudices—although they certainly can do this—but in the sense that they offer the imaginative means by which we explain ourselves and our situation. We orient ourselves toward others and toward ourselves by deploying these narratives. We do so whether we are explaining the past or anticipating the future. Without these narratives, we would not just be lost, we would have no world to be lost in. Indeed, we would not even have a self that was coherent over time. Those with whom we share these narratives constitute our community. The more we share, the closer the community. To share none is to be in the situation of the complete stranger.

The opinion persuades us when we come to see the situation as making sense in light of these large, organizing ideas that have already structured our understanding of ourselves and our communities. They include political narratives of revolution and war, of progress and decline, and of the rule of law itself. They include personal and moral narratives of family, friendship, growth, and care. There is no list and there are no sharp boundaries. The political narratives, for example, must intersect with the personal narratives through ideas of responsibility, rights, sacrifice, and duties. We come to public controversies with a sense of what it is that a citizen owes the state and vice versa. We don't have this sense independently of the way in which we narrate particular events in history or, perhaps even more importantly today, the way in which movies, television, and books have portrayed particular conflicts.[7]

We don't distinguish between fact and fiction in the sources of the imagination. Rather, the society is constantly reproducing this imaginative framework in and through all of its creative productions.[8] One form of these creative productions is the judicial opinion. We cannot really answer the question whether an opinion belongs in the category of fiction or nonfiction any more than we can answer that question with respect to much that we believe about ourselves, our nation, and our history. In an earlier era, we might have approached opinions as parables—archetypical precedents from which we derive morals by which we are to direct our own actions.

This literary form does not limit a court's creative capacities any more than the short story genre limits a fiction writer. There are always multiple narratives to which a court can appeal. There are always new variations to be worked on standard themes. We do not have a single account of ourselves but are apt to say different things as different controversies arise. We find our way forward as we choose one account over another. Similarly, a political project is not a logically organized scheme. We don't have a single set of values that are hierarchically arranged. Rather, we work with multiple norms and values, each of which can generate its own account. These different accounts can be in conflict. Often, however, we don't have to choose between them: different people can understand events differently. When we do have to choose, the conflicts can end up before the courts. Choosing to develop one narrative, a majority opinion does not eliminate the others. Often we see in dissents and concurrences just how rich—and problematic—the choices are. In future cases, those alternative narratives are likely to come back to inform the court's opinions. Narratives may fall out of fashion, but it is beyond the power of any institution, including a court, to eliminate them from the national imagination.

"The life of the law," Justice Oliver Wendell Holmes famously wrote, "has not been logic; it has been experience."[9] Experience, however, must be made to speak, to explain what the law is and why it is that way. To take up this task means choosing to write one story rather than another. That choice is not a matter of logic. At best, we can say that the choice is a matter of judicial character or what we might call "judicial ethos."[10] Judges reveal something about themselves in choosing one narrative possibility over another. They must choose from among narratives with which we are familiar, for they are not ruling over us but interpreting our law. Yet, differences within our community are evident in the competing narratives on offer. Choosing a narrative frame, the judge tells us where he stands. He reveals his character in these choices. We will respond to that character by either extending or withholding trust. This is the core issue behind our recurrent controversies over the role of judicial empathy: how the judge chooses among available narratives.[11]

A recent case that spawned multiple opinions offers a particularly good illustration of the way in which argument is situated within a larger project of persuasion that necessarily involves the choice of a narrative frame. In *Brown v. Entertainment Merchants Association*, the Court struck down a California statute that prohibited the sale or rental of violent video games to minors.[12] The Court held the statute violated the First Amendment's free speech guarantee because the state was not advancing a compelling interest through means narrowly tailored to that end. If we were to focus on the "legal reasoning" of the opinion, we would speak of the application of this abstract standard—the compelling state interest test—to the facts of the case—a statute restricting access to a form of expression. The Court holds that the end of protecting minors from the alleged harm of video games is not compelling and that the statute is both over- and under-inclusive, thus satisfying neither prong of the doctrinally appropriate test. That, no doubt, is how the opinion will appear in the casebooks. Nevertheless, to read the opinion is to see that this formal reasoning carries little of the burden of persuasion. The opinion holds our attention not because of its formal application of a rule but because of the narrative it offers.

The majority opinion casts the Court in the sympathetic role of defending the young against the old, the future against the past. At issue, the opinion would have us believe, is progress as a common value of our community. The new generation always strikes their elders as strange and threatening; the older generation is always dismayed by the youth culture. Video games, in this narrative, are only the latest in a long series of changing cultural forms of communication, each of which is resisted by the natural conservatism of the old. Tradition is a value and traditional values have a place in families and communities. But when the traditionalists seize control of the regulatory instruments of the state, when they try to use law to prevent innovation, they are undermining the healthy competition among ideas, which the First Amendment protects. This is how the majority would have us see the Court's role here. To persuade us, it must be more convincing than the competing narratives that are offered, including that of Justice Stephen Breyer, who inverts the story completely, casting the Court's intervention as itself the barrier to progress. Appealing to one particular theme—here, the idea of progress—does not resolve the issue of which side can best lay claim to that narrative. Who, we ask, has the more persuasive account to offer of how progress is advanced or hindered in this situation?

Consider our attitudes toward children—the deep issue here. We want them to grow into free, self-determining individuals, but we also want them to carry forward our own traditions. They embody our hopes but also our fears. We hope that they will be better than ourselves. We also fear that they are susceptible to bad influences and impulsive actions. Is the child at the computer screen practicing murder and mayhem or is he learning skills that will make him a responsible citizen in a high tech world that we may never understand? The opinions have to negotiate these many values, which means they must construct a narrative that makes us see this particular case one way rather than another. There is never just one story that can be told, and between the majority and the dissents we are offered multiple accounts.

For the majority, the relevant story is one of intergenerational conflict that begins with the introduction of "dime novels" early in the twentieth century. These offered young people stories of crime and passion. They were, for that reason, upsetting to the parents' generation, which remembered the "wholesome" stories on which they had been raised. Dime novels were followed by radio, film, comic books, and now electronic media. Always, the Court says, the reaction of the parents is the same: to fear the corruption of the youth by forces that, through the new medium, are released from traditional constraints. Had we followed our fears in the past, the path of progress would have been stymied. The Court portrays itself as the defender of progress. "For a time, our Court did permit broad censorship of movies because of their capacity to be used for evil, but we eventually reversed course."[13] The modern Court sides with youth and the future against the older generation's reactionary tendencies. We have seen this before, the Court tells us. The Court would reassure us by convincing us that it knows what to do. It exemplifies a certain sort of courage in the face of the always threatening demands of youth. We don't know the future, it tells us, but we must not fear it.

The rhetorical pose the Court strikes is broadly appealing, cutting across what might have been our expectations of factional, political division on the Court. Liberals and conservatives are both attracted to this ideal of a domain of free speech that must be kept current with technological innovation. Liberals may see it as keeping open the space for innovation, while conservatives may see it supporting a libertarian goal of keeping government away from the individual. They may, in other words, disagree on the deep grounds upon which the particular narrative rests.[14] The Court, however, is not asked to give a philosophical defense of the narrative upon which it relies. The object is to persuade, not to systematically demonstrate the truth of the matter. How exactly could it demonstrate that courage is more important than fear, progress more important than tradition, under the particular circumstances of this case? The only demonstration possible is a successful performance of persuasion.

The reader is indeed likely to be persuaded, for the opinion appeals to one of our deepest images of the meaning and nature of the American political project. It appeals to the idea of release from the dead hand of traditional authority; it picks up the idea of an ever-renewed promise to the next generation. The opinion reassures all of us that our community is not yet old and time-bound. With this image of the life of the nation as one of perpetual youth, we associate opportunity, innovation, and reward.

This is a narrative as old as America itself: a country founded on an idea of seeking a new place where one would be free from the constraints of tradition, whether in the form of religion, class, or political practice. Just as old as this idea of liberation from the past has been the fear that authorities will emerge in the new world who will replicate the sins of the old world. Toleration is, accordingly, a political and legal practice that every generation must take up as its own challenge. It begins in the home, for there is no strong distinction to be made between the political and the familial from this perspective:

a tolerant polity requires tolerant citizens. Playing video games subtly becomes a site for training in citizenship.[15]

The majority, accordingly, has a sound intuition of the available grounds of persuasion when it appeals to this narrative frame. It portrays itself as expressing our collective better self—indeed, setting forth the ideal of the nation itself. It is requiring the parental generation to live up to their own standards. We read the opinion and acknowledge that parents should not fear their own children, even when the children push in uncomfortable directions. Did the older generation not do this to their own parents? The same children who read dime novels and went to the movies grew up to be members of the establishment. Neither is it likely that today's children will be corrupted by forms of communication—video games—that are impenetrable to their parents and grandparents. Or, so the Court tries to reassure us. Is not this entire performance an expression of empathy and a demonstration of judicial ethos?

Justices who do not join the majority do not reject this narrative, explicitly or implicitly. Who could? Instead, they appeal to alternative narratives to which we are also sympathetic. The argument is over how to see the case. John Dewey famously said facts don't carry their meanings on their faces.[16] Indeed, the opinions illustrate the proposition that there are no facts apart from the narratives within which we frame them. The opinions, then, are a competition over how to understand the situation.

As we read further, accordingly, we come to see alternative narrative frameworks. We are likely to be no less sympathetic to these narratives, which place other values before us. This is exactly what makes the case difficult. If we all saw it one way, then it is unlikely the controversy would have made it to the Supreme Court. Because we are sympathetic to these alternative narratives, we cannot infer anything about their relative place in our political imaginations from the fact that they show up in the dissents in this particular case. Narratives are not defeated as a proposition of law might be. They have not lost their appeal; they have simply lost the competition to tell the master story about this set of facts. Structuring the arguments of the dissents, they actually gain strength precisely because they remain in circulation. A narrative is defeated not when it fails to gather enough votes but only when it does not receive any voice at all.

In dissent, Justice Thomas offers a narrative that focuses on the critical role of parental authority and parental responsibility in the long history of the nation.[17] Who could disagree with the importance of what, in a different political context, we might call "family values"? He does not see the case as one involving innovation in the technologies of speech but only the consistent social demand that parents take responsibility for their children's moral development. The California statute does not ban these video games; it does not prohibit minors from viewing them. Rather, it gives to parents the authority to decide whether their children will have access to the games. It says to the minor, if you want to play these games, speak to your parents. It says to the parents, take responsibility for what your children are doing. This narrative does not deny the value of progress. It does, however, suggest that progress may require some moral direction. This is the model of education generally: a progressive future does not simply leave it to the children; it offers them guidance in the form of adult supervision.

What could be wrong with the state trying to advance this interest in family responsibility? We are generally very sympathetic to the idea of strong families with watchful and responsible parents. We are likely to think the majority opinion borders on the frivolous when it seems to worry about the parent who might actually want his or her child to have unfettered access to video games portraying murder, dismemberment, rape, and hate crimes: "Not all of the children who are forbidden [by the statute] to purchase violent video games on their own, have parents who *care* whether they purchase violent video games."[18] Should we not support efforts by the state to encourage parental supervision—to send the message to the parent that, as parents, you should be paying attention. Do parents actually give these games to their children as Christmas presents? Are there really such parents? If there are, need the state respect this behavior?

THE OPINION AND NARRATIVE

That Justice Thomas receives no support from other members of the Court cannot be because the narrative of parental responsibility is itself unattractive. The problem is not the narrative but the legal conclusion that he wants to draw from it: minors have no First Amendment rights whatsoever. For the purpose of the First Amendment's protection of speech, Justice Thomas asserts that minors are simply nonentities existing only in the shadow of their parents. He casts the minor into a position little better than that historically occupied by the slave: members of a household with no legal identity and thus no legal rights. The majority opinion notes that there is no support in the precedents for this radical proposition: free speech rights have long been successfully claimed by minors.[19] Thomas would overturn a substantial body of judicial opinions, some of which have near-canonical status. Those cases have to do with recognizing the political and religious life of minors: high school students protesting the war in Vietnam or organizing prayer groups in school, for example.[20] Why would the Court want to dismantle this legacy of decisions? Apparently, they do not. What is Thomas telling us about his judicial character in choosing to throw these cases into issue?

Justice Thomas has hold of an important narrative, but he would use it to pursue an end dramatically out of line with contemporary understandings of the autonomy and respect due to a teenager. The narrative will not carry this weight for his colleagues or for most of the readers of the opinion. His legal conclusion that minors have no rights of freedom of speech hardly follows as a matter of course from his portrayal of the place of parental responsibility in our national history. Accepting the narrative, we might be convinced that the California statute is constitutional because it directly supports parental authority, which may appear here as a compelling state interest. One can reach that conclusion, however, without having to accept Thomas's broad denial of rights. Adults and children need not be set against each other everywhere and all at once. The state can recognize both interests and make context specific judgments as to how much weight to give to each. Indeed, there is no reason to see any conflict at all here, for the interest of the state is in advancing the growth of the child to become a mature, responsible citizen. This requires both parental responsibility and respect for the child. It means embracing the narrative of progress and that of parental responsibility. If both are fundamental, the Court could have said it is up to the state to balance them under the particular circumstances of this case.

To persuade us, Thomas must link his legal claim to a narrative, which is what he tries to do. But the narrative of parental responsibility can be used to support multiple legal outcomes short of his extreme claim. He is all alone because he asks too much, not because he has failed to find an attractive narrative. Of course, Thomas might be right in his claim that in 1787 few people would have thought that a child could have a legal right to speech independently of his or her parents' control. We know wives had few legal rights at the time, and children were no doubt treated much the same. But no one would think that the law should reflect the 1787 view of women, so why of children? There might be answers to this question—for example, women were extended the right to vote by constitutional amendment—but what does pursuit of such questions tell us about the ethos or character of the judge? Why put this on the agenda of judicial inquiry now? Part of the reason Thomas fails to persuade is because by overreaching he puts at issue his own character: we have no reason to trust a person who would use this case to go that far.

Thomas might insist that the Constitution requires us to live under eighteenth-century sensibilities even when they conflict with modern practices and beliefs. To the more general question of why we would bind ourselves to live under a regime that seems to us morally offensive, outdated, ill informed, and perhaps silly, Thomas offers no answer—except we must because that is the law. What the law is, however, is the question, not the answer. Thomas must try to persuade us that there are good reasons for this view.[21] He cannot appeal to the meaning of the Constitution itself, when that is what is contested.

Thomas is not the only lone dissenter in the case. Justice Breyer writes a dissent that offers yet another narrative. Like the majority, he too wants to establish a narrative of progress to which the Court can attach itself as a sort of adjunct or guardian. For him, however, progress is measured first by the advance of knowledge, and second by the deployment of that knowledge in government regulation. A progressive society encourages the development of the sciences and adjusts its regulatory regime to the facts that are discovered by the scientists. This is a powerful narrative in its own right, describing what we generally mean when we speak of ours as an enlightened age. This story too is as old as the Republic: the framers believed themselves to be designing a new political order under the principles revealed by the new science of politics.[22] They hoped that the government they designed would continue to be responsive to developments in this science as well as in other fields of knowledge.

A progressive government, Breyer suggests, listens to those with expert knowledge. When government refuses to listen, it creates problems for the regulatory regime. Today we are likely to think of the political problems created by the deniers of climate change; just a little earlier, the example of the deniers of evolution would have come to mind. The narrative of denial in the face of progressive insight is one to which the Court has appealed in confronting its own history. Many people understand the judicial crisis of the New Deal in this way: the Court refused to recognize the new forms of scientific expertise that were the ground of modern administrative authority.[23] That refusal led to the deepest legitimacy crisis in the Court's history. Justice Breyer appeals to this narrative of dangerous resistance in accusing the Court of a false progressivism in this case.

In the case of video game regulation, the relevant experts are the social scientists who have studied the actual effects of violent video games on minors. If American progress depends on the ability of government to keep current with the advancing path of knowledge, the danger is not so much from a fear of new forms of communication, but rather from judges thinking they know what they do not know. Whether new forms of communication raise special problems is a question to be answered by the social scientists, not by the arm-chair observations of the Justices. Breyer tells us that there have been many scientific studies of the issue and a state should be free to draw on them in formulating a regulatory response. "Social scientists . . . have found *causal* evidence that playing these games results in harm."[24]

The Court, Breyer suggests, thinks it knows about video games because it knows something about movies and novels. Really, however, it has no idea of what effects these new games might have. "Experts debate the conclusions of these studies. . . . I, like most judges, lack the social science expertise to say definitively who is right."[25] The Court does know the history of judicial responses to past regulatory efforts. Based on that, it claims to know something about different forms of speech: they are basically all the same. Breyer suggests that this is a position of ignorance; it is no more enlightened than that of those cultural traditionalists whom the Court imagines as the source of this statute. Perhaps this time the medium is different. One can only determine the truth of the matter by studying the evidence. That is project for scientific research. The effects of video games are not a matter for judicial intuition but for study by experts. A legislature that acts in response to that emerging body of knowledge should not be undermined by the Court.

Breyer and the majority appeal to competing narratives that imagine quite different roles for the Court. The majority looks to the past and tells a tale of the changing forms of media against which the single constitutional value of free speech must be upheld. It is telling us "we have seen this sort of behavior before and we must continue to stand firm." It casts itself in a heroic role. To do so it must disparage the idea that there is something new here. Breyer looks to the future and argues for a Court that holds itself open to the growing reach of scientific knowledge. His opinion canvases many scientific studies and ends with a four-page appendix listing those studies. We can be pretty sure that the majority has not read them. Are we equally sure that they are irrelevant? The Court's role, Breyer suggests, cannot be to condemn the society to governance under forms of ignorance that the Court justifies by virtue of an inflated sense of its own knowledge.

While Breyer appeals to a familiar narrative, the Court's response is also quite familiar: constitutional rights cannot depend on the changing and contested views of scientific investigators. But surely they must in some instances. The Court could not continue to hold to the idea that the earth is flat when everyone around them is saying it is round. It could not hold to this idea even if it were written in a text or even if it has repeated it on many past occasions. This, we saw, was just the problem with Justice Thomas's easy assumption that the status of children in the eighteenth century must determine the meaning of the law today. The persuasive power of a narrative is not independent of the context in which it is put forth. That context includes all of our ordinary beliefs—all that we take for granted.[26]

Read as a competition to persuade the reader, there is genuine excitement in the opinions. We find among them a battle fought out in the high rhetoric of our national project. The Justices are not speaking to an abstraction called "the law." Rather, they are speaking to us. If we take the time to read what they say, we see a conflict reaching to our deepest values. Those values are plural and they do not fall into any single order. If they were well ordered, there would be an easy convergence on what must be said. Only in theory do we find such a hierarchically arranged normative order. Real communities live with tensions and contradictions, with many different possibilities and many different public values. We are always writing and rewriting our history in order to imagine our future.

The three narrative frames canvassed stand in a kind of uneasy relationship to each other. Thomas appeals to the idea of tradition as the broad framework of his argument. He finds in that tradition a value of parental responsibility that is still appealing. Breyer casts tradition as the threat to progress. For him, constitutional governance must work to support the modern administrative state, the task of which is to keep its regulatory regime in synch with the advances of science. In between, we find the majority opinion, which seems to stand for the stability of a certain kind of sensibility even amid change. It will adhere to fundamental values in a changing world. We might call this an appeal to the idea of "a liberal tradition," which is a tradition of openness to the new—a kind of antitradition tradition.

Each of these narratives is well grounded in our common sense. All of us can imagine responding to or deploying each narrative, although we may each do so in different circumstances. We all want to encourage parents and defend children from harm. We all want to encourage the progress that comes with scientific research, while we also want to defend our common values in new contexts. We want to recognize difference but remain the same. The work of the opinion is to situate itself with respect to these broadly appealing narratives. Doing so, it offers us representations that we recognize as familiar and, more importantly, as true. Each opinion says the sorts of things that we would say if we were asked to make sense of the case before the Court. These opinions are not only speaking to us, they are speaking for us.[27]

Studying formal doctrine as it emerges from the Court's judgments barely reaches the work of the opinion. But what is the relationship of doctrine to narrative? We have no reason to think that judges first reach a legal conclusion and then pick a narrative within which to package this conclusion in the opinion. Rather, we have every reason to think that judges imagine different narratives as possible ways of explaining to themselves what is the right thing to do in response to the controversy. They too must be persuaded. They argue among themselves and they argue with themselves. They think through the competing positions, and to do so they must frame them within accounts that they find more or less convincing. Because there are multiple, appealing narratives that point toward different outcomes, the case is hard for them, no less than for us.

A judge may have an intuition of what she believes to be the appropriate outcome. It is wrong, however, to think of the narrative as something added to that intuition; it is rather the very structure of the intuition.[28] Just as we organize our physical perception of a situation—for example, asking who, what, where—we organize our normative perception of a situation. Examining her reasons for the intuition, the judge finds herself saying things that fall into one of these narrative patterns. In the end, of course, there must be an equilibrium between the narrative and the legal holding. The holding must, under these circumstances, be a reasonable conclusion to the story that the narrative offers. This is just what was lacking in Justice Thomas's effort: his conclusion went well beyond what the narrative would support.

Can legal doctrine help us to make the choice among these narratives? Not really, for the doctrine does not exist independently of the narratives. We see this clearly if we turn to the one opinion in *Entertainment Merchants* that has yet to make an appearance in my account: the concurrence of Justice Samuel Alito, which is joined by the Chief Justice.[29] This opinion tries to eschew any narrative structure at all by relying on a formal, technical doctrine of the law of due process: "void for vagueness." The California statute, Alito writes, fails because it is unconstitutionally vague. A reasonable person, he argues, would not know what forms of video violence are covered by the statute. This is a proposition that is somewhat difficult to believe given that the industry already imposes upon itself a regulatory regime that requires exactly this sort of judgment. As with pornography, the industry seems to have little trouble "knowing it when it sees it."[30]

Asserting that the statute is vague, however, is a way of encouraging the state legislature to try again.[31] Perhaps by that time, the scientific evidence will be more—or less—compelling. In any case, it puts off the issue of a real decision for the Court. Taking this formal way out, Alito is able to acknowledge the power of the competing narratives. Striking down the statute on technical grounds would have had the virtue of keeping the controversy alive in the public domain. As public opinion solidifies on this issue—in part in response to expert opinion—it may well be that a single vote would shift away from the five-person, majority position of the Court. Of course, the majority opinion was written in a way that makes that shift more, not less, difficult. Who is going to repudiate the image of the Court as the defender of the next generation?

Why, then, did a majority find one of the competing narratives persuasive with respect to this legal controversy? The answer cannot be that this position alone gets the law right, for the whole point of the narrative is to support one, among several, possible readings of the law. The very fact that there are multiple competing opinions tells us that it could have come out differently. Nor can we easily explain the outcome by looking to the personal values of the Justices. I am confident that all of them disapprove of these video games; all of them support strong family values; and all think of themselves as people who accept the idea of social progress under the guidance of scientific discovery. It is highly probable that none of them knew how they would decide the case until the arguments were presented and they were persuaded one way or the other. They are, moreover, not exercising a personal choice but rather their public function. Whatever they think personally about these issues, the accounts they offer tells us what they think the Court should do.

It may well be that the majority forms around the liberal/libertarian narrative at least in part because it casts the Court as the central figure in the drama. The Court's role, in this view, is that of defender of an important constitutional value that will be challenged by every generation. The Court appears as the defender of progress. This is a character—again, an ethos—that judges are no doubt eager to grasp for themselves when it is plausibly on offer. The character of the Court, then, becomes an image of the character of the nation at its best. The Court offers itself as a representation of our collective self. One problem with the dissenters' competing narratives is that they cast the Court as little more than an adjunct to a society in which the responsible center lies elsewhere: in the family or in the social scientist's laboratory. Sometimes the Court accepts that role, but there is no need for it to do so here. In this domain of freedom of speech, the Court has the least problematic claim to the starring role. For this reason as well, this narrative is able to overcome the breach we might otherwise expect to find between the liberals and the conservatives on the Court. This narrative strengthens the Court and does so on familiar grounds.

Of course, I don't know if any of this is true. The point, however, is that when we turn from holding to opinion, from doctrine to persuasion, these are the kinds of issues that become relevant to under-

THE OPINION AND NARRATIVE

standing the work of the Court. If your ambition is to persuade a court, then these are among the matters you must consider. If your ambition is to understand how and why the opinions persuade us to see the law one way rather than another, then you will have to consider these issues as well, for the law is not something apart from these narratives and the uses we make of them.

We cannot ignore these accounts when we speak of the law of the case. That law is not something separate from the opinion. We simply cannot know how far any proposition of law abstracted from the broader opinion will travel. Stripped of context, the abstract proposition will tell us very little about how the next controversial case will be decided. The very fact that there is controversy tells us that we are not sure how to understand the situation. We are likely to feel the pull of competing narratives as we try to answer the question of how a precedent applies or fails to apply. Each of these competing narratives makes a claim on what the earlier cases meant. Nothing is ever settled once and for all. Of course, we are not arguing about every case all of the time, but not because the legal doctrine somehow stands clear of narrative. Rather, when a case is uncontroversial, we all understand the situation in the same way, that is, we all tell the same story about facts and law.

A court may have the authority simply to pronounce a legal conclusion, but were that authority exercised in the absence of persuasion, it might not last for long. This is why we cannot simply transfer abroad our own judicial practices as if the function of the courts were something like that of a professional association. Lacking the legitimacy that is visibly embodied in the electoral process, courts must create their own legitimacy. Judges sometimes suggest their authority arises from their expertise, rather like doctors and engineers have authority because of their claim to knowledge.[32] But the doctor's knowledge is visible in work that is easily evaluated: we get better or we do not. The same with the engineer: the bridge that fails does so spectacularly. We have no similar measure of the work of a court. Worse, judges are themselves deeply split over what the law is. They could not agree among themselves on the legality of the California statute. The issue was not complicated in the ordinary sense. Rather, it was controversial. Professional expertise simply does not look like this. Doctors may, on occasion, disagree on their diagnosis of an individual patient's problem, but if they disagreed regularly, we would no longer think of medicine as a field of expert knowledge.

There are parts of the law in which expertise is important, but the judicial opinion is not one of them. Judges are not just deciding upon a means to reach a commonly understood end—for example, healthcare. They are also telling us what the ends are. In *Entertainment Merchants*, we don't know in advance whether our end is support for the family or liberation of youth from the constraints of the older generation. The Court's burden is to persuade us that the way forward in this situation is as it sees the case. There is no logic by which it can compel us to take its point of view, for the case presents a clash of values that if not exactly incommensurable are surely in tension. If we think of politics as the domain within which we collectively give order to the multiple values circulating in our community, then the judiciary is a deeply political institution.[33]

The courts, accordingly, have no choice but to try to persuade us to accept their understandings of the law. They do not do this in the abstract. Judges do not write treatises on political theory. Judges are neither political philosophers nor philosopher kings. They are not even leaders in the field of jurisprudential thought. Few judges have been legal academics. Their task of persuasion is taken up in a lawerly fashion: one case at a time. Opinions express the manner in which lawyers imagine the world in which they are engaged as participant-advocates. This is exactly why students learn to be lawyers by studying opinions.

Of course, courts have been around quite a long time and our own Supreme Court has been an ongoing project for some two hundred years. The best measure of an institution's success is its endurance. We might disagree with the terms of that success—for example, if it were built on force or coercion. Success, accordingly, does not necessarily imply some quality of moral goodness or political justice. But the Supreme Court has succeeded without "the sword or the purse;" it has succeeded through persuading us to accept its decisions.[34] Suc-

THE OPINION AND NARRATIVE

ceeding, it has built up a certain surplus of legitimacy. For this reason, we don't have a crisis each time a gap emerges between persuasion and authority. Thus, even when people are unpersuaded in a particular case, they continue to accept the institution. They trust it.

Nevertheless, when a serious gap between persuasion and authority emerges, there can be a genuine political crisis. Lincoln and his party were not persuaded by *Dred Scott*.[35] Roosevelt and his party were not persuaded by those decisions that declared unconstitutional major elements of the New Deal legislative program.[36] Perhaps we are moving toward a similar political crisis with respect to the Supreme Court's recent decisions striking down federal and state legislation regulating campaign spending.[37] The Supreme Court, Alexander Bickel famously wrote, "labors under an obligation to succeed," by which he meant the Justices either succeed in persuading us or they must change their position.[38] Fear of this possibility of failure haunts the Justices themselves.[39]

One of the most famous examples of narrative failure in recent years was *Bush v. Gore*.[40] In this extraordinary case, the Court told a waiting nation who would be the next president of the United States. Virtually everyone in this country thinks that we elect the president. They think that the legitimating source of presidential authority is victory at the polls, and they think that victory means getting the most votes. But Bush did not get the most votes. We don't even know for sure whether a majority of voters in the state of Florida believed they were voting for Bush.[41] *Bush v. Gore* left us in the puzzling situation in which virtually no one in the country could explain why it was that Bush was president. The democratic failure was not at the voting booth but in the judicial opinion. Citizens could not explain what exactly was the source of Bush's claim to legitimately represent the American people. All that could be said was that the Supreme Court had announced that this was the case. That was an extraordinary exercise of power.

Not just ordinary citizens but law professors too could not explain the decision.[42] Most law professors thought the Court would never presume to intervene, let alone decide the election. The controversy was not clearly within the Court's jurisdiction, so why would it get involved? It did not have to: the case fell within the Court's discretionary, certiorari jurisdiction. If the Court were to take the case, most academics thought the Justices would allow the political process to go forward under some general guidelines. Virtually no one thought the Court would stop the vote count and declare Bush the winner on the basis of an indeterminate and incomplete vote.

Behind this professional judgment that the Court would never do this, and would surely not do so on the basis of a five-to-four vote split between the conservatives and the liberals, was a sense that here the line between politics and law was just too indistinct. A judicial intervention would be judged in political terms, and that would amount to a failure on the part of the Court. There were no available grounds to persuade the country that something other than a political intervention had occurred. Partisans would be pleased or angered, but there would be no narrative that could persuade anyone to see the outcome as a matter of law, not politics.[43]

The dissenters expressed this fear directly. The Court itself, they said, would be the "loser," because no one would hear the court speaking the law.[44] Instead, citizens would hear only the voice of the political contest. They would hear this because it was indeed the voice with which the Court would be speaking. There simply was no legal argument that was sufficiently compelling to overcome this political reading. Thus, we find the dissenters writing that there is not even a "substantial" claim for the Court to address, that the situation is politically, but not legally, complicated. The Court, they said, should never have taken the case because there is nothing for it to say.[45]

When one turns to the actual opinion of the Court, virtually no one will defend it and most can barely understand it. Even the Court seemed uncertain of what it was saying about the law, leading to an extraordinarily unusual statement suggesting that the decision is not to serve as a precedent for any other situation.[46] The opinion offers the law of this case only, but the very idea of such a limited judgment undermines the principle of the rule of law.[47] Whatever else one might think, the rule of law begins from the idea that like cases are to be treated alike, that the particular is to be decided under a rule of general applicability. We argue over the nature of that rule and its reach; we argue, as well, over the characterization of the facts. Uncertainty does not itself undermine the idea of law, but it borders on lawless to announce in advance that nothing more is to come of a decision. Politics overwhelms law when a court declares that whatever it says in the particular case is to go no further. Here, vote over voice is expressed almost as purely as if the majority could say nothing coherent at all—nothing beyond the command, "Bush wins."[48]

There are many problems with the legal arguments the Court and the concurrence put forth. The majority relies upon an equal protection claim; the concurrence upon a claim that the federal Constitution assigns a unique authority to the state legislature, which protects it from the state's own courts. That these arguments are rather transparently insubstantial has been argued in many places.[49] I will not renew these arguments. Even if one were to give them some weight, they had little bearing on the remedy the Court ordered, which was to stop the vote count.[50] My point, however, is different and deeper, for the Court's largest failure is not doctrinal. Rather, it is a failure of narrative.

The Court offers no grand narrative at all at this moment of national political crisis. Instead of taking up this rhetorical task of persuasion, it appeals to the technicalities of law, as if the question of presidential selection is actually determined for us by the technical details of electoral machinery. Choosing the president, however, is hardly a technical matter—even if the Court exercises a technical expertise in good faith. Instead, the disregard of the obligation of voice suggests a bad faith effort to obfuscate.

Nowhere in the opinions does the Court offer us a narrative to make sense of the situation. It does not try to persuade us to see the deep political values at stake and to see its own intervention as a vindication of those values. We are left with an incomplete election and the appearance of an arbitrary action by the Court. The counting must stop, we are told. But why? How does this advance democratic values, the integrity of the election, the legitimacy of our politics, or any other important political value? There is no suggestion that the Court is intervening to prevent fraud or abuse. At most, the Court suggests there is confusion and inconsistency among the vote counters. Perhaps there is partisanship, but it is after all an election. No one claims that anyone has acted in an illegal fashion. The Court acts in utter disregard for this persuasive burden, as if it need not convince us because it rules us. The democratic failure extends, accordingly, from the legitimacy of the president to the legitimacy of the Court.

How might a Court aware of its obligation to persuade have handled this situation once it chose to get involved? There were at least three grand narratives available to the Court. We can call these the narrative of the individual voter, of federalism, and of political responsibility. In each version, the role of the Court would not have been to cast itself as the authoritative voice regarding the decision on the outcome of the election but rather to direct our attention elsewhere in the political process. Instead of vote over voice, such an opinion would have emphasized voice over vote.[51]

The first narrative was surely the most easily accessible. It points to the values upon which the Florida Supreme Court relied when it decided that the standard that should guide the vote count was "the intent of the voter." If a ballot conveyed the intent of the voter, then it should be counted regardless of whether it had any technical problem. How might the federal Supreme Court have picked up this narrative? It could have written an opinion that put electoral democracy at its center. It could have said that the will of the voter is the basis of our contemporary understanding of the source of legitimacy of political authority. Regardless of what might have been thought in 1787 with the invention of the Electoral College, today every state has electors chosen directly by the people. There is a reason for this: there is no other ground available for political legitimacy. This is why the right to vote has been deemed "fundamental."

If the right to vote is the fundamental principle involved, the Court could have used its own authority to make sure that right was vindicated in Florida. Such an opinion would have reassured the nation that there is no crisis and there is no ticking clock that limits what can be done—as if we are hostage to clerks and administrators. The Court could have assured us that while the situation is difficult, it can be resolved in a democratic fashion for our law makes provision for situations in which an election has yet to produce a determinate outcome: the Presidential Succession Act provides that the Speaker of the House can temporarily serve as president.[52] The Court would have written an opinion organized around the fundamental importance of counting every vote in a democratic society. It would have told Florida to make every effort to count every vote, to do it expeditiously but fairly. The rest of us can wait precisely because the Supreme Court is there to make sure that the legal order remains effective. Such a narrative might have persuaded the nation that this was not a moment of crisis but one in which we collectively rose to the challenge of showing ourselves committed to the democratic values upon which the nation is founded.

Instead of taking this narrative path, the Court began by writing that the fact that we elect members of the Electoral College is merely a historical contingency—a choice made by state legislatures that they are free to reconsider.[53] Having immediately discarded the narrative of democracy, it could have adopted a narrative of federalism. Given other decisions of this Court, this might have been an attractive line to take. Moreover, Americans generally understand that our political system is built on a notion of dual responsibility in which governmental roles are divided between the federal and state political communities. Perhaps citizens could have been persuaded that the issue involved not the vindication of the individual voter but rather of the individual state. One can imagine an opinion that explained the importance and responsibility of the state in the selection of the president. This is, after all, a theme that must be reached once one acknowledges that Bush had already lost the national popular vote.

In this federalism narrative, the theme would have been that the state of Florida must take responsibility for settling this dispute. That might not mean following the state supreme court. Perhaps the state legislature needed to intervene and choose a slate of electors. Arguably, the state election had failed to select a winner: the outcome was statistically a tie. There may have been no nonarbitrary way of determining the winner of the vote. The Court could have written an opinion that placed the burden of responsibility clearly on the state legislature, explaining to the rest of the nation what was entailed by this constitutional responsibility and why we must wait for Florida to perform this function. Again, the theme of the opinion would have been to assure the nation that there was no crisis, that the electoral system was working its will within the boundaries of law. The opinion would have sought to persuade us that the process has its own integrity and that by allowing it to go forward we are adhering to our common constitutional values: not, in this instance, individual liberty but state responsibility.

We can describe these two narratives as the choices that might have been made by a great liberal court or a great conservative court. A great national Court might have adopted yet a third narrative in which the point was to emphasize that Congress has all of the authority and responsibility to deal with the problems arising from Florida. Congress has dealt with such problems in the past; it can do so in this instance as well.[54] It has already specified a set of procedures for settling conflicts. It is not bound to any particular dates, all of which are of its own making. There was no real risk that Congress would disenfranchise Florida, no risk that Congress could not resolve whatever controversies remained after Florida filed its electoral slate. The Court's role would have been to remind us of the history of prior controversies and the way in which Congress resolved them and learned from them. Citizens could have understood that a political problem requires a political solution, and that Congress is the national political institution best situated to resolve the controversy in a legitimate fashion.

Under all of these possible opinions, the chances were very substantial that George W. Bush would have become the president. The Florida legislature was Republican, as was its governor. The Congress was also Republican. We don't know what the Florida recount might have produced had the state been given the time to count all the votes, but it could easily have been the case that Bush would have maintained his lead. Of course, predicting the political outcome is not the business of the Court. If that is all we see, the legitimacy of both the president and the courts suffer. The Court needed to explain the controversy and what was to be done about it by reminding us of who we are and what was at stake for the nation. It needed to rise to the occasion and take up its burden of persuasion. This was a high, dramatic moment of American political life. We looked to the Court and we heard nothing more than a proclamation—"shut down the election"—as if it need not explain itself. We got a technically implausible reading of the legal situation instead of a rhetorically persuasive narrative or our national life. Some of us might have been happy with the outcome, but no one was convinced.

Bush v. Gore, all seem to agree, is best forgotten about.[55] It stands for nothing except the extraordinary power of the Court. It has barely any presence in the casebooks. It will emerge in the long run as one of the low points of the Court's history: a perpetual embarrassment like *Dred Scott*. There is an important lesson here, however. The embarrassment of the case is not in its formalistic manipulation of the Florida statute and its misreading of the federal safe harbor provision. Rather, it is in the Court's failure to write an opinion. The words it spoke do not even attempt to persuade; they don't offer a sensible reading of the situation. We cannot return to the opinion in order to understand how that difficult election fits into our national story. The Justices offered vote without voice, when what the nation needed most of all was voice. The failure of the case has nothing to do with the failure of authority: Bush does become president after the decision. He does so without further objection even from the loser, Vice President Al Gore. The failure of the case is that no one could understand why he was the president.

three
UNITY: THE JUDICIAL VOICE

All of the criticism of *Bush v. Gore* came to little politically. Even before the Court pronounced its decision, Vice President Gore had concluded that whatever the Court decided, that would be the end of the matter.[1] There were to be no protests, no mobilization of the popular majority that had supported Gore at the polls. Individuals did accuse the Court of partisanship, but few went on from there to challenge its authority or to suggest resistance. There was not even symbolic resistance. No boycott of the inauguration by Democrats, no refusal by the Clinton administration to cooperate in the transfer of power. Nor did the decision begin a sustained reexamination of the power of courts, or even of the Supreme Court.

Bush v. Gore reveals a central fact about our national political culture. We listen to the courts and we obey. We don't read an opinion and then decide what to do. Like Vice President Gore, we believe in the courts even before we know what they will say. *Bush* shows us that we continue to obey even when we are not persuaded. We were not persuaded because the opinion offered very little by which to persuade us.

The last chapter made clear that we cannot read opinions looking for proof in the form of logical deduction or practical syllogism. A well-crafted opinion works by offering a convincing narrative that brings facts and law together in a persuasive account. *Bush*, however, suggests that judicial authority remains even when the narrative fails. The courts can rely upon a sort of reservoir of belief. From where does that arise, if not from proof or narrative? To answer this question, we have to broaden our perspective and ask not just *what* the opinion says, but *who* is saying it.

Often we are persuaded not so much by an argument but because we trust the speaker. The same words spoken by a different speaker would not persuade us. Trust might be based on character: we trust the person who has, over time, shown himself to have good judgment with respect to issues that matter to us. The same might be true of institutions. For example, thinking that courts have generally performed their adjudicative function well, we trust them to resolve our disputes. Their past performance has built up an ethos of trust, upon which we rely even when we disagree with a particular outcome. The dissenting Justices in *Bush* had this view in mind when they asserted that such an important decision, without a persuasive opinion, would drain the reservoir of institutional trust.[2] They were right to think that trust earned can also be lost: a friend who betrays us will no longer have our trust. Once an institution is shown to be corrupt or incompetent, we will withdraw whatever trust we had in it.

Trust might also be based on institutional structure. We trust some strangers because of the role they play within an institution that has mechanisms to enforce its norms. Think of referees in a sports competition or the teachers in a school. We don't know who is going to referee the particular game; we may not know who is going to teach a particular course. Nevertheless, we may trust that the calls will be fair and the material will be covered. There may be some range in the performance of particular individuals, but we trust the institution to police itself in order to accomplish its ends. We can be disappointed in the particular instance, but we will maintain our trust if we believe that the institution generally self-corrects. The elaborate system of appellate and collateral review of judicial judgments is an example of this sort of institutional self-correction.

No doubt trust in courts rests in part on judicial character and in part on institutional integrity. Some people romanticize the work of judges; some think the institutional structure of the judiciary is the best we can do. We can tell a story of judicial performance that places judges repeatedly at the center of national efforts to realize justice and fairness. We might, depending on our own values, highlight their role in the civil rights movement, their protection of individual liberties, or their creation of a property regime supportive of economic growth. Sometimes judges defended these principles at substantial risk to themselves.³ Alternatively, trust might rest on a sense that the institution has reliably and fairly settled our disputes and that its structure of appellate review effectively corrects mistakes.

Arguably, *Bush* put these two sources of trust in some conflict. On one hand, the decision could be seen as an instance of institutional self-policing. Clearly, a majority did not trust the judges on the Florida Supreme Court. Reversing the state court decision, the majority opinion suggests that the state court judges had been moved by partisanship. On the other hand, the dissenters thought that the Supreme Court's own judgment would be received by many citizens as a political, rather than a legal, act. Institutional self-policing may create trust, but political opportunism by judges will destroy trust. That these sources—personal and institutional—can so easily be put in conflict suggests that something more is involved when we accept the authority of the courts. In this chapter, I will argue that one place to look for that additional element is in the narrative voice of the opinion. I offer a democratic theory of the opinion by linking that voice to popular sovereignty. My aim is not to justify any particular opinion, least of all *Bush v. Gore*. It is, rather, to describe the normative order within which our practice of writing opinions occurs. Any particular opinion can fail to meet this norm.

Authorship and Legitimacy

About any speech act, we can ask both *what* is said and *who* is saying it. We can read an opinion and ask about the rule or rules that it puts forth. About those rules, we can ask whether they are just or efficient. We need not know their author to engage in this discussion. We are likely to be more concerned about their effect than their source.⁴ We can have this conversation about a foreign state's law even if we know nothing of the origin of that law. When we study "black letter" law, this is our approach to legal texts. Our relationship to law in many of our daily activities has this character. We want to know what the speed limit is. Authorship seems beside the point.

We may think the limit too low or too high, but that judgment is not likely to turn on issues of authorship.

Often we think our laws have missed the mark of justice, but we nevertheless think them legitimate. Despite our objections, we use the rules to guide our own conduct. We do so not because we are worried about punishment or because we feel compelled but because we believe this to be an obligation of citizenship in a democratic political order. We don't say that this felt obligation excuses injustice; we continue to want to reform the law to make it more just. Nevertheless, we think the law is binding on us. I pay my taxes even when I think the government is using some part of these funds for unjust ends. Most people pay even if they believe that the government is asking for an unjust share of their income. At some point, our sense of injustice may overwhelm our sense of legitimacy, but things must get pretty extreme before we arrive at that point.

We want our laws not only to be just but to be our own. We think they are our own when we can imagine ourselves as their author. The point is actually quite familiar: the laws in a democratic political order are legitimate because their author is, in some sense, the people themselves. Of course, all of the difficulty—and interest—is in understanding in what sense this is true. Since we don't all vote on all laws, and even when we vote there are many who disagree with the outcome, how do we maintain an idea of self-authorship? More specifically, for our purposes, how does this idea of legal self-authorship help us to understand the judicial opinion?

When you visit a foreign country, you ordinarily comply with its law. You may do so because you don't want to get in trouble with the police. You may also think this is the respect due a foreign community. As a visitor, you are not concerned with the authorship of the law but only with its content. This is not the relationship you imagine with respect to your own law. Compliance here is informed by ideas of responsibility and accountability. I am not only responsible to the law but accountable for the law. Because I am accountable for the law, I can be asked to defend it. I might think that the law of Canada is more just than the law of the United States. I may prefer their rules to our own. Their law, however, is not mine. I do not hold myself accountable for it. This is not just a matter of the reach of the two nations' police forces. I am responsible to our law, not to our police.

The sense that the law is our own rests on a set of beliefs about authorship. The author of a text is not necessarily its writer, and, conversely, the writer cannot always claim authorship. Sometimes the distinction between writer and author points to the collective nature of a project: a committee authors a report even if it is drafted by one member. Sometimes authors have assistants who help them with the writing of a text. To draft is not to author, because the drafter is not held accountable for the text. Authorship points to accountability and accountability to authority.[5] For this reason, it is not acceptable for a professor to blame his research assistant when problems emerge with a published text that the assistant drafted. Similarly, a judge cannot blame her law clerk for what an opinion says. The clerk may have drafted the opinion, but he is not the author.[6] He is not the author even if he wrote every word of the opinion. No one wants to know what the clerk thought when he drafted this text.

Authorship is not the act of drafting but a social practice of accountability. That practice varies across fields. In the sciences, articles list as authors all members of the team, from highest to lowest; in the humanities, individuals doing the same kind of work as coauthors in the sciences appear only as assistants thanked in a footnote; in government, persons doing that same work—staff—make no appearance at all. Paradoxically, authorship is less about writing than about reading: readers attribute authorship.

Readers ordinarily attribute authorship just as the text directs them. Readers, drafters, and authors are all engaged in a common social practice.[7] When we deny the text's attribution of authorship, we are often making an accusation of plagiarism. There has, in that case, been a violation of some norm within the social practices of authorship. No one accuses a judge of plagiarism because a clerk wrote the text of an opinion. Just the opposite: if a law clerk claims authorship, we think he is violating the norms of the practice.

Surprisingly, when we examine the opinions of the Supreme Court, we discover that authorship is not readily apparent. The Justice whose name appears at the beginning of the text is explicitly denied authorship. He or she "delivered the opinion of the Court." The Justice who "delivers" the opinion may have drafted it—with more or less assistance from others—but authority and accountability lie elsewhere. Two possibilities of authorship come to mind. Is the opinion a text jointly authored by all the Justices who join it? Or, is the Court as an institution the author?

The former view is hard to sustain. The particular Justices who join are not themselves held accountable for the opinion. It is not theirs in any meaningful sense. They are no more bound to it than any other judge or Justice, including those who may have dissented. They have no special claim on its meaning. A Justice who dissented may have no trouble subsequently speaking of what "we" did in and through that opinion. Is it, then, the Court that is the author? It is after all "the opinion of the Court." This view is more plausible, but it is not satisfactory. We turned to authorship to understand the surplus of authority with which decisions are received. If we can say nothing more than that the Court is the author, then authorship cannot possibly add anything to the persuasive character of the opinion. The opinion of the Court is better thought of as itself a sort of draft that gains legitimacy when we imagine its author as the people themselves acting as the popular sovereign. The successful opinion does not just persuade us to obey; rather, it persuades us to hold ourselves accountable for the law that it sets forth.

Authorship in Political Practice

Every text constructs an idea of its own narrator. The narrator is not necessarily the author. This is readily apparent in fiction; it remains true even if the fictional text speaks in the first person. Some postmodern literary critics have observed this distinction of narrator from author and concluded that we really don't need to think about authors at all to study texts.[8] To consider the author is to approach the text from the outside—appropriate perhaps if we are studying history or biography. One way in which legal texts are not literary texts is that authorship matters.

While literary critics caution us not to confuse the narrator with the author, certain sorts of texts want us to make precisely this identification. The social practice of reading these texts may go so far as to deny any other possibility of authorship, asserting that there can be no access to the author outside of the text. Religious texts are important examples. If you believe the Bible to be literally the word of God, then you believe the third-person, omniscient narrator of the text to be God the author. Of course, this does not mean that there was no human drafter.[9] Similarly, Muhammad wrote the Qur'an, but he is not its author. He too was scripting the word of God.[10]

Readers of these religious texts don't have these beliefs because they have some sort of independent access to God by which they check to see if he really was the author. Asserting divine authorship reflects a social practice of reading, not a fact independent of the text's narrative. When a Christian reads the Qur'an, he sees the same words as the Muslim, but he is likely to attribute authorship to Muhammad rather than to God. Christian and Muslim do not share in the same practice of reading, that is, of finding meaning in the text, for meaning is constituted in part by locating authorship. To deny God's authorship does not otherwise leave the text alone.

Similarly, legal texts cannot be understood apart from social practices of reading that include an attribution of authorship to the narrator. For us, that narrator/author is We the People. This is a common practice across our legal texts because all have the same problem of legitimacy: each must convey a sense of why it is law *for us*. The construction of the author is a practice of holding ourselves accountable.

Consider the Declaration of Independence. We know as a matter of historical fact that Thomas Jefferson drafted much of the Declaration. If we were writing a biography of Jefferson, we might attribute authorship to him. Doing so, we would hold him accountable for the text as a matter of character, learning, skill, and foresight. We would ask from where he got his ideas and what motivated him to write as he did.[11] We would be curious about where he compromised, for what reasons, and with whom. We would discuss the moral dilemma he faced as an owner of slaves. From the perspective of our political practices, however, Jefferson is not the author of the Declaration. The political meaning of the text does not turn on anything that Jefferson may have thought in the process of drafting. Politically, we do not hold him accountable for this text.

Is it the case, then, that all those who signed the text that Jefferson drafted are its authors? Is it simply a matter of collective authorship? This is not quite right either, for they were acting as representatives of their communities. They could no more declare independence as a collection of individuals than each could do so on his own. They describe themselves as "the Representatives of the united States of America, in General Congress, Assembled."[12] They act "in the Name, and by Authority of the good People of these Colonies."[13] And what they do is "solemnly publish and declare, That these United Colonies are, and of Right ought to be Free and Independent States."[14] The authority they exercise, accordingly, is that of the people of these colonies: only the people could declare themselves free. It is the people who are accountable for this act of authorship: they suffer the burdens and the injuries of the war. If the British had managed to hang every one of the signers for their act of treason, the colonies would be no less free.

Understanding the people as the author allows us to see an important inversion of the relationship we ordinarily conceive between author and text. We think the author precedes the text, that the author brings the text into being. We ask an author, "What are you working on?" But with the Declaration, the text precedes the author. The people who declare through their representatives are not a subject existing in the world prior to their act of collective authorship; they do not first decide and then author a text. They are not to be located on a map or a calendar. The text is successful when it is received as the work of the people. Declaring in their name, this text calls the people into existence. That author exists only as long as belief in the agency of the people is maintained. If we lose that belief, we might come to see this text as authored by a privileged elite who deployed a populist rhetoric to advance their own interests. As long as the belief remains, however, we don't receive the text merely as a gift from a now-dead author. Rather, reading the text we acknowledge authorship.[15] We hold ourselves accountable for this text. In part, accountability means that this text's narrative of revolution is one that we adopt as our own. In part, it means that we are responsible for the continued presence of this text as a part of a political practice. The latter point makes clear that the beliefs at issue are not subjective states of mind. Rather, they are elements of a social practice. A private politics makes no more sense than a private language.[16]

This act of authorial self-creation is inseparable from the text's continual reference to a narrator, "We"—as in "We hold these truths to be self evident."[17] Who is it that holds that "life, liberty and the pursuit of happiness" are "unalienable rights"?[18] Surely this does not refer to the drafters, as if the text were telling us what a particular group of individuals in Philadelphia late in the eighteenth century happened to believe. The text is not recording their beliefs but rather is pronouncing a kind of communal creed. The We, then, is each of us as we read this text together. At that moment, we affirm our political identity as part of this We that narrates the text. *We say this.*

The step from the narrative We to the authorial We the People is blurred in the practice of reading. The We that *holds* becomes the We that *declares.* The rhetorical accomplishment of the text is to lead the reader from holding to declaring: because I believe, I declare. Precisely here we see that the justice of the claims set forth is not irrelevant to the issue of legitimacy. Rather, the arguments from injustice (the king's abuses) contribute to the persuasive character of the text. Someone who believed its claims to be false would likely have remained a loyalist. Today, someone who reads this text and believes its claims to have been false is likely to give a historical explanation of its creation. He will attribute authorship elsewhere than to the people. Of course, such a reader might find other grounds—other texts—through which to identify with the political project of We the People. That he is not persuaded here does not mean that he is not persuaded anywhere.

The same distinctions and connections are at work in the Constitution. We distinguish between what the Constitution says—for example, "nor shall any State . . . deny to any person within its jurisdiction the equal protection of the laws"[19]—and who it is that we hear when reading that text. About the text we can and do ask whether the law it creates is just and fair. Similarly, we argue about whether the institutions it establishes are efficient and democratic. We could have similar arguments about the constitutions of other nations. We pursue projects of comparative constitutionalism with exactly these ambitions. In contrast, our political relationship to the Constitution is not constituted in the first instance by its justice or efficiency. Rather, that relationship arises out of beliefs about authorship.

If we ask who is the author of the Constitution, we are not asking who are its drafters. The drafters met in Philadelphia. They, however, had even less authority than did the signers of the Declaration. The text of the Constitution still had to be approved by special assemblies in each of the states. Nor is it the case that reading the text today we imagine those assemblies of delegates to be the authors. Drafters and delegates were causal conditions of the emergence of this text, but were we to assign authorship to them, we could not easily explain why we continue to be bound by their text. How are they not simply the dead hand of the past? The law they authored might be just, but it is hard to see how it is mine.

Like the Declaration, the text of the Constitution creates a narrator: "We the People . . . do ordain and establish."[20] Prior to ratification, this narrator had no more claim to authorship than the narrator of any fictional text. Any one of us can draft a text that presents itself as if it were written by We the People. Suppose the draft had not been ratified: would anyone attribute authorship to this narrator, despite what the text said? Ratification begins a practice under which we read the narrator as the author. Once again, the authority of the text is linked to our relationship to this collective, transgenerational agent that appears as narrator and author. Because we are authors of this text, it has authority over us. The legitimacy of the Constitution, but not its justice, is located in the maintenance of this practice of reading.

The pattern continues with legislation. We know that legislators don't actually draft the text of legislation, but even if they did, they would not be the authors of the law. They are not the authors because they have authority only as representatives. Indeed, the nature of our federal lawmaking process guarantees that it is difficult to localize authorship in any institution. Congress acts, but then so does the president. Many of the legal rules that actually apply to us are drafted by administrative agencies. Are they the authors? If that is all we see when we ask about authorship, then we are likely to worry about an unconstitutional delegation of legislative authority.[21] We must see through the regulation to the statute and through the statute to its author, who is us.[22]

No less than with the Constitution, we have to distinguish between the causes that bring an ordinary legal text into being and the attribution of authorship. The former is a matter of fact; the latter is a normative, social practice. A drafter is a cause of a text; authorship is a practice of social accountability. Individuals must take certain steps to make the law—including written steps—but that does not make them the authors.[23] They might be voted out of office for what they have done, but holding them electorally accountable has no effect on the way in which we read the law. Individual legislators may disappear from social memory, but the law continues to be our own. This distinction runs so deep that even when legislators are convicted of corruption, of taking bribes for their votes, the law they drafted remains our own.[24]

Because representatives are not the authors, when courts investigate legislative history, individual legislators are never called to testify about their intentions. When there are different intentions expressed in a legislative history, courts do not call the representatives to testify and then make an evidentiary determination of the truth of the matter. Courts do not do so because it is our law, not that of the representatives, no matter how active they were in the drafting or how important their votes were. The point here is not that the meaning of a text may be beyond the control of its author—the reader of a novel may understand it differently than the author. Reading a legal text, we do want to attribute meaning to an author. We do not say it is the reader's reception that creates the meaning of the text. Without the attribution of authorship to the people, the legal text would no longer be part of a project of self-government. When a court investigates legislative history, it ignores individual intentions and looks instead to reasons that the people could adopt as their own—statements of general policy aimed at a public good.

Statutes do not adopt the same narrative voice as the Constitution, "We the People." Legislation does not speak in the first person at all. Rather, the legislative text creates an idea of a third-person, omniscient narrator. Omniscient here does not mean quite the same thing as in fiction, where an omniscient narrator can know the thoughts and feelings of characters. Rather, it means a knowledge of the entire legal order.[25] No one thinks that the same third-person narrator appears in different works of fiction, but in law that is exactly what we think. Every statute has the same narrator, because each is part of the single project of the law.

Reading a statute, we take up the point of view of this third-person, omniscient narrator.[26] This narrator is a purposive, rational agent with a comprehensive view of the entire legal order. Attributing purposiveness to the narrator, we affirm the unity of the entire legal order, for a single narrator cannot intend a contradiction.[27] The narrator is a kind of reification of this unity that our practice of reading finds in the law. This unity of meaning is imagined as a unitary agency; the agent is We the People. We hold ourselves accountable for our law—all of it. Doing so, we move from narrator to author.

A representative—for example, a lawyer, agent, or parent—can act not only for me, but in my place. When I recognize him as my representative, I hold myself accountable for those actions. He exercises my authority and, in some circumstances, I will consider myself the author. In law creation, Congress's role is representational, not authorial. There are many different Congresses, each with a different specific intent responding to the circumstances it faces. The specific intent of a representative makes no difference to the meaning of the act attributed to the represented. My lawyer may be acting for his personal gain or out of hatred of his brother-in-law, but that intent has no bearing on the meaning of the act for which I hold myself accountable.[28] Congress stands in the same relationship to self-authorship by the people. It does not matter what it thought; what matters is what the people did.

Those who cannot see in the law their own self-authorship are outside of the democratic community, even if they have the vote. Conversely, those who cannot vote will believe that they are part of this community if they imagine the law as a product of their own authorship.[29] We are all in this position with respect to that body of law that preceded our entry into the community. An important part of the work of a legal text in a democracy, then, is to persuade us that we are its authors. Self-government begins here, rather than with the vote, which legitimates political acts over a much more limited range—for example, electing a representative or passing on a referendum.[30]

Self-authorship is not simply a matter of looking at the text to see how it constructs a narrator. The text alone does not carry the social practice. We have to consider popular opinion formation, political organization, historical narratives, and circulating ideologies, as well as political rituals. We have to consider what can be said and what cannot be said within different political contexts. To do so is to try to understand the working creed that establishes the boundaries of political belief. Legal texts are produced by, and in turn contribute to the maintenance of, this entire web of practices and belief.[31] For this reason, the study of legal doctrine can never teach more than a part of the law.

Understanding representatives as drafters rather than as authors bears on contested questions of statutory interpretation. Those who purport to be strict textualists in the interpretation of legislation correctly note that the text of a statute is often the result of compromises among representatives acting on behalf of particular interest groups that have contributed in one way or another to their election. They are also correct when they argue that the text alone receives the vote of Congress. There are no congressional votes on committee reports or floor statements. From this they argue that to go beyond the text is to go beyond the legitimate warrant of democratic authority, which arises from the process of electoral accountability. On their view, judges or administrators who stray from the legislative text are taking on to themselves the responsibility for lawmaking, but they lack democratic legitimacy.[32]

If we believe that representatives draft but do not author the law, then we may take quite a different position on the scope of statutory interpretation. On this view, we are no more ruled by legislators than we are by courts. Both must persuade us to see their texts as products of our own self-authorship. The emphasis shifts from bargaining among interest groups to identification of a public purpose. Ronald Dworkin makes a similar point when he speaks of the impermissibility of a "checkerboard statute," by which he means one that distributes a benefit or burden in a manner that could be explained as a political compromise but is arbitrary with respect to any principle capable of public affirmation—for example, imposing a tax on only those whose names begin with a letter in the first half of the alphabet.[33] Such a statute may be rational if we think of legislatures as authors, but it is not something that can be imagined as the product of popular self-authorship.

An elected legislature can come to seem as alien to us as an institution with no electoral accountability. We might think that way, for example, of past legislatures that produced laws that continue in place.[34] We can see those laws as the dead hand of the past. We might experience a similar alienation if we judge the texts a legislature produces to be outrageously unjust. We would speak, then, of electoral failures or social pathologies, but the point would be the same. Whether we continued to comply with the law would depend on political judgments about the likely consequences of resistance. We would, however, be in a potentially revolutionary situation—that is, a situation in which the sovereign people no longer recognize their authorship of the law.

The perspective of self-authorship is not the only framework from within which we understand our institutions of law creation. We are perfectly capable of counting votes and of analyzing historical influences. We can speak of the power of the farm lobby or of Wall Street. This, however, is not what we are doing when we interpret law. That interpretive process is normative in the dimensions of both justice and legitimacy.[35] If I interpret the law to be the product of a bribe, I cannot simultaneously see myself as its author. If I interpret it to be the result of a corrupt, backroom deal between self-interested legislators, I cannot see myself as its author. Only when I interpret the law in light of a public purpose that extends to the entire community can I maintain a belief in self-authorship by the people. That public purpose, in turn, necessarily reflects contemporary ideas of justice. We cannot will injustice upon ourselves.[36] Accordingly, turning to authorship hardly means abandoning questions of justice, although it is not exhausted by these questions.

Today, an element of our perception of justice includes citizen participation in the lawmaking process through free and fair elections. We go wrong when we confuse these participatory elements of a conception of justice with the concept of self-authorship.[37] Most obviously, these participatory elements will not speak to the legitimacy of prior law, including the Constitution. Here too, however, imagining self-authorship is the ground of legitimacy.

That legitimacy rests on self-authorship is an old idea in political theory. Hobbes's idea of sovereign authority was based on this idea: the sovereign represents everyone in the state. He has been authorized to act for them, which means that the citizens are to understand themselves as the authors of his acts: "The Essence of the Common-wealth . . . is *One Person, of whose Acts a great multitude, by mutual Covenants one with another, have made themselves every one the Author.*"[38] To oppose his actions is to contradict oneself. Hobbes speaks of the act of authorization as the "social contract," which has nothing to do with electoral politics, but with the emergence of a political community from the state of nature.

When we speak of representative government today, we have something of the same idea in mind—even if we don't go as far as Hobbes in thinking that everyone is bound "to Own, and be reputed Author of all, that he that already is their Soveraigne, shall do, and judge fit to be done."[39] Making law, representatives act not just in our interest, although we hope they do, but also *in our place*. Representative government, on this view, is to be self-government. If we follow the Hobbesian thought here, we will find ourselves saying something like the authority is our own or, more simply, we govern ourselves through law. When we try to explain why the losing minority in an election is nevertheless bound by the legislation produced by those against whom they voted, we find ourselves appealing to this idea. We don't say that losing an election is like losing a battle: they must subordinate themselves to the victors. Rather, we say that they too are represented by those elected. Because they are represented, they are no less the authors of the law than anybody else. We distinguish between a procedure by which we select representatives (voting) and the nature of the representatives' responsibility to make law. They write, but they do not author. We hold ourselves accountable for what our representatives do, because it is our authority that they exercise.

Hobbes grasped a central truth of the modern state when he wrote that citizens will take up the law as their own as long as they see the sovereign as acting with the authority of the entire body politic. They must see the product of representative government—law—as if they are its author. Contemporary political and legal theorists have considered the procedural conditions under which such an identification with the law is possible. Jürgen Habermas, for example, has focused on public opinion formation as a critical mediation between citizen and law, while Robert Post elaborated the implications of this view for First Amendment law.[40] What these theorists have not done is consider how this need for self-authorship should figure in the construction of the judicial opinion.

We need to explain how the judicial opinion contributes to our social practices of reading the legal order as a product of our own authorship. How do we maintain the capacity to see our own identity in a collective, transtemporal agent that is We the People? The legitimacy of the democratic project as one of self-government depends not just on elections but on this broader and deeper idea of popular sovereignty. The judicial opinion is precisely the place where we can see how this idea of authorship is constructed and maintained through the narrative voice.

Marbury v. Madison: *The Voice of the People*

If asked, most Americans would no doubt say that the basis of governmental legitimacy is some sort of democratic credential. They are thinking of elections. We certainly measure other nations by their electoral practices. We believe that authoritarian regimes are in need of democratic reform. At every level of government—national, state, and local—we practice a politics organized around periodic elections. But most judges are not elected. Even if we thought the judicial appointment process provides some indirect democratic legitimacy for judges, surely that is not enough to ground a lifetime appointment. No reputable democratic system would elect officials for life; periodic review by the voters is just as important as the initial choice.[41]

Judges are not the only unelected officials in a democratic state. No one elects military officers, heads of administrative departments, or civil servants. These other officials, however, are ordinarily subject to supervision, direct or indirect, by elected officials. The more important a role that an official plays in setting policies, practices, and norms, the more we expect some sort of electoral check. This is the reason the president is also the commander in chief. Yet, the most controversial issues regularly end up before the courts. Their decisions, especially in constitutional cases, are not easily subject to an electoral check.

One response of academics has been to try to reassure us that it is not as bad as it looks. Democratic politics, they argue, is there, but we must learn where to look. Some try to locate that democratic element in the appointments process; others in the pressures on judges to "mind the polls." For the former, there is generally enough judicial turnover to keep courts in synch with changing political sentiments.[42] For the latter, the judges' own sense of vulnerability to public opinion is enough.[43] Neither suggestion is very persuasive. First, modern judges tend to serve a very long time. Second, while opinion polls allow judges to track public support, most of the issues judges decide are not going to affect the polls one way or the other. Only rarely does a case appear that could potentially have such an impact. *Bush v. Gore* may have been one; *National Federation of Independent Business v. Sebelius*, the Obama health care case, another.[44] There were, however, twelve years between the two.

Some academics turn from elections to the personal qualifications of the judges. No one—least of all the judges themselves—seriously argues that it is the wisdom and moral character of judges that makes elections unnecessary.[45] Some scholars do argue that judges bring to bear professional habits of deliberation and a commitment to fair procedures independent of their individual preferences.[46] Appointed to a jury, you will do your best to decide the case under the law; you will not consider the interests of yourself or your friends. Judges, no doubt, do the same. Still, you don't get appointed to a jury because of your beliefs and political attachments. That, however, is often the path to a judicial nomination.

We find a curious juxtaposition of politics and law in the process of appointment, which for the more important judicial posts has become a highly ritualized affair. Essential to the ritual is a denial of the obviously political character of the process. Participants do not speak in partisan tones. Respect is given to an idea of law as a professional field of knowledge apart from politics. A nominee, nevertheless, knows that she has been selected for partisan, political reasons. She also knows that regardless of the apolitical language expressed by everyone involved, the disputes over a nomination are rooted in political disagreements over the meaning of law.

The confirmation process is a sort of rite of passage, ending when the new judge puts on the black robes.[47] The judge is never again to participate directly in that political world. If we nevertheless say that the courts are "political," we mean something other than that they operate alongside the partisan institutions of government.[48] While we regularly appraise judicial outcomes along a political scale ranging from conservative to liberal, we don't think that judges formulate their positions by consulting with party operatives or sitting politicians. Judges don't call the White House or the governor's office.

The ritual of the confirmation process puts on display the need to move from politics to law. To use a religious analogy, the judge who emerges has been "born again," leaving behind her prior life as a political actor. The courtroom too has rituals that signal an order of law, not politics, for those who are present. For most of us, however, the weight of this transition has to be carried by the opinion. Reading the opinion for the court, we are not to hear the particular judge with his or her personal history of partisan, political participation. We are not to hear the voice of a particular judge at all, whether it is that of the drafter of the opinion or that of the swing vote.[49] We are, instead, to hear ourselves as popular sovereign. To see how the opinion accomplishes this shift from narrator to author, we need to return to the origins of judicial review in *Marbury v. Madison*.[50]

In no case, not even *Bush v. Gore*, has the brute political reality of factional contest been more at issue than in *Marbury*, which arose in the aftermath of the bitter election of 1800 between Thomas Jefferson and the incumbent, President John Adams. This was the first real party conflict in American history, pitting Federalists against Republicans. The election was thrown into the House when Jefferson and his running mate, Aaron Burr, tied in electoral college votes.[51] It took the House some thirty-six votes before it settled on Jefferson. *Marbury* arises against the background of this electoral contest between the outgoing Federalists and the incoming Republicans.

Marbury seeks an order from the Supreme Court directing Madison, President Jefferson's secretary of state, to deliver to him the commission, signed by President Adams, making him a justice of the peace in the District of Columbia.

Consider Chief Justice John Marshall himself. Marshall served as John Adams's secretary of state right up to the end of his administration. Indeed, he continued in that role even after he was appointed Chief Justice in the last months of Adams's term. Among other things, that means that all the talk in the opinion about the signing of the commission and the circumstances of the failure of delivery of the commission directly involved Marshall himself. He was the official who applied the Great Seal of the United States to the commission; he was the figure responsible for filing and delivery.

It gets worse. Marbury was appointed a justice of the peace in the final days—and even hours—of the Adams administration. His was one of numerous judicial positions created by the holdover Federalist Congress in the period between the November election and Jefferson's taking the oath of office. The whole point of these appointments was to create a number of sinecures to which Federalist operatives could retreat after losing the election, in order to harass the incoming Republican administration. It is no accident that the statute creating the new position of justice of the peace established a five-year term of office.

Not only justices of the peace, but federal circuit court judgeships were at stake, for that same holdover Congress had significantly expanded the federal bench. These positions too were all filled by Adams on his way out: the "midnight appointees." And then there was Chief Justice Marshall himself, also appointed after the election, the most prominent of all of these last-minute, partisan, judicial appointments. Strikingly, when Jefferson and the Republicans took office in 1801, there was not a single Republican on the federal bench.

Jefferson had targeted federal judges in his campaign for president. He argued that they had abandoned the meaning of the Revolution by applying English common law, as if independence did not mean a new beginning in law as well as politics. Worse, federal judges were doing the work of Federalist politics by applying the Alien and Sedition Acts against their Republican opponents—particularly against Republican newspaper editors. When Jefferson called his election the "Second American Revolution," he had in mind taking the government back from the courts, which were working to undermine the significance of the first American Revolution. The Federalist effort to pack the courts after the election made Jefferson's point only that much stronger.[52]

With Adams so explicitly politicizing the courts, why should the new president respect these last-minute appointments? Why not get rid of the lot of them, which is indeed what Jefferson tried to do? He adopted a variety of strategies for the different sorts of judicial appointees. He managed congressional repeal of the Circuit Courts Act, which had created the new federal appellate judges appointed by Adams. He targeted some judges, including one Justice, for impeachment. He refused to deliver the commissions that remained in the office of the secretary of state—Marbury's problem. Where he could not get rid of the judges, he harassed them. Supreme Court Justices were again required to take on the onerous task of riding circuit. Even more pointedly, the new Republican Congress passed a law simply cancelling the next two terms of the Supreme Court's sittings. Where he could do nothing else, he ignored them. Thus, when Marbury filed his lawsuit against Secretary of State Madison, no one from the administration bothered to show up. They would not dignify this process with the appearance of law.

Marbury blocks from our vision all of these political machinations. Jefferson's "Second American Revolution" does not even appear in the opinion. Events—the failure of delivery—are stripped of their political context, as are legal structures—the five-year term. Without the help of a history textbook, we could not read the opinion and learn anything about the political contest out of which the case emerged. We are told that Madison never appeared, but we are not told why. We do not see the actual officeholders, only the offices. This is true not only of the executive branch but also of the Justices themselves. Because we do not see the officeholders, we are never told that the secretary of state and the Chief Justice were the same person. We are told of actions by the president but not that the holder of that office changed between the moment of signing the commission and that of the refusal to deliver it.

Marbury is an early expression of what was to become the conventional American legal imagination. This is as much a matter of not seeing as it is of seeing. We are not to see the midnight appointments; we are not to see an election fought over judicial role; we are not to see Jefferson or Marshall at all. Both disappear: one into the "presidency," the other into "the opinion of the Court." Instead of the historian's account of politicians acting for partisan ends, we see offices, causes of action, and remedies; instead of a political power to act, we see jurisdiction or a lack of jurisdiction.

The *Marbury* opinion is full of the language of appearance, but the Court insists that the Constitution be viewed with open eyes:

> Those, then, who controvert the principle, that the constitution is to be considered, in court, as a paramount law, are reduced to the necessity of maintaining that courts must close their eyes on the constitution, and see only the law [passed by Congress]. This doctrine would subvert the very foundation of all written constitutions.[53]

Not just the Justices, but we, the citizen-readers, are to look at the Constitution. Following the Court's gaze, we are no longer to see the Justices as authors of the text that is the opinion. Instead, we are to see only the object of our mutual attention: the Constitution. Thus, Marshall does not appear as the author of the opinion; it is not his. Instead, he "delivers" the opinion of the Court. Delivery here refers to a literal act of narration, for the Justice read the text from the bench. The failure of delivery of Marbury's commission is matched by the successful delivery of the opinion. Both texts—commission and opinion—are not the law but evidence of law.

The commission, *Marbury* tells us, is not itself empowering, as if possession of the commission created the office of justice of the peace. Possession may be nine-tenths of the law, but not in this case. The commission attests to, is evidence of, an authorial act. The act that makes Marbury a justice of the peace is wholly that of the president, not of the man who happens to be president. Thus Jefferson cannot revoke Marbury's commission, even though he is now president. The actual person—Jefferson—is completely effaced when the opinion states that since the president "cannot lawfully forbid" this act of delivery of the commission, he is "therefore . . . never presumed to have forbidden [it]."[54] In short, it does not matter what Jefferson has actually done, for the opinion sees a world of law, not politics. In that world, Marbury is a justice of the peace regardless of a political reality that will prevent him from ever acting in that role.

The Court's opinion has a structure parallel to that of Marbury's commission. The text does not claim any power for the individual justices. They have no authorial power. A Justice cannot change his mind and revoke an opinion. He cannot do so even if he was the critical fifth vote. The opinion, like the commission, points beyond itself to a source of authority. The judicial opinion is not authority but evidence of authority. The opinion presents itself as an interpretation of the law. Formally, we can say that the Justices claim no discretion for themselves; they are not acting but only looking at the law. *Marbury* never speaks of choice but only of what is necessary.

The Justices, accordingly, exercise no responsibility for governance that requires evaluation of the circumstances and a choice for the public good. The opinion would have us believe that the Court does not exercise a collective judgment to decide what the law should be. Rather, it tells us only what the law is. This collapse of the normative into the descriptive is a critical feature of the opinion's voice. *Marbury* sets forth what rights have already "vested."[55]

A classical Greek idea can help us to understand what is going on here. Plato, in his famous divided line, distinguishes among levels of understanding.[56] Knowledge, he argues, is necessarily of the truth. We cannot have knowledge of something that is false. If we think we know something that is, in fact, false, we don't have knowledge but error. Below knowledge stands what Plato terms "doxa," which we translate as "opinion." I can have opinions about many things, which may or may not be true. What then is the object of an opinion? In Plato's scheme, the object of an opinion is a kind of image of the truth. Images can be better or worse. This is a good way to understand the opinion of the Court: it offers an image of the truth. Today, we would call it a representation. As a representation, it never claims the authority to make law but only to make clear to us what the law already is. If the opinion is a representation, then the law itself stands apart from the judicial text: it is that toward which the opinion points. If we fail to see the through the opinion to the law, then we will think that the Court is itself authoring the law.[57]

The judicial opinion is delivered to us as if it were the image created by the written text of the law. The opinion offers the reader a way of standing with the Court as it looks to the law—in this case to the Constitution. Thus, the opinion is not itself the authority of the law but an image of that authority, which always lies elsewhere. The opinion, accordingly, is persuasive just to the degree that it does not appear at all. As soon as we see the opinion as the authored act of the Justices, we will ask with what authority they rule in our democratic polity. There is no answer to that question, for they have no such authority.

The most successful opinion is one that is completely transparent to another text. The opinion's role is only to make us see better that authoritative text. Drawing an analogy to interpretation of the Bible can again help us. A biblical interpretation has no authority in itself but only insofar as it makes us see better the biblical text. Of course, one interpretation can place itself in relationship to another; it can build on it or distinguish itself from it. Not every interpretation begins from the authoritative text itself. Yet, the interpretation fails if we come to privilege it over that of which it is an interpretation.[58] Structurally, every interpretation is subject to this vulnerability. Someone can always accuse the interpreter of mistaking the image for the truth, the interpretation for the authoritative text. This is just the form of criticism to which courts are always subject: judges are accused of falling into the trap of taking their own text as if it were authoritative and not just a representation. When that happens, the court is "making" law rather than representing the law. The court has no more authority to make law than the biblical commentator has to create the holy word.

It is easy to confuse this position with a formal textualism. Indeed *Marbury* gestures in this direction when it tells us that we need only to open our eyes to the constitutional text. Recognizing the opinion as an image—a representation—has nothing, however, to do with textualism. The idea of representation does not tell us anything about the nature of that which is represented; it does not tell us anything about the usefulness of prior interpretations—precedents—in understanding the law. We might think the law itself evolves over time or that it is located in changeless moral principles; we might think the true Constitution is an unwritten text.[59] The burden of the opinion is to persuade us that its representation does indeed convey to us what the law is. It fails if we see the opinion as only an expression of the Justices' opinions. Such a failure is just as possible for the textualist judge, for we can easily believe that textualism is only his opinion.

Near the end of *Marbury*, we read that ours is a nation in which the written Constitution has always been viewed "with so much reverence."[60] That reverence is to shine through the opinion. The only way to accomplish this is to offer a writing that is transparent, that puts into plain view the Constitution. The opinion is full of the language of looking and seeing. The opinion is an appearance, but the Constitution is the thing itself. Thus, *Marbury* states that the Constitution is written in order that the law that it creates "may not be mistaken or forgotten." The opinion of the Court is only a sort of reminder. It is, again, a "delivery" bringing the Constitution back into our field of vision.

Marbury can be likened to a great magic act. The trick of the opinion is to make its drafter disappear, leaving us staring at the Constitution—or, more accurately, persuading us that we are staring at the Constitution. We will think this only as long as we fail to see Chief Justice Marshall locked in a political battle with President Jefferson. The opinion must speak in a way in which we no longer hear

Federalist or Republican voices. Ironically, Marshall follows Jefferson's lead from his inaugural address where he proclaimed:

> We are all Republicans, we are all Federalists. . . . I believe this . . . the strongest Government on Earth. I believe it the only one where every man, at the call of the law, would fly to the standard of the law, and would meet invasions of the public order as his own personal concern.[61]

The Court effectively takes this language as its own. Its voice is to be "the call of the law," and it speaks to all citizens in a way that is beyond their partisan identity. Its opinion is to be "the standard of law." Not the law itself, but a representation of the law that always stands outside of or beyond the opinion. Like the standard on the battlefield, the opinion is a flag or sign of national identity.

The text of the opinion is, then, only an image of another text: the Constitution. When you read a successful opinion, you come away persuaded that you now understand the Constitution. The opinion has only helped you to see the Constitution better. If you are not persuaded, then you go away wondering what the court was up to. As soon as you shift your attention to the judges, the opinion has failed in its legal task, for judges can never claim authority for themselves. If you are counting votes, then you are not reading. And if you are not reading, law has become simply a continuation of politics by other means—exactly Jefferson's view of what his cousin, John Marshall, was up to.

To understand why *Marbury* still persuades, we have to return to the question from which we began. If Marshall is not the author of the opinion, who is? It is not enough to say "the Court," for the opinion works hard to suppress this idea of authorship as well. We are not to hear the Court speaking to us—that is the whole point of the visual metaphors deployed in the opinion, of the idea that we are to look through the opinion's text to see the Constitution. If what we see is the Constitution, then the author of the opinion merges with the author of the Constitution. *Marbury* works this transition through a kind of play on the word "opinion." At the critical juncture, in which the opinion is explaining the very nature of constitutional government, it offers the following: "That the people have an original right to establish, for their future government, such principles as, in their *opinion*, shall most conduce to their own happiness, is the basis on which the whole American fabric has been erected."[62] We are at the imaginative foundation of the whole fabric that is the American idea of the rule of law. The opinion of the Court is nothing less than the opinion of the people. The people are the author of both opinions because there is to be no gap between them. That is the sole source of authority for the government. Between the opinion of the people and the Constitution there is only an act of will, "a very great exertion" by the people themselves.[63] There is no other measure of legitimacy; no test of right reason, or, for that matter, of divine reason.

The opinion would persuade us that the author of the constitutional text is the people exercising their original right to rule themselves. Reading this judicial text, then, we are to hear the voice of the people willing their own continued presence. As long as we believe this, we will continue to view the Constitution with reverence. We are not bound by the dead white men who drafted the Constitution; we are not bound by the Justices. Rather, we are bound by the people. The people, however, is us. This belief in membership in a collective, transgenerational agent is at the foundation of the whole. This is why the Supreme Court can tell us that Bush is the president of the United States and we accept it.

Does Marshall win his battle with Jefferson? There is no simple answer. Jefferson goes on to eight successful years as president. He strengthens the populist element of our national political life, which certainly remains strong. But Marshall sets forth an imaginative framework of the meaning of America, which is not just about democratic majorities but about the rule of law. He creates the role for the Court, which continues to this day. Even today, when the Court confronts the most difficult of issues, we are likely to see their opinions returning to *Marbury v. Madison* as the foundation for the judicial role. That role is to write, but not to author, opinions. The authority to author remains with the people.[64]

What about Statutory Interpretation?

You may be willing to listen to the music of *Marbury* but still wonder what this has to do with opinions that focus on statutory, rather than constitutional, issues. One might believe that the Constitution was authored by "We the People" but also know that statutes have their origin in hard bargaining among interest groups. Not all politics is constitutional politics, and not all law is constitutional law.[65] If that is so, can this idea of popular self-authorship help us to understand the judicial opinion in cases of statutory interpretation?

A modest reformulation of what it means for a court to declare a statute unconstitutional suggests that there is good reason to pursue this line of thought. We imagine courts making sure that the legislature does not exceed constitutional limits. Courts exercise a sort of policing function to keep the legislature within constitutional borders. The appeal is to spatial imagery, as if a legislature operated within a bordered domain. At least with respect to federal statutes, however, we can learn more by focusing again on the idea of self-authorship.[66] When a court declares a statute unconstitutional, the opinion seeks to persuade us that we cannot simultaneously imagine ourselves as authors of the Constitution and of the statute.

This recharacterization sets a direction for thinking about statutory interpretation even in cases in which no constitutional issue arises. Democratic legitimacy is no less at issue in reading a statute. We are not "sometime democrats." A proper judicial reading, accordingly, works toward the end of persuading us that we, the sovereign people, are the authors of the statute. The opinion must show us the reach and character of our own will.

Democratic legitimacy is not something that precedes the work of interpretation. As I explained above, the election of legislators does not guarantee that legislation will not represent "majority tyranny" or powerful special interests. In the absence of a public purpose, the people cannot see such laws as the product of their own authorship. In such cases, we say that there has been a failure of representation: the public cannot hold itself accountable for such laws. A democratic interpretation, accordingly, cannot simply point to election results. Rather, it reads the statute in such a way as to persuade us of our own authorship. Reading the opinion, we are to understand what we have done, not what was done to us.

Courts have no other rhetorical technique for accomplishing this than to persuade us that we are hearing ourselves when we listen to the opinion. The opinion represents the law to us. If we read it as telling us what the judges think, then we will see them as the authors. Their voice will have occluded our voice. For this reason, the contemporary debate over statutory interpretation replays the same fears of judicial activism that we saw in the debate over constitutional interpretation.[67] Here too a court's task is to offer a reading of a legal text that does not draw upon the preferences, norms, and beliefs of the individual judges. The judge cannot assume the authorial voice without inviting the accusation that she is making law. A judge has no more authority to author statutes than to author the Constitution. The controversy in statutory interpretation has been over how best to represent the meaning of a statute without crossing the line into judicial authorship.

The techniques of statutory construction are means to accomplish a coincidence of voice between narrator of the opinion and the author of the statute. Thus, the opinion presents itself as the space within which the meaning of the statute clearly appears. The narrator is to say nothing that the author would not acknowledge as its own.[68] We easily fall into a pattern of thought under which the ideal opinion would simply set forth the text of the statute, followed by the word "see!" If this is the ideal, then everything beyond "just looking" is the result of a failure of the author of the statutory text to speak clearly. The work of the opinion must be remedial: to render in the text of the opinion that which is missing from the text of the statute. The opinion's text becomes a representation of the statutory text. Standing in its place, it has the same author.

The opinion is a "speaking for" that makes no claim to legitimacy apart from the original authorial voice. We are to come away understanding the statute better; we now see what it is trying to do. The authority on display is that of the people to govern themselves, not that of a court to add to or subtract from law. After the decision, when we ask what the statute means we read the opinion in place of the legislative text. We are not free to "prefer" the original. Thus, the ambition of the opinion is to persuade us that we are not hearing the voice of the judge, but rather we are hearing more clearly the people as author of the statute.

To understand the opinion, therefore, we have to ask what are the conditions under which we can maintain the belief in popular self-authorship of statutes. These conditions are not so different from those that make it possible for us to understand ourselves as authors of the Constitution. In both cases, we imagine a transgenerational, collective subject with a temporal extension that fills the past and future of the nation. It includes the dead, the living, and the not yet living. This is not a universal subject or an abstraction. It is rather a collective subject with a unique history and a particular future. This collective subject acts only to advance a public purpose, which is to say it acts with a belief in the public good. That public purpose must make sense in light of a contemporary morality and a common set of expectations about the public interest.

A successful opinion represents the statute as the product of this author. Thus, there is much that cannot be said in an opinion, even though we might know it otherwise to be true, and even though we might appeal to this knowledge in other contexts. The opinion rarely speaks of a statute as if it were the product of successful action by the farm lobby, the oil industry, or any other special interest.[69] The opinion rarely speaks of deals cut, contributions made, promises of support, or threats of political retaliation. All of these factors may be causes of the laws coming into being, but they do not represent actions by the author of the law.

Just as authorship of law is not seen from the perspective of the individual motives of those who happen to be involved in that process—whether officials or lobbyists—opinions do not report on the judge's own decision-making process. An opinion does not explain how a judge happened to come to his or her beliefs. Judges don't use the occasion to talk about the evolution of their particular opinions; they don't look back across all of their judicial work and explain how it all makes sense from their point of view.[70] We don't hear about the works in philosophy, political science, economics, or religion that have had an influence upon the judge. This is no more appropriate than writing of political affiliation or party platforms. Any such references would cause us to think of the judge as the author.

No one would deny that all of these matters influence a judge's actions and beliefs, just as no one would deny that lobbyists and interest groups influence the legislative process. If we were to write a biography of a judge, these are just the sort of things that we would want to investigate. They don't appear in the judicial opinion, because the persuasive character of the opinion hinges on its ability to attribute authorship elsewhere. We are not to hear the judge's voice but only that of the lawmaking power, which is the people as popular sovereign.

The successful opinion does not interpose itself between the reader and the statute. Its aim is to be transparent to the statute. We are not to stumble over the words of the opinion on our way to the statute. Rather, the text of the opinion must keep the statute before the reader.[71] If we were to conclude that the text of the opinion and the text of the statute could not have the same author, then the opinion fails. The authority to which both texts refer is that of the people.

Neither a judge nor a legislator can claim personal authority; neither can say that he exercised power for his own sake. Both labor under an obligation to represent the same collective subject: the people authoring their own law. At stake again is the threefold identification of the narrator of the opinion, the author of the statute, and the reader. As I explained above, this threefold identification does not work the same way in the constitutional case as in the statutory case. In the latter case, the people appear in the form of the third-person omniscient narrator—no longer the first-person plural of the

Constitution. This third-person narrator represents the popular sovereign as the background condition of a democratic state.

Think of the distinction this way. You can look back at actions that you took deliberately. They stand out in your memory because they mark important turning points in your life. You think, "I did that." That is, you think of yourself in the first person. But you can also call to mind the whole of your life: the things that are memorable and those that are not. When you attribute the whole course of events to yourself, you are imagining yourself not from inside the decision but from the outside, just as someone else might see you. You may come to know much about yourself from others. About these events too you hold yourself accountable; you are their author. They too express who you are, even if you did not engage in a process of decision that stayed with you after the event. When, for example, you look at old pictures, you acknowledge yourself even if you have no independent memory of the events. The distinction here is that between a first-person and a third-person account of the self.

About the collective subject too we say something similar. We authored the Constitution; we acknowledge authorship of statutes. The statute must be seen as our own, but we see ourselves from a third-person point of view. If we cannot attain this position of authorship, we will experience the law as something done to us.

Self-authorship imposes a number of positive demands upon an opinion interpreting a statute. Most important, a public purpose must be attributed to the statute. One cannot hold oneself accountable for an unintelligible act, but an act only gains intelligibility when it is seen from the perspective of a purpose. Stripped of a purpose an act is only an event with a cause, just like other events in the natural order. When we cannot attribute a public purpose to legislation, we explain it in terms of causes: the farm lobby or campaign contributions. About such a statute, we might say it is "an abuse" of the legislation process; it is not something we have done.

Just as a legislative act is not an event, it is not an abstract expression of beliefs. A proof is not an act. A statute is trying to do something, not prove something. Thus, a statute is not just a norm that appears as if from nowhere. Statutes are authored; they are not simply statements of natural law. Justice Holmes famously made a similar point about authorship even with respect to the common law: "The common law is not a brooding omnipresence in the sky, but the articulate voice of some sovereign or quasi sovereign that can be identified."[72]

Authorship requires unity of purpose, even for a collective subject. A single author can have multiple, but not inconsistent, purposes. This is a substantive, not a formal, point. A single piece of legislation might have a number of different purposes; it could have been passed as multiple Acts. Collective authorship fails only if the ends undermine each other. Authorship thus brings with it requirements of rational coherence and consistency, although not completeness. A statute might address only a part of a problem; it might envision multiple steps. There is nothing irrational or inconsistent about proceeding one step at a time.

These are minimal requirements, but the same demand for self-authorship will take us considerably further. The third-person point of view constructs the agency of a community defined by membership and belief across time and space. The popular sovereign has a history of action and belief, as well as a territorial locus.[73] Without this, we could not identify with this agent. Accordingly, the opinion must read the statute as if it were the product of a single agent with a comprehensive awareness of community norms and membership. The author of a statute always "knows" the nation's past history of authoring law.

If we are to see ourselves as author, the substantive norms held forth in the opinion must be ones that we can see as our own. Accordingly, the text of the statute must be read in light of our common beliefs with respect to the norms of justice, dignity, liberty, and autonomy that inform our politics. Ordinarily we cannot simultaneously see an act as unjust and ourselves as its author. We can in the exceptional case, but then we need to be offered some sort of excuse: for example, necessity or mistake.

These abstract values are themselves the subject of considerable interpretive dispute. For that reason, merely citing them will not resolve disagreement over the meaning of a statute. An opinion must convince us that this is the right way to see the values at stake—right, at least, under the circumstances. It makes that argument to us, which means that it must begin with the practices and beliefs that we actually have.[74] An opinion is usually not trying to persuade us to change our minds about the meaning of particular norms, but trying to show us how a statute has given order to the multiple values that are at issue in a case.

The opinion must offer a reading of the statute that allows us to see that the author's purpose was to realize some conception of these values, and that this conception is "close enough" to our own that we can share in this authorial intent. An opinion that spoke, for example, of a conception of justice founded on patriarchy would not be persuasive. Even if we thought that the judges were doing an adequate job of expressing the intent of the actual legislators, about such legislators we would ask what gives them the legitimate authority to rule us.[75] If it were recent legislation, we would offer accounts of the pathologies of contemporary politics that allowed capture of the democratic process by unrepresentative elements who are seeking to advance their own factional interests and values. We could not take authorship of such legislation.

What we might do about such pathology is another question. We might very well come to think that the problem is with the court, for its role is not simply to present what certain legislators thought but to present the statute in such a way that we can see it as our own. This can require going considerably beyond the statutory text and beyond the record of the beliefs of particular legislators. The right reading is not one that is "true to the text," as if the text simply makes an objective demand on the reader. The right reading is one that accomplishes the political function of sustaining the democratic project, which rests on belief in the self-authorship of law.

When no such reading consistent with self-authorship is available, then the work of the courts is to demonstrate the illegitimacy of the statute.[76] We are not the authors of that law; that text offers only a false representation of law. In that case, we may indeed believe the law to have been authored by an elected legislature, but that is only another way of saying it was not authored by us. Some elementary doctrines of constitutional law further just this sort of reading. Thus, any law or regulatory act must pass a minimal, due process standard of rationality. A law that is arbitrary cannot be seen as the product of that single collective author that is the people. An arbitrary law is not one without any purpose; rather, it is one without a *public* purpose. It is a rare case that fails this test, but the point is important, for it tells us that pluralist politics alone are not constitutionally adequate politics.[77] The legislative process is not necessarily due process because by itself it does not guarantee that we can read a statutory text as the product of our own self-authorship.

To focus on self-authorship gives us a new way of understanding what is at stake in many of the formal canons of statutory construction—for example, the presumption in favor of the ordinary meanings of terms,[78] the effort to read a statute as a coherent and consistent whole,[79] the presumption of continuity in the law and against implied repeals,[80] and the presumption that while legislative history can confirm the meaning of a text, it cannot displace the plain meaning of that text.[81] The last point, in particular, suggests that the subjective intention of individual legislators—or even all of them—is not the point of judicial interpretation. Rather, the point is to construct the objective purpose of the statute. If we ask whose purpose it is, the answer points to the collective agent that is the people. The opinion is to show us what we are doing in and through the statute—not what is being done to us.

The same idea of self-authorship is apparent when we look to the substantive canons of statutory interpretation. Their aim is to support an interpretation such that the statute can be seen as coherently authored by the same agent who authored the general order of our law, including constitutional and common-law norms.[82] Since the underlying issue is to imagine collective agency, the rules of statutory construction do not just preclude constitutional contradiction but also direct courts to steer clear of close cases.[83] Coherence of purpose does not have sharp lines but gradual frontiers where coherence may be strained even if not broken.

The substantive norms that inform the canons also include presumptions about due process and equality, which are taken as central to the American project. In part, these are constitutional norms, but in part they are common-law norms. Thus, the canons urge adherence to the common law, unless the statute explicitly rejects such norms.[84] The same point can be made about large principles of government structure—for example, federalism and separation of powers.[85] While these are constitutional norms, their reach in statutory construction goes further. The opinion's ambition is not to show us this structure as a set of limits that the courts apply. Rather, using these canons, the opinion shows us the statutory arrangement of power as a form of self-organization. The statute is interpreted in a way that affirms this structure. We are not "changing our minds" when we write a statute. Rather, we are again expressing ourselves.

A typical case of statutory construction illustrates how some of these rules work to sustain an idea of self-authorship. Consider *Babbitt v. Sweet Home*, which involved a provision of the Endangered Species Act that made it illegal for any person "to take" any endangered or threatened species.[86] The statutory definition of "take" included the word "harm," and the secretary of the interior issued a regulation that prohibited "habitat modification or degradation," even on private property, when it "actually kills or injures wildlife." The question was whether the statutory prohibition on taking could support the regulation's prohibition on habitat modification: was the regulation implementing or rewriting the statute? The Court, over a vigorous dissent, upheld the regulation.

The opinion goes to some effort to suggest that it is directing its attention solely to the statutory text: "The text of the Act provides three reasons for concluding that the Secretary's interpretation is reasonable."[87] The first of these reasons appeals to the ordinary, common understanding of the word harm, as set forth in dictionary definitions. Choosing among these definitions, the opinion expresses a reluctance to adopt a reading of harm that would render the word "surplusage," that is, to read it as failing to add anything beyond the other elements of the statutory definition of the word "take."[88] Surplusage avoidance has nothing to do with what individual members of the legislature might have intended: they might have repeated themselves for emphasis or out of carelessness or confusion. Rather, it is about how we imagine the author of the statutory text. The no surplusage rule suggests an omniscient author who makes no mistakes. Interestingly, this same perfect author, who never engages in surplusage, appears in *Marbury*'s interpretation of the constitutional grant of original jurisdiction to the Supreme Court.

From dictionaries, the opinion goes on to consider "the broad purposes" of the statute. The main source that the opinion brings to bear in determining this purpose is its own precedent, *TVA v. Hill*.[89] *Hill* was the famous snail darter case, which described the Endangered Species Act as "the most comprehensive legislation for the preservation of endangered species ever enacted by any nation."[90] Notice the shift in the attribution of authorship that accompanies the broadening of purpose. The "nation," not a legislative majority, enacted the statute: we did this. Broader still, the nation was acting on a world stage. We are to see ourselves as others see us. We see ourselves being seen, and we take responsibility for what is seen. It is our law, not Congress's, and we must all hold ourselves accountable.

The final element in the *Sweet Home*'s interpretation of the Endangered Species Act focuses on a permit provision that Congress added in a subsequent amendment. That permitting provision, the opinion tells us, makes sense only if harm is read in the manner that the controverted regulation assumes. The argument assumes that the subsequent Congress drafts in a manner consistent with the original purpose of the statute. The amending Congress is not simply adding on a new element. Rather, the entire act constitutes a single, coherent project. The opinion's expression of the purpose of the statute is to make sense of all of its provisions, understood horizontally (across the whole act) and vertically (across the various temporally distinct interventions).

Only after the interpretation is complete does the opinion go on to discuss legislative history. It shows that the secretary's reading is in accord with some particular statements of intent expressed on the floor. This is not a favored source of interpretation precisely because it turns our attention away from self-authorship, as if the particular acts of will of these individual representatives are themselves constitutive of the meaning of the statute.

When we look to the overall structure of the opinion, we see a progression from reader to author that reminds us of *Marbury*. We begin as the ordinary reader: the dictionary stands for this reader who is a sort of passive recipient of the law. That reader rapidly assumes her place as a part of the sovereign people, as we observe the nation acting and being seen in the world. Finally, sovereign agency to create law enters time as the history of the nation itself. We are a part of a single historical project. The opinion is filling out for us the meaning of our third-person point of view on the collective agent that is the people. Reading the opinion, we are led out of our ordinary selves as recipients of law and come to see ourselves as authors of our law.

Conclusion: Charismatic Courts

The argument of *Marbury* does not lack reason. Nevertheless, we misunderstand the stakes if we ask whether the conclusion follows logically from the premises. Taking that perspective, we would question whether the opinion "cheats" by delaying the discussion of jurisdiction until the end; whether it misreads section 13 of the 1789 Judiciary Act; and whether a failure to pursue judicial review would really render the idea of a written constitution "an absurdity."[91] Each of these questions could easily be answered in the opposite way from that presented in the opinion. The formal reasoning of *Marbury* simply cannot carry the weight of the opinion. It is not so different in this respect from the ordinary work of the courts. Opinions don't offer proofs. There is almost always much about which we can disagree. The dissents are there to remind us of these disagreements.[92]

If it is not the argument, what is it about *Marbury* and countless other opinions that persuades us? The answer lies, at least in part, in the relationship between the narrative voice and the authorial voice. We can use a term from modern sociology to get a better grasp of this phenomenon. The judicial voice aims to speak not with the abstraction of reason but with the fullness of charismatic presence. Charisma originally meant "divine gift."[93] Max Weber took this idea of the "gifted" individual and developed a sociological category of authority that he deliberately set against traditional and bureaucratic authority.[94] Since Weber's time, "charisma" has become a term of popular psychology, applied as much to rock stars as to political leaders. I want to emphasize the original sense of the word.

One who has charisma stands between the sacred and the profane.[95] In Christian terms, he has received the gift of God's grace. While not himself divine, he is a locus of the showing forth of the sacred. "Gift" seems just the right word, for it draws our attention to the relationship between the giver and the receiver.[96] Once again, we confront a sort of delivery. This is a gift that can only be received by those who share a faith: grace does not appear to the nonbeliever.[97] To the nonbeliever, the Eucharist remains a wafer and the wine remains only a drink. To this we can add that to the nonbeliever the judicial opinion looks like a text authored by a particular person who happens to be a judge.

Weber was interested in drawing broad categories of social organization. He constructed the category of charismatic authority to stand in opposition to an order of law with its bureaucratic reasoning and its appeals to tradition, including precedents. Yet, when we turn to American practice, we find judges maintaining a relationship of reciprocal support between the transcendent authority of the people and the legal order as an ongoing social practice. The persuasive character of the opinion points to the charismatic quality of the court that speaks in the voice of the author of the law: the people. This judicial charisma—unlike Weber's category of charisma—does not release the court into a sort of exceptional domain in which it can exercise its own will. Rather, its charismatic role is to show forth the action of

We the People. The opinion bears the gift of law—a gift that the American people imagine they have given to themselves.

The judge's charismatic role is to renew the faith that the source of law—the popular sovereign—bears the qualities of the sacred. Lincoln spoke of "reverence for law" and understood this as a way of commemorating—literally remembering together—the sacrifices of the Revolution.[98] Those sacrifices marked the presence of the popular sovereign. His point remains: we read law reverentially when we see it as the text authored by that now-withdrawn sovereign. Without this belief that law is a remainder of sovereign presence, law becomes a matter of habit at best and coercion at worst. Following the law can become a hollow ritual—a point about which Weber worried.[99]

Charismatic authority appears in the judicial call to live under the law as the truth of the self.[100] For this reason, courts can strike down every law or official act that is not consistent with that truth. Courts persuade us of their access to this truth not by logic but by the rituals and beliefs that go into the production of the opinion. If we knew nothing but the text of the opinion, we would actually know nothing at all. We need to read the opinion as it shows itself in our social practices, which begin with the judicial rite of passage that is the confirmation process, continue in the symbolism of the courtroom, and then bring forth the opinion that takes us from the position of reader, to that of narrator, and finally to that of author. The charismatic claim succeeds when we read through the judicial opinion to the opinion of the popular sovereign. Hearing that voice, we solve the puzzle of how popular sovereignty and the rule of law can be one and the same.

Courts speak the law not because judges are more reasonable than the rest of us, and not because they have a special expertise in the law, but because they stand in a charismatic relationship to the sovereign source of law. The life appointment has its foundation here, rather than in a worry about independence. Judges are to have no other life than that of the law. Because our belief is in a *popular* sovereign, every American stands in exactly the same relationship of identity to the sovereign authority as that modeled by the judge. Law asks us to imagine ourselves as part of a single community in which the public good displaces our particular interests. Thus, even when a party loses a case, the law continues to unite him with the entire community.

If this all seems mysterious, it is because it is. It is a matter of faith and belief, of rituals that maintain that faith, and of rhetoric that gives it expression. The charismatic function of the judge is enacted, not represented. It is not something that stands apart, that a judge can get right or wrong. We either see through the opinion to the popular sovereign or we hear the voice of the finite person who happens to be the judge. If we hear only the latter, we will assess his or her reasons according to our own well-considered judgments. The judge is likely to be no better at reasoning than the rest of us. We will say she got it wrong or that she simply expressed her personal views. Then law becomes politics, and politics becomes a competition among interest groups. Many people intuit the distinction of law from politics, yet they are hard pressed to explain their sense of the distinction. They have lost the language of charismatic authority; they see the politics that surrounds the Court without seeing through the opinion to its author.

Only when we understand "reverence" for the law and how it has filled the American imagination can we understand the exceptional nature of the judicial opinion. This practice of writing and reading often looks to the rest of the world like a fetishism of the legal text. Of course this looks strange to those who believe that the authority of a court arises out of its capacity to apply reason to conflicts among different interests groups.[101] We will never find a European judge looking back over two hundred years to their *Marbury*. The idea makes no sense in a legal order in which judges pursue a legal science rather than the sovereign voice. Indeed, the political order of post–World War Two Europe is grounded in the rejection of charismatic authority. The rest of the world may be concluding that sovereignty is an increasingly anachronistic concept, but Americans do not generally share that belief.[102] Popular sovereignty has not yet been displaced here by a new cosmopolitanism.[103] Whether that will happen and whether that would bring about a more just legal order are not questions I can answer. All I can reasonably predict is that if such a change occurs, the meaning of the rule of law will no longer be the same.

To learn this lesson of popular sovereignty and the charismatic voice, you must carefully read the opinion itself. You must allow yourself to fall within the grasp of the opinion and then reflect on its persuasive power. What you will discover is that the world of law is like one of those Russian dolls that continually open up to reveal yet another doll. Each moment that we think that we have hold of *Marbury*, it eludes our grasp, referring us back to something else. We are to keep seeing through: first, through Chief Justice Marshall, who only delivers but does not author the opinion; then through the opinion of the Court, which is only a holding forth of another legal text, the Constitution; then through that text to its drafters; and then through them to the authors. When, finally, we see those authors whose opinions are the foundation of the whole, we see only ourselves. If it works, we will have been persuaded that ours is a government of the people, by the people, and for the people.

four
LEGAL DOCTRINE: BETWEEN ERUDITION AND FUNDAMENTALISM

The paradox of the judicial opinion is that while it draws attention to itself, it is most successful when it is not seen. It is to be transparent; we are to see right through it to the authoritative legal text. When an opinion succeeds, we don't say "the court says . . ." Rather, we say "the law is . . ." Instead of seeing judges authoring a text, we see law authored by the people. The successful opinion shows us the law as a text that memorializes an act of the popular sovereign. This begins with the Constitution, but it continues through the entire national enterprise of lawmaking.[1] This hardly means that every opinion succeeds in bringing together narrator, author, and reader. Sometimes we are not persuaded.

Nevertheless, if the ideal of self-authorship were to disappear entirely, judicial practices would likely shift. The legitimacy of the courts would have to be grounded in a claim to expert knowledge or in a unique capacity peacefully to resolve disputes. Courts would come to be seen as similar to administrative agencies, deploying their own form of technical reasoning or making their services available for dispute resolution. This is a familiar phenomenon elsewhere. Arguably, it characterizes the continuing common-law adjudications of our own courts—particularly of state courts. But notice the way Chief Justice Roberts ended a recent, emotionally wrought case involving a lawsuit brought for intentional infliction of emotional distress (a common-law action) against a conservative church that organized antigay protests at a veteran's funeral:

> Speech is powerful. It can stir people to action, move them to tears of both joy and sorrow, and—as it did here—inflict great pain. On the facts before us, we cannot react to that pain by punishing the speaker. As a Nation we have chosen a different course—to protect even hurtful speech on public issues to ensure that we do not stifle public

debate. That choice requires that we shield Westboro from tort liability for its picketing in this case.[2]

The last three sentences move from the we of the court ("we cannot react") to We the People ("we have chosen") and then back to we the court ("we shield"). The elision of We the People and we the court is deliberate and characteristic. It is also not available to a court that grounds its legitimacy in sources other than self-authorship.

In much of the world, judges are bureaucrats on a professional career path. They have neither the status nor the political responsibilities of an American judge. Even in those countries that have recently created constitutional courts, the judges on those courts tend to think of themselves as experts in a form of reasoning—proportionality review.[3] Our judges generally speak as interpreters of texts, not as experts in a science of law. The American judicial opinion aims to persuade us that the narrator's voice coincides with the authorial voice of the people. Listening to the courts, we are to hear ourselves. When we do, the rule of law and the rule of the people, or legality and democracy, converge.[4]

From Legitimacy to Justice

In chapter 3, I focused on the "who" of the judicial opinion. Who is the author? In this chapter and the next, I focus on the "what." What is it that the opinion says? To separate the who and the what is to open a space for two distinct normative categories: legitimacy and justice. Sometimes we find ourselves in a situation in which we simultaneously believe that the law is legitimate yet nevertheless unjust. These are the circumstances under which we pursue reform, not revolution. Recognizing the law as the product of our own self-authorship explains the citizen's belief that law makes a legitimate claim on him or her. Whether that claim is just depends on its content. An illegitimate government can produce just law; a legitimate government can produce unjust law.

The who and the what—authorship and content—while analytically distinct do have a necessary relationship to each other. We cannot ordinarily see ourselves as authors of an opinion that sets forth norms with which we are in fundamental disagreement. At least we cannot sustain such a position of normative dissonance for long. This does not mean that judges read the opinion polls.[5] As we saw in chapter 2, about many controversies there is no settled, popular opinion. A range of attractive or potentially attractive values are at stake. That some things are ruled out by our normative commitments does not leave just one option standing.

The logic of the relationship of self-authorship to the content of the rule of law was played out in the abolitionist debate.[6] When some radical abolitionists described the Constitution as a "devil's pact," they were not just condemning its content but disavowing any claim of collective self-authorship. It was not a pact—a social contract—that they had made or could imagine themselves having made, for they would have nothing to do with the devil.[7] When other abolitionists argued that the "true reading" of the Constitution—despite the appearance of its text—was that slavery must be illegal, they too were operating with an idea of self-authorship: if it is our text, then it must say this.[8]

There is a regular impulse—indeed a necessity—in American political life to find in the Constitution our deepest moral beliefs. Consider the contemporary debate over abortion. Those who are deeply opposed to the practice find in the Constitution protection for the fetus; their opponents find protection of the woman's right to choose. Neither side can imagine the Constitution as a product of their own authorship in the absence of these norms. Or consider our debate over gun control. The National Rifle Association claims to be the oldest "civil rights" organization in America, defending a core constitutional liberty. This is not just an abstract value for them but a symbol of their own identity—a symbol through which they understand the whole of the constitutional order as their own.[9] Many of their opponents have trouble imagining a Constitution that would extend protection to individual gun ownership. Were the Constitution to say that, they could not imagine themselves as the authors.

LEGAL DOCTRINE

Whenever a judicial opinion reaches for a moral principle unmentioned or left indeterminate by the words of the text, it is repeating this movement: it is asking what are the necessary moral constraints implied by a belief in self-authorship. We see a clear example of this movement in *Griswold v. Connecticut*, which held unconstitutional a Connecticut statute making use of contraceptives illegal.[10] The moment of greatest force in the opinion amounts to little more than an exclamation: "Would we allow the police to search the sacred precincts of marital bedrooms for telltale signs of the use of contraceptives? The very idea is repulsive to the notions of privacy surrounding the marriage relationship."[11] There is nothing in the text of the Constitution that speaks of the marriage relationship, nor even of a right to privacy. The Fourth Amendment protects against warrantless searches, but it says nothing about what can and cannot be a crime. If there is probable cause to believe a crime is being committed in the marital bedroom, the Fourth Amendment is no barrier to obtaining a search warrant. Nevertheless, it is inconceivable that *we* could have authored a text that authorized actions we find "repulsive." The "we" that begins as the narrative voice of the opinion—"Would we allow"—becomes the We of popular self-authorship.

Self-authorship cannot require that we—meaning each of us—agree with every opinion issued by the courts, just as we take different views of the merits of various legislative acts. There is a considerable distance, however, between finding something "repulsive" and simply disagreeing with it. Affirming responsibility in the face of disagreement is quite common. I might be outvoted in a faculty meeting with respect to an issue of school policy, but still I take responsibility for it. The same thing happens in businesses, on teams, or in volunteer organizations, families, and congregations. Indeed, it is true of our relationship to elected politicians, who represent us despite our disagreements on particular matters of policy. I don't insist that I get my way in these group enterprises, and I don't disavow my part of the collective responsibility when things don't go my way. I recognize that unanimity is often not possible and the group must be capable of acting in the face of disagreement. About some things, however, I do take a stand: I might abandon the group if it goes in a direction with which I deeply disagree.[12] These are choices that each of us would characterize as personally "repulsive." I cannot affirm my identity and support that choice at the same time.

Short of such choices, we have many ways of reconciling ourselves with disagreement. Sometimes there are multiple values at stake in a controversy and we are uncertain how they should stand in relation to each other. We understand in such cases how it was reasonable to come out as the court did, even if we might have come out otherwise. Sometimes, we are convinced that the courts are "on the path" to the right outcome: we think they will get there one step at a time. Sometimes, we think an opinion is just wrong, but we understand that anyone, including ourselves, can commit an error. Sometimes, we realize that we hold a minority view about an issue upon which others might reasonably disagree.

Reconciliation is not, however, always possible. Sometimes the issue is important and our alienation from the opinion is extreme. We may then offer a "political" reading of the opinion. We accuse the court of "making," rather than "applying," the law. We accuse the judges of abandoning the law for politics. In these cases, we are unlikely to conclude that we were simply mistaken about the law. That is as difficult as saying we are mistaken about who we are. It is as difficult because it is effectively to say the same thing. We do not, for example, expect right-to-life groups to acknowledge they were wrong when the Court reaffirms *Roe*, nor are groups committed to campaign finance reform likely to change their minds on the constitutional issues after *Citizens United*.[13]

We may not expect the morally committed to change their minds, yet the opinion is directed at an ideal reader whose mind is open. Our practice of writing opinions puts persuasion at its center. Indeed, the typical Supreme Court opinion performs a kind of contest in persuasion, for the majority opinion is presented alongside dissents and concurrences. The Justices are trying to persuade each other, but more broadly they are trying to persuade us. Such a competition in persuasion is not an essential characteristic of the law. Opinions do not always accompany legal decisions. Juries, for example, don't explain themselves. They must be persuaded by the evidence, but they don't take up a burden of persuasion. Traditionally, the civil law courts of Europe expressed themselves in a fashion that was closer to that of the jury than to an American-style opinion. Their opinions were little more than conclusory statements of the outcome. There were no dissents. The opinions were not meant to persuade but to set forth the application of the law through what purported to be a demonstrable proof.

Although there is a considerable distance between the form of a jury's decision and the form of a continental court's decision, both reflect an idea of truth. The jury expresses an idea of factual truth: something happened or it did not. The civil law court opinion expresses an idea of demonstrable truth: a proof is true for everyone. Neither juries nor civil law courts allowed a space for public dissent. American appellate courts have always allowed dissent. In this, they are importing the method of the democratic assembly into the judicial forum.

If judges publicly disagree among themselves, it cannot be the case that disagreement undermines confidence in the courts. It does not do so because truth, either as fact or demonstration, is not at issue. Rather, the opinion offers an interpretation of a legal text. An interpretation succeeds when it persuades us. For this reason, it is sometimes argued that dissents contribute to the production of more persuasive opinions.[14] A dissent can force the majority to respond to arguments that might otherwise be passed over. It can also, however, alert the reader to weaknesses, making the burden of persuasion for the majority that much harder.

When judges disagree, they are arguing over the meaning of the law or the characterization of the facts—or both. In this chapter, I'm concerned with legal disagreement; in the next, with disagreement over facts. Disagreement over the law expresses itself in arguments about doctrine. The practice of dissent, accordingly, gives us a point of access for thinking about the way in which legal doctrine works within the opinion.

Unpacking the imaginative possibility of dissent is the problem of the first part of this chapter. Of particular interest is the judge who continues to dissent even after his or her position has been rejected. That judge effectively proclaims in response to the majority position that "the authoritative text does not say this." There is no alternative, for the judge cannot proclaim that the text means whatever she happens to believe. Nor can she rest on a personal preference for an interpretation set forth in a prior opinion, for the majority is free to overrule or reinterpret their own case law. A prior opinion has no authority over a contemporary opinion—unless the dissenting judge asserts that the precedent correctly sets forth what the constitutional or statutory text says.

Disagreement over the law raises the broader issue of doctrinal development. A dissent argues that the majority interpretation of an authoritative text is in error. The continuing dissent announces a hope that in some future case the majority position will be reversed. A practice of dissent, accordingly, is inevitably linked to claims about the role of *stare decisis*. More broadly, disagreement raises issues of doctrinal innovation, maintenance, and reversal: the life cycle of doctrine. I will address these issues later in the chapter.

The two parts of this chapter are united in their investigation of the relationship between legal resources and outcomes in the judicial opinion. Judges do not author law; they tell us what the law is. Yet they disagree among themselves. Out of those disagreements comes the development of legal doctrine. Because disagreement is always possible, nothing in the law is ever settled forever.

Interpretation as Argument: Vertical and Horizontal Dimensions of Interpretation

If you read only *Marbury* you might be convinced that the Court had identified the foundation of its authority in popular sovereignty, but you might still be puzzled as to how that foundation can support an ongoing system of governance that must be responsive to changing beliefs and circumstances. *Marbury* speaks a language of permanence, but law is as much about doctrinal change as it is about permanence. Change must be possible even as the authoritative text remains the same. Were that not the case, we would be overwhelmed by the task of constantly rewriting the law to account for new developments.[15]

Because an opinion is an interpretation, it links change to permanence. Consider interpretations of *Hamlet*. We do not expect a nineteenth-century interpretation of the play to be the same as contemporary interpretations. We don't expect either to be the same as that with which the play was first greeted. Each generation reads the play again—the text remains the same—but each new reading is informed by prior interpretations. We cannot choose simply to stop with nineteenth-century interpretations, as if they got hold of the "truth" of the play. Because of this history of readings, new readers are never in the same position as earlier ones.[16] A modern reader may "go back" to an earlier interpretation, but he brings to it a different context that inevitably influences his understanding. The uses he makes of it, the connections he sees, are not the same as those of the earlier generation.

Just as interpretations of fictional texts change over time, so do interpretations of legal texts. And just as the interpretation of fiction will refer both to the original, authoritative text and to past interpretations, so will an interpretation of a legal text. Opinions are in an endless discussion with both authoritative texts and past opinions interpreting those texts. Doctrinal change, in the absence of drafting new law, is the product of this two-dimensional conversation. An opinion interpreting Congress's power under the Commerce Clause, for example, will move back and forth between reading the constitutional text and discussing prior opinions that bear on the issue. Again, just as with *Hamlet*, we might bring other resources to bear in interpreting these two sources: for example, we might think the earlier opinions have to be understood in terms of their historical context, or we might think that the original text should be read in light of its place within the overall structure of the Constitution.

LEGAL DOCTRINE

Metaphorically, we can think of any single argument as occupying a position on a line that reaches toward the words of the authoritative text in one direction and toward other opinions interpreting that text in the other direction. Because an opinion is generally made up of many arguments, we can imagine a two-dimensional graph with the vertical axis representing the relationship of the opinion to the authoritative text itself, and the horizontal axis representing engagement with other opinions. An opinion that focused its arguments entirely on interpreting other opinions would be far out on the horizontal dimension. A good example of such an opinion is *Shelby County v. Holder*, in which the Court struck down a provision of the Voting Rights Act that specified the conditions under which a state or political subdivision is subject to preclearance procedures.[17] The opinion shows tremendous erudition in its reading of the cases—a reading that we may, nevertheless, find unpersuasive. At no point, however, does it offer a reading of a constitutional text that Congress is said to have violated in passing the act. It relies in large part on a principle that requires the federal government to treat each of the states equally. Whatever one thinks of this principle, it is not set forth in the constitutional text itself. The majority opinion is entirely an argument about what previous opinions—lots of them—mean. Not surprisingly, the dissent responds, in part, by arguing that *the text of* the Fifteenth Amendment assigns remedial responsibility to Congress, to which the Court should therefore defer.

The horizontal dimension represents a conversation—wider as one moves along the axis—among those who have engaged in interpreting the same authoritative text. Contrariwise, an opinion climbs the vertical axis as it considers a variety of resources (apart from other opinions) as aids in reading the authoritative text itself. The simplest argument on the vertical axis is a plain-sight reading of the authoritative text. In *TVA v. Hill*, which I discussed in chapter 3, the Court held the snail darter to be protected because the text made no exceptions to its category of endangered species.[18] Unreasonable as this position might seem, this is what the text "plainly" said. An example of an opinion far up the vertical axis is *District of Columbia v. Heller*, which held a local gun control ordinance violated the Second Amendment.[19] The opinion is devoted to a close textual analysis of the words of the Second Amendment, using multiple historical resources to get at what the words meant to those who first received them. It consults contemporary dictionaries, looks to handbooks on rhetoric, and examines contemporary usage, including parallel state efforts with respect to the right to bear arms. We still might not be persuaded by its historical claim or we might not be persuaded by its methodology, in which case we are likely to look to later judicial readings of that same text, which had come to the opposite conclusion.

These two dimensions provide the basic argumentative tools for the doctrinal positions of a judicial opinion. Reading an opinion, you will find it parsing the words of an authoritative text or explaining the meaning of prior opinions (precedents). Most opinions contain some combination of these arguments. Accordingly, the opinion lies somewhere between the two axes. We can, nevertheless, generalize. An opinion that reverses an earlier opinion is often high on the vertical axis: it rejects the prior interpretation by returning to a reading of the authoritative text itself. An opinion elaborating a rule or establishing an exception to a rule is likely to fall far out on the horizontal axis. The more elaborate the doctrinal position, the further out on this axis the opinion is likely to be.

While we should not take the spatial imagery too seriously—it is a metaphor, not a precise tool of analysis—it does give us a way to parse the legal arguments of an opinion. Horizontal movement will represent interpretation as the navigation of an increasingly complex network of opinions. Horizontal arguments are characteristically erudite: the legal expert knows all the relevant cases and has a view of how they relate to each other. This erudition can move very far from the words of the original text. Erudition can be, but is not necessarily, linked to the development of complex legal standards or tests. Consider, for example, levels of scrutiny in equal protection doctrine.[20] Or consider that there is no mention of privacy in the Fourteenth Amendment. To argue the law with respect to levels of scrutiny or privacy one must know the cases. Reading the authoritative text itself will tell you very little about the law in these domains—unless, of course, your interest is to reverse the precedents precisely because "the text does not say this."

Erudition, as I use it, refers only to a technique of persuasion. That an expert in the law can argue from multiple cases does not put him in a position similar to a scientist who knows the results of multiple experiments. Scientists tend to agree on fundamentals and disagree at the margins; legal experts, including judges, may disagree even on the fundamentals. Erudition in the law, unlike in science, is not connected to truth. The better analogy is to literary criticism or biblical studies, where equally erudite scholars disagree among themselves. Erudition may be a ground of respect, but we can disagree even with those we respect.

Vertical arguments claim to rely on the authoritative text itself and thus to be free of the encumbrances of prior opinions. One should not confuse this claim with a position that denies that any interpretation is required at all—as if the text carried its meaning on its face. That is only one possible interpretive position. We have already seen that vertical arguments can be every bit as sophisticated as horizontal arguments. There are always different possible ways of reading the text; a choice for one approach is a choice against others. These choices have to be defended, and that defense takes us deep into the argument of the opinion.

Vertical arguments then are not somehow noninterpretive. Indeed, there are multiple forms of vertical arguments. Sometimes the claim is that we need only place the text in plain sight to understand the law; sometimes it is that we must read the text as it was originally understood. These two positions can yield quite different results. Consider, for example, the Eleventh Amendment: "The Judicial power of the United States shall not be construed to extend to any suit in law or equity, commenced or prosecuted against one of the United States by Citizens of another State. . . ."[21] The plain-sight reading says that the amendment does not bear on suits brought by citizens against their own states; the originalist reading extends the amendment to cover such suits.[22]

Different areas of law tend to fall into different regions of this two-dimensional graph. Constitutional law often develops through the judicial formulation of tests: strict scrutiny, rational basis, undue burden, substantial effect, endorsement, or accommodation.[23] Some of these tests apply in multiple areas; some are unique to particular domains. None of these tests are in the authoritative text; their endless elaboration is a matter of horizontal argument. Often the entire argument of an opinion that elaborates, distinguishes, and applies such a test is a discussion of precedents. *Casey* argues about the meaning of *Roe*; *Carhart* about the meaning of *Casey*. *Lawrence* overruled *Bowers* but did so by rereading *Casey* and *Romer*.[24] Criminal procedure cases too are far along the horizontal axis. The jurisprudence of a right to counsel, the suppression of evidence, or the administration of the death penalty is enormously complicated but not to be found in the text itself. That does not mean that they are without a basis in text, since the precedents discussed are themselves interpretations of the meaning of the text. It does mean that an explicit appeal to the text is likely to be used to deny the authority of the prior line of doctrinal development.[25]

If we turn to opinions involving statutes, we generally move up the vertical axis. The attractions of vertical arguments here are twofold. First, we are more likely to agree on how to read a recent text. Because we agree, we think that the text "needs no interpretation." We have it in plain sight.[26] Second, because statutes are more easily revised by a subsequent Congress, courts are more likely to leave doctrinal change to the representative branches. Congress did indeed respond to the Court's extension of endangered species protection to the snail darter; it created an exception.[27] We can say that Congress changed its mind or that the Court misinterpreted the earlier statute. On either view, the opinion effectively told Congress to say what it means.

These alignments on one axis or another are only generalizations. Constitutional cases often lie close to the vertical axis. A claim to plain sight of the text was already deployed in *Marbury*. The Court holds unconstitutional Congress's expansion of the Supreme Court's original jurisdiction because the statute conflicts with Article III's narrow enumeration of cases that fall within that jurisdiction. To reach that conclusion, the Court had to explain why the Constitution's explicit grant to Congress of a power to make exceptions to the specified original jurisdiction did not apply in this case. Is an expansion properly read as "an exception"? Appealing to an interpretive rule that every word of the authoritative text must be given an operative meaning, the Court holds the exceptions clause inapplicable.[28] To adopt this "no surplusage" rule is to insist that a reading must keep the text—all of it—in plain sight.

Just as constitutional cases can climb the vertical axis, statutory cases can move along the horizontal axis. For example, the disparate impact test of Title VII, which was set forth in *Griggs*, has been elaborated in a line of opinions, each building on what came before.[29] Scholars have recently written of "super statutes," examples of which include the Sherman Antitrust Act of 1890, the Civil Rights Act of 1964, and the Endangered Species Act of 1973. These statutes have a status close to that of constitutional provisions in framing the public order for citizens, officials, and judges.[30] Characteristic of such statutes is that their provisions are subject to continuing elaboration in opinions.[31]

The point is not to decide between the vertical and the horizontal but to see how they facilitate doctrinal contestation and thus development. Vertical movement represents a potential counterpoint to the complexity that can arise from the proliferation of opinions in the horizontal dimension. Vertical arguments can dismiss erudite interpretations as "only the opinions of judges." This is where we find the persistent dissenter.[32] It is also where we find reversal.

Conversely, horizontal arguments will always counter that the impulse to return to the text itself is naive. We cannot determine, for example, what the Sherman Antitrust Act means by a "restraint of trade" by looking to the text itself. Similarly, the text of the Fourth Amendment will not tell us what to do about surveillance in cyberspace. Justice Potter Stewart, who dissented in *Griswold* because the constitutional text says nothing about marital privacy, voted with the majority in *Roe*. He explained himself this way:

> [T]he Connecticut law [in *Griswold*] did not violate any provision of the Bill of Rights, nor any other specific provision of the Constitution. So it was clear to me then, and it is equally clear to me now, that the *Griswold* decision can be rationally understood only as a holding that the Connecticut statute substantively invaded the "liberty" that is protected by the Due Process Clause of the Fourteenth Amendment. As so understood, *Griswold* stands as one in a long line of pre-*Skrupa* cases decided under the doctrine of substantive due process, and I now accept it as such.[33]

He is saying that he moved from the vertical ("the text does not say this") to the horizontal axis ("a long line of cases") in shifting his position from *Griswold* to *Roe*.

The competition between the different axes of argument is visible in *District of Columbia v. Heller*.[34] The Court's opinion explicitly relies upon an originalist reading of the text: "In interpreting this text, we are guided by the principle that '[t]he Constitution was written to be understood by the voters; its words and phrases were used in their normal and ordinary as distinguished from technical meaning.'"[35] The voters to whom this plain text was to make sense were those who originally received it. The opinion concludes that the Second Amendment's prefatory clause, referring to "a well regulated militia," is not a limit on the substantive right "to keep and bear arms." Accordingly, the plain text statement of the right extends to guns kept for private, self-defense. The principal dissent counters the majority's vertical argument with its own claim of plain sight: "[N]ot a word in the constitutional text even arguably supports the Court's overwrought and novel description of the Second Amendment...."[36] It also emphasizes the importance of horizontal arguments: "Since our decision in *Miller*, hundreds of judges have relied on the view of the Amendment we endorsed there; we ourselves affirmed it in 1980."[37] Indeed, the dissent gives a priority to horizontal arguments: "Even if the textual and historical arguments on both sides of the issue were evenly balanced, respect for the well-settled views of all of our predecessors on this Court, and for the rule of law itself, would prevent most jurists from endorsing such a dramatic upheaval in the law."[38] The rule of law is no less at stake in horizontal than in vertical arguments.

Such arguments are not limited to the pages of the *United States Reports*. As I write this, I read in the paper an argument that a woman cannot be president because the constitutional text uses the pronoun "he" some twenty times in referring to the office. That is an originalist, but not a plain-sight, argument. Today we read "he" as a neutral with respect to gender. On plain sight, we know that the constitutional text "says nothing" about the gender of the president. The newspaper commentator is relying on what he takes to be pronoun usage in 1787. There is, however, nothing about the structure of interpretation that binds us to antiquated, offensive meanings, even though there is something about interpretation that supports the return to the text. We cannot silence the critic with a copy of the Constitution in his pocket by telling him that its meaning is too complicated for a layman to understand without studying the history of judicial opinions interpreting that text. It is, after all, his text.

While he cannot be silenced, he may not persuade us. If an interpretation, including an opinion, effectively represents the authoritative text as nothing more than a product of historically contingent views and the distribution of political power in 1787—or even 1868—we would simply stop caring about that text. This is one of the lessons of *Dred Scott*, which was a deeply originalist opinion, canvassing the implicit and explicit views of the founders on slavery and the possibility of black citizenship.[39] This made the decision less, not more, persuasive.

Vertical and horizontal arguments follow from the nature of interpretation. We can speak of their analogues in many fields. Is the art critic in conversation with other critics or is he looking at the work itself? The most important analogy, however, is to theological argument. The Protestant Reformation begins with the rejection of the church's claim to an erudite knowledge that had been built up through a long history of doctrinal development.[40] The reformers were able to undermine this tradition of erudition by effectively claiming that the Bible—the authoritative text—"does not say this." To the Protestant fundamentalist, faith requires plain sight of the biblical text. Of course, even Protestantism will build up its own history of erudite interpretation, which will itself be vulnerable to the criticism that the text does not say this. The erudition of the scholar must always contend with the revolutionary fundamentalism of the prophet. To those who pursue the work of erudition, the fundamentalist claim appears dangerously naive. To the fundamentalist, naiveté is the virtue of the uncorrupted.

Multiple interest groups in America claim ownership of the constitutional text as the source of their own political legitimacy. We find a constant effort to translate political claims into constitutional claims, as if winning that argument will settle a dispute.[41] Success translates what might have appeared as a contentious political claim into the voice of We the People. Not surprisingly, fundamentalism has certain political advantages over erudition in this popular politics of constitutionalism. The pocket-size constitutional text plays the same role of immediate accessibility that the biblical text plays for the fundamentalist. Holding up the text, the citizen can challenge the judicial opinion. Conversely, it may be difficult to mobilize ordinary citizens around an erudite reading of the text.

That both horizontal and vertical moves are available means that every opinion begins with a choice.[42] This choice can be extremely dramatic, for it always includes the possibility of overthrowing an entire doctrinal field. We might think that the memorialization of law in a positive text is a way of stabilizing doctrine. *Marbury* suggests this: "The powers of the Legislature are defined and limited; and that those limits may not be mistaken or forgotten, the Constitution is written. To what purpose are powers limited, and to what purpose is that limitation committed to writing, if these limits may at any time be passed by those intended to be restrained?"[43] *Marbury* actually has it backward, for every legal text requires interpretation and every interpretation can be reversed in the name of the text itself. It is not possible to argue that our text-based constitutionalism has had more stability than the British, textless, common-law constitutionalism.

The Life of Doctrine

Parties to a dispute can seek peaceful resolution through bargaining, mediation, or arbitration. The aim of these procedures is to resolve the dispute in such as a way as to allow all parties to move forward without a sense that they have been treated unfairly. Courts can serve this same purpose. We see this clearly when cases settle. An appellate court issuing an opinion, however, is in a different position. It must bring the private dispute into contact with public values.[44] The opinion links the resolution of the particular dispute to a systematic representation of the law. What looks like a particular dispute to the parties, whose interests may go no further than winning, appears now to the larger public as a statement of the law. Metaphorically, the parties read the opinion starting from the end, where the judgment is announced. The rest of us read from the beginning; we come to the opinion to learn the law, not to learn who won.

Because private dispute resolution aims to satisfy the interested parties, it is singular.[45] Conversely, judicial opinions are never a one-shot deal. Rather, they fall into doctrinal domains with indeterminate borders.[46] A court cannot write about a Fourth Amendment or an antitrust claim, for example, without looking at the opinions that have already spoken to the meaning of the authoritative texts, just as it cannot write without some regard to the authoritative text itself. If it is a lower court, it looks to higher court opinions as authoritative statements of what the law is. A higher court too must look to its own prior opinions, even if it plans to reverse them. Professionals tend to share an understanding of which texts and which opinions form the legal horizon against which the present dispute is to be resolved. Of course, sometimes there is a disagreement about the horizon, which the court must resolve.[47]

To have a common legal horizon is not to agree on the proper outcome of the case. Legal doctrine exists as a network of multiple connections, operating in both the vertical and horizontal directions. Some of these connections are emphasized and others fall into the background in any particular argument. The case is an occasion for restating the law; every such restatement is an interpretation.[48] The range of cases across which that restatement must work is indeterminate in the abstract. The only requirement is "far enough to persuade." The opinion should not leave us asking, "But what about . . . ?"

Across this range of resources, the argument operates under a demand for doctrinal coherence. In part, this is a function of the simple intuition that justice at law demands that like cases be treated alike. Of course, the work of the opinion is to identify what counts as likeness and what as difference with respect to the legal norms at issue. In part, the demand for coherence arises from the intuition that legitimacy rests on a sense of self-authorship: we cannot imagine ourselves authors of an incoherent law.[49]

The demand for coherence has important implications. Most obviously, doctrine cannot appear to contradict itself. We cannot understand ourselves as author of a rule and its opposite. This hardly means that rules apply without exceptions. Just the opposite: every legal rule comes with a doctrine of exceptions. The coherence demand means that the opinion must explain the exceptions—for example, they all pass a test of satisfying a compelling state interest. Even without obvious contradiction, incoherence can arise if the legal background seems to be "all over the place." We often speak of the law as balancing a number of purposes. Doctrine becomes incoherent if the balances drawn are wildly inconsistent from case to case. Law cannot appear as arbitrary.[50] Unlike courts, Congress may have no reason for its actions other than shifting constellations of power. Congress, however, is not trying to persuade anyone by offering reasons.

A legal argument, accordingly, must achieve a kind of double coherence: it must provide a coherent representation of the legal background, and it must resolve the current controversy coherently with respect to that background. These are not two separate steps, even if the opinion formally presents the argument in this way. The background will be seen through the application, just as much as the application will be viewed against the background. This means that every opinion puts at issue the background of legal doctrine even as it appears to accept that doctrine as something given. Because the background is at issue, every opinion occupies a point in the development of legal doctrine. Thus, a judicial intervention can resolve one conflict but nevertheless disturb the larger doctrinal network. Entire areas of law become active as networks are disturbed. One opinion leads to another, and pretty soon there is something like a judicial campaign to work out what the law is.

We have recently seen such a campaign with respect to federalism doctrine. The New Deal settlement in favor of the national government has come apart: what had been settled has become very unsettled. Federalism concerns have recently raised controversies under the Commerce Clause,[51] the Eleventh Amendment,[52] the spending power,[53] the Tenth Amendment,[54] and the Fifteenth Amendment,[55] as well as with respect to issues of statutory interpretation.[56] That state sovereignty claims would be at the forefront of constitutional controversy at the beginning of the twenty-first century could not have been predicted sixty years earlier, when the Court declared the Tenth Amendment a "truism."[57] For decades, it was thought that such controversies had been left behind when the Supreme Court upheld the New Deal program of centralization and regulation.

These campaigns of doctrinal contest can last decades. They can involve many parties inside and outside the courts. Eventually, the area of law settles back into a steady background state. Lawyers operate with an intuitive sense of what is currently open to contestation and what is settled. The opinion addresses a reader who expects to be told how this case fits within these ongoing contests. Sometimes he is told to abandon what has come before and to start over.

Ronald Dworkin analogizes the process of judicial interpretation to writing a chain novel: when the judge writes an opinion, he or she is to write the next chapter in an ongoing project among courts and across time.[58] The metaphor emphasizes that each new chapter is the point of access to the prior chapters. The new chapter must sustain a belief in coherence of the whole project, but that does not mean that it is bound to any particular view of the past opinions. It can, for example, overrule some of them; it can announce some aspects mistaken; it can check a line of development; it can return to an earlier point as the best expression of the law by which we are to measure what came later. Still, the chapter must offer a credible reading of all that has come before. It is not free to act as if it were writing on a clean slate; it is not free to ignore that with which it disagrees; it cannot appear arbitrary.

The chain novel metaphor should not be pushed too hard. The law is not developing as a single novel—chain or otherwise. There is no single end or even multiple, coordinated ends. We disagree about whether the end should be efficiency or justice; we disagree on how to reach these ends. Our disagreements are both general and particular as specific texts come into issue. The interpretive aspiration for coherence does not change this. There is not a single principle—substantive or methodological—that we have already agreed to and around which we can organize claims of doctrinal coherence. Portraying the law as coherent, the opinion represents its own conclusion as if it were the necessary outcome of the law—anything else would be "incoherent."[59] It succeeds when it persuades, but every such success can be unsettled in the future.

Laboring under the burden to persuade, the opinion uses the tools of horizontal and vertical interpretation to make one of three possible doctrinal moves.[60] First, it can attempt a new beginning. Borrowing from Hannah Arendt, I call this the moment of "natality."[61] Second, it can offer an incremental step in the progressive development of existing doctrine. Such a step may include reversing other opinions, which are now seen as having taken a step "in the wrong direction." Third, an opinion can attempt to destroy an existing line of doctrine. These three categories describe the range of formal possibilities because they correspond to the beginning, middle, and end of a line of doctrinal development. Speaking very generally, we can say that a destructive opinion is likely to rely on vertical arguments; a progressive opinion on horizontal arguments; and a natal opinion on a mix of vertical and horizontal. There is nothing about the facts of a case or the authoritative text to which it appeals that can tell us in advance whether the argument of an opinion will take the course of natality, incrementalism, or destruction. Together they make possible the shaping and reshaping of doctrine.

Natality

Students sometimes report that they can find no precedents relevant to a problem they have been assigned. They are told to keep looking, for the position they report is literally impossible. There is always law; there are no lacunae.[62] There is always an answer to the question of whether some act—official or private—is legal. Law builds answers by locating connections within proliferating networks. Those connections are built as the argument draws analogies, makes distinctions, offers general propositions, or asserts exceptions. Nevertheless, the students may be pointing to something important: there are instances in which we feel something new is at issue. To say that there is always law is not to deny the possibility of judicial innovation.

NEW BEGINNINGS OF LIBERTY *Griswold v. Connecticut* is a case in which we can observe the difficulties of bringing forth the new.[63] The issue was whether Connecticut could prohibit Planned Parenthood from providing contraceptives to married couples. Connecticut had an old law prohibiting the use of contraceptives; the defendants were accused of aiding and abetting the violation of this statute. While Connecticut did not generally enforce the prohibition, the state did move against the staff of Planned Parenthood. *Griswold* declares the underlying statute unconstitutional, but the opinion demonstrates considerable uncertainty as to what to say in support of this conclusion. This is characteristic of the arguments in natal opinions: there is a groping for support, precisely because the law was not leading to this outcome.

The difficulty of *Griswold* arises from the dark shadow still cast by the Court's earlier use of substantive due process—specifically a right to liberty of contract—to strike down much of the progressive welfare legislation of the early part of the twentieth century.[64] Those decisions, along with the Commerce Clause decisions striking down New Deal legislation, brought the Court to its greatest political crisis: Roosevelt's threat to pack the Court.[65] The Court averted the crisis by abandoning these doctrinal limits on government regulation.[66] *Griswold* faces the problem of finding a constitutionally protected liberty interest without resuscitating these earlier decisions. *Lochner*, it declares, will not be "our guide."[67] What then is?

Formally, *Griswold* relies on constitutional text—lots of it. It cites the First, Third, Fourth, Fifth, and Ninth Amendments. About each of these, it says that the amendment has a textual core and a "penumbra."[68] The latter extends the reach of the amendment to activities that contribute to the accomplishment of those at the core. For example, the First Amendment's protection of speech extends to the protection of association even though no mention is made of association, because without the penumbral extension, the core right of speech would be less than fully realized. The opinion notes that all of these penumbras protect private activity from state regulation. Together, they protect a zone of individual liberty that is beyond government intervention—a zone that includes the marital bedroom. The last step is quite a leap.

Of course, there is nothing surprising in noting that the Bill of Rights creates zones of privacy: every right can be described as creating a zone of privacy into which the state may not intervene. To claim a civil right is to claim some sort of independence from the state— an independence that the state has a duty to acknowledge. This independence, however, hardly equates with our ordinary sense of privacy, as in the privacy of the bedroom. Some constitutional rights are about privacy in this ordinary sense, but many are or can be asserted in public. They protect forms of public behavior, particularly political behavior. The important work of the legal argument, one might have thought, would be to connect contraceptive practices to the protected zones of rights. On this point, the opinion falls dramatically short.[69]

If by itself no constitutional right protects sexual activity, it is hard to see how aggregating a number of rights will cross the bedroom threshold. The real work of the opinion is done when it turns directly to moral intuition, which leads to the passage I quoted above asserting that it would be unthinkable to allow the state to search the "marital bedroom."[70] One might reasonably respond that the state was not suggesting any such search; it was regulating services offered by doctors at Planned Parenthood, not invading homes.

Justice Hugo Black, in dissent, points out that the case does not involve constitutionally protected speech, but only a doctor-patient relationship, and the Constitution nowhere prohibits state regulation of that relationship. This is the classic fundamentalist move: "the text does not say this." Justice Stewart's famous dissent makes the same sort of move. He writes that the Connecticut law is "uncommonly silly" but is nowhere addressed by the constitutional text.[71] Black and Stewart both see the opinion as a sort of relapse to the pre–New Deal law rather than as a doctrinal innovation.

At stake is a radical shift of the site at which citizens expect to realize liberty and dignity. This is a shift from contract to family. It is not just any bedroom that is protected but the "marital bedroom." In the decades after the Civil War, it made sense to think that contract was the site of constitutionally protected liberty. Slaves could not contract; the war had been fought in substantial part under the ideology of free labor.[72] The right to contract was, accordingly, a sign of political liberty and civic dignity. The idea of contract as a site of liberty could not survive the Depression. Citizens now needed state regulation just to "hold their own" against market forces that threatened oppression, not liberty. Markets were now about power, not liberty.

A liberal, democratic state, however, still needs an idea of meaningful self-construction outside of the political order; it needs an idea of the private. If not contract, what? Traditionally, we might have pointed to religion, but by the 1960s, this was no longer a sufficient answer. In place of markets and church, there was a new appearance of the family as the protected zone of private liberty.[73] Family had not been absent earlier: the economic and religious orders assumed familial organization. The modern home, however, gains a sort of autochthonous meaning: family now represents intimacy as a source of private meaning that must be respected by the state.

Griswold arises at this moment of cultural transition. The new site of liberty is symbolized by the bedroom. Indeed, we come to speak of the suburbs as "bedroom communities." Contract gives way to intimacy as the source of meaningful self-construction. This new concern with the liberty interest in marriage grounds a new attitude toward divorce: *Griswold* appears just as divorce rates are beginning their rapid rise.[74] Marriage is no longer a site of constraint "for better and for worse," but the site at which an autonomous agent can realize his or her own truth. Not surprisingly, this new association of marriage with liberty brings with it a turn to no-fault divorce law, starting with California in 1969.[75] If marital exit is just as important as marital entrance for conceiving of the marital bedroom as a site of liberty, then *Griswold* adopted a very unstable position in relying on the ethos of marriage: "the sacred precincts of marital bedrooms." It is not the formal relationship of "being married" that matters but the choice for intimacy.[76] Accordingly, the rights of *Griswold* are rapidly extended to the unmarried in *Eisenstadt v. Baird*.[77]

Griswold is certainly doing something new in shifting the site of constitutionally protected liberty. To accomplish this shift, the opinion uses the jurisprudential tools at hand. First, it suggests a reliance on the constitutional text: not just one but at least five different amendments are cited. Second, it invokes a sophisticated, interpretive methodology: constitutional provisions must be read in light of their penumbral reach. Third, it flatly denies the obvious continuity with the earlier substantive due process cases. These three arguments are, in themselves, so unsuccessful that they do little more than mark this as a natal moment. But for the appeal to the self-evident moral intuition of the sanctity of the marital bedroom, the opinion is entirely unconvincing. In no post-*Griswold* opinion does the Court deploy the concept of penumbral rights. Similarly, post-*Griswold* there is a frank acknowledgment that the case rested on substantive due process.[78] If *Griswold* persuades, it is because we cannot imagine that we would author a text protecting an autonomous individual from state intrusion without protecting this form of privacy. We cannot imagine that, for this is the privacy that has come to matter most to us moderns.

Griswold's reliance on the crutch of marriage to persuade us to accept doctrinal innovation is itself short-lived. It turns out that we cannot imagine the police invading anyone's bedroom. Thus, *Griswold* begins a line of doctrine that quickly moves from married to unmarried couples,[79] extends its reach to a right to abortion,[80] stumbles over gay sex,[81] before it reverses itself to recognize that the same ideas of liberty and autonomy rights extend to gay couples.[82] At each stage, *Griswold* is relied upon and thus its precedential value becomes continually stronger. It becomes a necessary case, in the sense that anyone who questions it is outside of the mainstream of constitutional understanding.[83] When we finally get to *Lawrence*, which declared state sodomy laws unconstitutional, we find spoken what could not yet be said—because no one knew how to say it—in *Griswold*: "The petitioners are entitled to respect for their private lives. The State cannot demean their existence or control their destiny by making their private sexual conduct a crime. Their right to liberty under the Due Process Clause gives them the full right to engage in their conduct without intervention of the government."[84] That, now, is what *Griswold* means. *Griswold* has become quite literally a new foundation for liberty in a world in which everything beyond the choice for intimacy can seem to be a function of forces beyond our control.[85]

NEW BEGINNINGS OF EQUALITY   *Griswold* is one natal point for modern doctrine; *Brown v. Board of Education* is another.[86] Reading *Brown*, we again find a weak argument that gives little indication of the direction in which doctrine will develop. A reader of *Griswold* alone would likely think she was at the beginning of a line of cases about marriage and family; a reader of *Brown* alone would likely think she was at the beginning of a line of cases about education. After all, the holding of *Brown* is that the doctrine of separate but equal has no place "in the field of public education."[87] The opinion says nothing about the continuing place of segregation elsewhere. In neither *Brown* nor *Griswold* would it be right to think that the Court was hiding its intention. Rather, a characteristic of the natal opinion is that the Court does not yet know the direction in which doctrine will develop. Marriage really was as far as the Court could see in *Griswold*, just as education was the horizon in *Brown*.

Since doctrine does not develop according to a plan, the natal opinion cannot offer a blueprint. Rather, it achieves its position as a foundation only through its repeated use as a precedent. That it will be so used cannot be known at the moment of decision.[88] Looking back on a natal opinion, we have a sense that the doctrinal shift was necessary but that the opinion could not find the words to justify the shift. This is captured in the ambiguity of the word "unprecedented," which simultaneously suggests importance and an absence of support.

While these natal qualities are no less true of *Brown* than they were of *Griswold*, there is a significant difference in the setting of the two opinions: no one thought the state laws requiring segregated schools were "silly." The *Brown* Court understood that it was taking a very controversial step that would trigger popular resistance. This put an even larger burden of persuasion on the Court. It dealt with this pressure procedurally, not doctrinally. It extended its period of deliberation: the case was argued three times over three years. Relief was delayed even further when the lower courts were ordered to work out the nature of any remedial orders and to proceed with "all deliberate speed."[89] Whether this strategy of delay had any effect, for good or bad, is unknowable.[90] Nevertheless, it does illustrate the inherent tentativeness of the natal opinion.[91]

The architectonic shift worked by *Brown* is seen in the radical slippage between the argument and the conclusion. Doctrinally, *Brown* places itself as the successor to a line of recent cases about segregation in public education.[92] Those cases had involved graduate education, unlike *Brown* itself which involved primary and secondary education. All had resulted in orders requiring termination of separate facilities for white and black students. *Brown* might, accordingly, be thought of as an extension of the doctrine developed in these cases to primary and secondary schools.

The earlier cases, however, were understood to involve adults, not children. These adults had voluntarily chosen to pursue a course of higher education. They had choices; they could go elsewhere. Adults making choices did not raise the same fears and popular resistance as compelled integration of children. More importantly, the earlier cases had reached their conclusion through the application of the doctrine of separate but equal: the graduate programs failed the test requiring separate schools to be equal. Failure was, in each case, a fact-based judgment.[93] It remained possible, at least in theory, for a program to try to make a showing that it did indeed provide equal benefits while maintaining segregation.

No such argument is possible after *Brown*. This new opinion is not extending the old doctrine but putting in place an entirely new position. The Court cannot rely on the prior education cases to work the doctrinal elimination of separate but equal, for those cases had relied upon this doctrine. Seeking some more persuasive ground, the argument begins with a move in the vertical dimension. Indeed, the Court had scheduled reargument on the question of what the original intent of the Fourteenth Amendment had been with respect to segregated schools. Yet, little comes of this originalist inquiry: "[A]lthough these sources cast some light, it is not enough to resolve the problem with which we are faced. At best they are inconclusive."[94] The opinion then turns from the vertical to the horizontal dimension, from text to precedents, looking, however, to cases that precede the recent education cases:

> In the first cases in this Court construing the Fourteenth Amendment, decided shortly after its adoption, the Court interpreted it as proscribing all state-imposed discriminations against the Negro race.

LEGAL DOCTRINE

> The doctrine of "separate but equal" did not make its appearance in this Court until 1896 in the case of *Plessy v. Ferguson*, involving not education but transportation.[95]

There is a suggestion, not quite explicit, that *Brown* is an erudite exercise in the recovery of earlier doctrine, after a series of interpretive errors. This indeed might be the best reading, but it is not what the opinion goes on to argue. It turns instead to education and concludes that the *Plessy* doctrine of separate but equal has no place in the public schools.

The lower courts had decided the cases before the Court in *Brown* under the doctrine of separate but equal. Following the reasoning of the graduate education opinions, the lower courts inquired whether it is possible to achieve equal primary and secondary education through separate schools. They answered that question through an evidentiary inquiry regarding the facilities, faculty, students, programs, and what the earlier opinions referred to as the "intangible" factors that contribute to educational success. *Brown* seems to adopt this style of reasoning as well.

The opinion, accordingly, moves in the direction of a factual inquiry on the effects of segregated education. It quotes an opinion from below: "Segregation with the sanction of law, therefore, has a tendency to [retard] the educational and mental development of Negro children and to deprive them of some of the benefits they would receive in a racial[ly] integrated school system."[96] It bolsters this "finding" with reference to the growth of "psychological knowledge" in the modern age.[97] We now know what could not have been known in 1896 when the doctrine of separate but equal was adopted: education in segregated schools affects the "hearts and minds" of black children. Yet, the argument does not rely on these findings of fact in any ordinary sense.

Reading *Brown*, we understand that these are no longer contestable findings of fact. The opinion is settling, rather than opening, a debate about psychological or educational facts. It actually offers very little in support of the truth of these empirical claims: one footnote, citing a small number of studies. Nevertheless, post-*Brown* the lower courts are not invited to consider evidence to the contrary. It does not remain open to a school district to offer to make a showing that its separate schools are in fact equal. Nothing will turn on such factual claims, even though it is the actual effect of segregation on education that seems to be at the heart of the opinion.

The opinion is actually establishing something that is better characterized as a constitutional harm, which has little to do with the factual claims of educational harms that the opinion explicitly discusses. At stake is not an inferior education but the dignity harm that arises from segregation. To be segregated is to be treated unequally, full stop. After *Brown*, the offense to this right no more depends on showing some other injury than does the offense to the constitutional right to speech depend on showing some harm apart from the restriction on speech. The Equal Protection Clause will now be interpreted to mean that the state cannot segregate. It cannot do so, even were it to promise a superior education.[98] This, however, is not yet what the opinion says, although it is what the opinion will come to mean.

Instead of articulating this new harm, *Brown* focuses on the importance of education in today's society. This is treated as a changed circumstance arising since the text of the Fourteenth Amendment was written. Education has become "perhaps the most important function of state and local governments," because without an adequate education a child cannot succeed economically, culturally, or politically.[99] For this reason, educational opportunity, "where the state has undertaken to provide it, is a right which must be made available to all on equal terms."[100] Reading this in the mid-1950s, one might have expected a line of cases to follow filling out the meaning of equal educational opportunity in multiple dimensions apart from race. Instead, *Brown* is followed by a line of cases applying the prohibition on segregation wherever it occurs.[101] Providing all children an equal education proves to be exceptionally difficult, but education has no particular relevance to the constitutional norm for which *Brown* comes to stand.

Hannah Arendt's paradigm of political natality is revolution.[102] Those who make a revolution rarely know where they are going; they know only that something must be done. They can fail, in which case there was no revolution at all. The same is true of the natal opinion. It has a tentativeness, uncertainty, and a sense of openness about it. It does not know the future but gathers meaning retrospectively. The opinions that follow will lay claim to the legacy of this foundation. Doing so, they give the opinion its foundational quality. Even today, we are still arguing about the meaning of *Brown*, for whoever appears as the inheritor of this opinion speaks with a certain legitimacy.[103] For one thing we do know is that *Brown* speaks for all of us.

Neither *Brown* nor *Griswold* can be judged by the quality of its arguments because we do not read opinions one at a time. We read across time and in entire fields of doctrine. These opinions refound fields of law. An opinion can always say more than its writers intend or even understand, for it is appropriated over time as the authorial act of the people giving the law to themselves. Thus, *Brown* and *Griswold* cannot be disavowed, for they have become transparent to the Constitution. Through these opinions we believe we see the Constitution itself. In terms of the double axes of interpretation, these opinions might be thought of as themselves taking their place as texts on the vertical axis.[104] We argue about their meaning not as two opinions among others but rather as if they are themselves the authoritative source of doctrine.

The Growth of Doctrine: Erudition

When one has authority to make law, one does not need to interpret. Congress does not interpret its laws to determine what should be done. It passes a new law. A court claims no such authority; instead, it offers interpretations. The opinion binds us because the law binds us, not because a judge happened to think this would be a good result. Judges are not to think any such thing, and often they tell us that their personal views are irrelevant.[105] We can be skeptical of that claim, but there is no argument available by which judges can claim the authority to make law independent of interpretation.[106]

The rhetorical task of the opinion is to narrow the gap between the interpretation and the text that is the object of interpretation. To be fully persuaded is to think there is no gap at all: the opinion tells us what the law means. Critics will always allege a gap. They will say that judges are claiming a power to make law in the guise of interpreting the law. These critics include dissenting judges. The presence of dissent is a constant reminder of the possibility of the gap. Worry about the charge that a judge is making law operates as a source of judicial self-policing. *Bowers v. Hardwick*, for example, expressed this fear: "The Court is most vulnerable and comes nearest to illegitimacy when it deals with judge-made constitutional law having little or no cognizable roots in the language or design of the Constitution."[107] That *Bowers*, which upheld a Georgia criminal sodomy statute, was overruled by *Lawrence* just seventeen years later suggests that sticking close to the "language or design of the Constitution" is not in itself sufficient.[108] *Lawrence* accuses the earlier opinion of failing to read correctly the considerable work of erudite interpretation that had already been accomplished in the precedents concerning the constitutionally protected right to privacy. Those opinions, according to *Lawrence*, tell us what the Constitution means. There is no gap.[109]

The natal opinion suppresses the gap by virtue of its subsequent use: the opinion becomes the reference point from which to view the authoritative text. As long as the natal opinion is accepted as such, we can think of subsequent opinions as unable to move further on the vertical axis. This is another way of saying that the text of this opinion comes to stand in for the legal text itself; it has become the starting point from which argument begins in subsequent cases. Those cases generally represent incremental additions to doctrine. They move out along the horizontal axis. Cumulatively, the opinions can move considerably beyond an original position. This is what makes the doctrinal line of development eventually vulnerable to the vertical challenge of a threat of reversal: "the text does not say this."

LEGAL DOCTRINE

To understand incremental movement along the horizontal axis, it is not enough to observe that the opinions are all interpreting the same text. Precedents can be grouped together in any number of ways, whether or not they refer to a common authoritative text. Do we think, for example, of *Brown* as a schools case or a case about a broadly applicable antidiscrimination principle? Do we think of *Griswold* as about sexual intimacy and family, or is it about liberty in general? We answer those questions when we place the opinion in relation to others. To do so is to draw an analogy or to make a distinction.[110]

Consider a familiar controversy raising issues of the meaning of the constitutional norm of equality. The Equal Protection Clause states that no state shall "deny to any person . . . the equal protection of the laws."[111] How does that language apply to programs of affirmative action? An abstract norm will not apply itself. Indeed, the problem arises because we are uncertain over the meaning of equality in this context. If we say that the principle is that we must "treat like cases alike," what follows? How do we know what is alike and what is different? How do we proceed to argue the case?

If we had no examples in mind—if we had no idea of what equality meant under any circumstances—we would not know how to begin. In the abstract, we might conclude that the norm of equality is meaningless because every person and every situation is different. Conversely, we might conclude it imposes an impossible burden because it forbids making distinctions that are necessary to any legal regime. An effective rule must lie somewhere in-between, which is to say that the norm must be negotiated as we make judgments of likeness and difference. Since those judgments change over time, there is no way that the rule can be changeless if it is to continue to operate in a way that makes sense to us. But then, who else should it make sense to?

In the case of affirmative action, we start with a shared understanding that race-based categories cannot be used to deny benefits to people who belong to historically discriminated against groups—particularly black people. Of this we are already convinced. Is the use of race-based categories in an affirmative action program, then, like the use of such categories in traditional acts of discrimination?

The judge might think the answer to be "sometimes." To determine when, she draws her analogies more closely. She wants to know what it was about the past cases that made them instances of inequality. Was it the reasons for the behavior, the history of the behavior, the social meaning of the behavior, the questionable politics that led to the behavior, or something else? Did it have to do with the benefit or burden at issue? She is trying to identify with more precision the norm that serves as the premise common to the cases. How exactly are the cases similar? They are not similar "in themselves." Nor are they similar in their relationship to an established, abstract rule applied in each case. The rule and its application are reciprocally constitutive. We don't know the rule until we have interpreted the meaning of the case.

The judge must move along the horizontal axis, which means to analyze how the norm of equality has been interpreted in past cases. She must read the cases and then construct an argument using analogies and distinctions. She needs to determine which are the relevant cases, but she doesn't arrive with a list. Rather, one case leads to another as she tries out different arguments. She finds likeness and difference only as she makes the arguments. She might say that the cases rely on a conception of equality that bars discrimination against disadvantaged groups. In that case, advantaged groups have no special claim. Or she might argue that what is common to the cases is that they condemn any use of race at all. If so, whites are similarly situated to blacks. Other possibilities exist: for example, a majority group cannot discriminate against a minority. She formulates a hypothesis and then tests the cases against that norm. Of course, she might decide that some particular case was in error—just as *Bowers* was in error. Or, instead of denouncing the outlying case as an error, she might try to find some way to distinguish it from the others with which it seemed at first to belong.

The judge does not construct analogies aimlessly but rather with an eye to determining what matters. She too reads past cases in light of the present controversy. To clarify the meaning of past opinions, she will use hypotheticals to artificially construct analogies and distinctions. A hypothetical allows her to focus on one particular element and to ask whether it accounts for the legal conclusion across some range of precedents. Of course, it is something of a misrepresentation to say that the judge is discovering the common, doctrinal premise of the cases. It is not there like an object in a box. It is there like the theme of a poem. The principle for which we are looking is not independent of our looking.

If we are persuaded by the opinion, the argument has shown how the cases are analogous or distinguishable, for in themselves they are neither. Once we are persuaded, we will find ourselves saying things like affirmative action is "racial discrimination, plain and simple"[112] or, conversely, that there is a difference between a "No Trespassing sign" and a "welcome mat."[113] These are not descriptions or observations; they are conclusions signaling that our minds are now made up.

Short-lived as it was, *Bowers* can still teach us a good deal about erudition as a source of doctrinal development. The opinion does not simply announce that the constitutional text does not speak to the Georgia sodomy statute. It does not turn to the text itself, because that move would have challenged the whole line of substantive due process cases that gained a new foundation in *Griswold* and led to *Roe*. This the Court was not willing to do. Instead, the opinion deploys erudition in support of an interpretation that makes the precedents irrelevant to the controverted Georgia law: the situations are not analogous.

Bowers helps us to see how the process of analogical reasoning works. The opinion's concern is to identify the common principle for which the "privacy" cases stand. Its account of the course of doctrinal development begins in the early part of the twentieth century with *Pierce* and *Meyers*—cases involving childrearing—and then continues to *Skinner* and *Loving*—cases involving procreation and marriage.[114] These substantive due process cases, dating from the *Lochner* era, were still too toxic to be mentioned in *Griswold*, although they were used in Justice Black's dissent to taint the majority's position.[115] These opinions are recovered in *Bowers* because they fit within a re-reading that places family at the center of this entire doctrinal field.

Pierce and *Meyers* were about the parental right to make decisions regarding their children's education: whether to attend private school and whether to learn a foreign language. *Prince* affirmed this notion of constitutional protection of the parent/guardian-child relationship, while nevertheless upholding application of child labor laws against the guardian's wishes. *Loving* struck down a state antimiscegenation law.

Placing *Griswold* against these earlier cases shifts the focus away from the sexual relationship to the familial relationship. *Griswold* now appears as an incremental extension of the constitutional protection of the family—a move from raising children to having children. The controversy over access to contraceptives is reread as one about family planning. We are no longer focused on the intimacy of the bedroom but on the household unit. No longer about sex, *Griswold* has become analogous to the earlier cases protecting private decision making in the family. The cases following *Griswold* are also read as matters of family planning, not sex and not lifestyle. Thus, *Eisenstadt* made clear that the liberty interest in deciding whether to have children is not limited to married couples. Finally, *Roe*'s protection of a right of access to abortion is also seen to involve family planning. In *Bowers*'s account of the cases, they all involve the legal protection of the parent-child relationship—whether to have children and how to raise them. For the state to interfere in these decisions requires a compelling state interest. This is the principle that all of these cases share. Of course, we did not know this was the principle until the opinion drew the analogies in this way.

Turning to the Georgia sodomy statute, the Court finds that this principle simply does not reach this case:

> [W]e think it evident that none of the rights announced in those cases bears any resemblance to the claimed constitutional right of homosexuals to engage in acts of sodomy that is asserted in this case. No connection between family, marriage, or procreation, on the one hand and homosexual activity on the other has been demonstrated.[116]

There is, accordingly, nothing to which to apply the norm derived from the earlier cases. The earlier cases were not about the law of sexual intimacy but about the law of the family. Formally, we might say that the erudite reading of the cases provided the major premise of the argument: there is a constitutionally protected liberty interest in decisions regarding the creation and maintenance of a family. The facts of the present controversy provide the minor premise: homosexual activity does not touch on matters of family creation.[117] The conclusion follows: therefore, criminal prosecution of this conduct does not violate the Constitution.

Bowers goes through the same sort of doctrinal exercise a second time at a higher level of generality—again expressing the same anxiety about interpretation become lawmaking. Shifting its focus from particular precedents bearing on family to those articulating more general principles, the Court writes:

> Striving to assure itself and the public that announcing rights not readily identifiable in the Constitution's text involves much more than the imposition of the Justices' own choice of values on the States and the Federal Government, the Court has sought to identify the nature of the rights qualifying for heightened judicial protection. In *Palko v. Connecticut*, it was said that this category includes those fundamental liberties that are "implicit in the concept of ordered liberty," such that "neither liberty nor justice would exist if [they] were sacrificed." A different description of fundamental liberties appeared in *Moore v. East Cleveland*, where they are characterized as those liberties that are "deeply rooted in this Nation's history and tradition." See also *Griswold v. Connecticut*, 381 U.S. at 506.[118]

The opinion draws what it takes to be an easy conclusion from these premises: the claims made against the Georgia sodomy statute are neither implicit in the concept of ordered liberty nor deeply rooted in American history. The Georgia prohibition does not threaten "ordered liberty" and is not inconsistent with our "history and tradition."[119]

The dissent disagrees because it interprets the precedents to establish a different principle. For the dissenters, the cases are about intimacy between consenting adults. The norm that makes the cases analogous, on this reading, is a prohibition on state interference with such intimate relations. This principle arguably falls within the concept of ordered liberty and is deeply rooted in our nation's history. It is also at stake on the facts of this case. How do we know which is the correct description of the principle that is to serve as the premise of the argument in *Bowers?* There is no abstract answer to this question. We don't first determine the norm and then apply it. Which norm we see in this conflict of interpretations depends more than anything on how we view homosexual couples. How we see them, however, depends on a good deal more than the law alone.

Bowers focuses on the derivation of a common norm from a series of cases. Just as important to the development of doctrine, however, is the creation of exceptions to a rule. Once again, we see a reliance on analogy, for a court cannot declare exceptions absent a reason that applies generally: one exception must be like another in some respect. To study this, we can turn to another much maligned opinion, *Lochner v. New York*, which held unconstitutional a New York statute limiting the hours of employment of bakery employees.[120] The question addressed by the opinion was whether these employees constitute an exception to the general rule that the Fourteenth Amendment prohibits a state from interfering with private contracts—including contracts of employment—freely entered into by both parties. *Lochner* answers this question by identifying the principle that grounds the exceptions; the exceptions are analogous by virtue of this shared feature. Once we know what that is, we can answer the question of whether bakery employees share that feature.

Past cases have held minors, women, and those of diminished intelligence to be exceptional. What they share is some sort of deficiency that undermines their capacity to pursue their interests through ordinary bargaining in a free market. That deficiency lies outside of and prior to the market outcome; it is brought to the transaction. All of these protected groups are, according to the opinion, constructively "wards of the state": they require state protection.[121] Exceptions, accordingly, are not random or arbitrary; they are not a reflection of political power. Dissatisfaction with the market outcome—the contract—is never itself an adequate ground of state intervention. Workers cannot use their political power in the state legislature to supplement their market power. Contracts between *sui juris* adults cannot be disturbed by a political intervention.

Bakery employees fail the test because they are in no sense exceptional. Rather, they are just like the rest of us. Doctrinal erudition is supported by our ordinary intuitions. Here too we see immediately how the argument will fall apart in the future: everyone will come to seem more like the exceptional cases. Once contracts appear to be a function of power rather than liberty, the exceptions swallow the rule. None of us enters the market on equal footing with corporate power. Analogies fail or succeed within a changing historical context.

In these examples, we see the way analogy works. We articulate the general norm only after we group cases together on the basis of intuition. These cases, we feel, belong together. Drawing them together, we operate with a felt sense of the relevant rule, with what Ronald Dworkin called a pre-interpretive sense.[122] In the legal argument, we have to explain why that is—or should be—the rule. Often we are uncertain or in disagreement—not because there is no such rule but because there is more than one possibility. We reason forward from this point. Generally, we move in both directions at once, grouping and separating cases by intuition and formulating general propositions that we test against the cases. Additional cases will sometimes require us to modify the rule: the cases we say were not about family but about intimacy. Or, new cases may require us to draw an additional exception: we didn't mean that kind of contract.

We misunderstand the situation if we think that we are simply "clarifying" the rule at work in the cases. Rather, we are coming to agree upon what the rule is. Analogy is, for this reason, inevitably a normative and not just a descriptive practice. The argument is an effort to persuade, even as it claims only to describe. The alternative to analogical reasoning is to stick close to the "language or design" of the text, as *Bowers* put it. That is not an alternative, however, by which we can avoid the problem of persuading each other as to what the law means. The return to the text is rather a countermove within a contest over persuasion. It is a move from the horizontal to the vertical dimension.

Doctrinal Destruction: Fundamentalism

The fundamentalist critique of precedents is not grounded in nostalgia or in hopes of return to a purer past. Rather, the argument relies on the powerful claim of return to an authoritative text; it does not matter when or in what context the text was produced. Such a text-based argument can operate without regard for earlier opinions because it claims to have hold of the only truth that matters. The persistent dissenter, on or off the bench, is likely to make such a claim. The text is put forward as "the truth," while the judicial precedents are dismissed as "only opinions."

Today, fundamentalist arguments tend toward conservative positions because the doctrines attacked generally emerged during a period of liberal judicial interpretations. The form of an argument, however, does not tell us anything about the substantive content of the argument. In the mid-twentieth century, for example, Justice Black urged a fundamentalist return to the text in support of liberal positions regarding freedom of speech.[123] The independence of form from content becomes very evident when we look at the way in which the New Deal Court dismantled the erudite doctrines of Commerce Clause jurisprudence developed by conservative judges earlier in the century.

Congress began actively to assert its power "to regulate interstate commerce" only at the end of the nineteenth century. With the growth of the national railroads came the Interstate Commerce Commission; with more interstate commerce came efforts to regulate trusts and monopolies.[124] Courts generally upheld these innovations, but in 1918, the Supreme Court drew a line. *Hammer v. Dagenhart* sustained a challenge to a federal statute that prohibited the shipment in interstate commerce of goods produced by child labor.[125] *Hammer* has many of the characteristics of a natal opinion: it cannot convincingly distinguish the earlier cases in which federal legislation was upheld; it purports to offer a plain-sight reading of the constitutional text of the Commerce Clause. That reading asserts that manufacture is not commerce; prohibition is not regulation. These categorical distinctions are hardly in the constitutional text itself; rather, the Court is reading the text through the lens of nineteenth-century political economy. The statute, it says, is not a regulation of commerce but a prohibition on manufacture; the constitutional text permits only the former. *Hammer* was followed by the erudite development of a rule—regulating the conditions of production is a state, not a federal, function—and a doctrine of exceptions.[126] This doctrinal line came to a crisis when the Court declared unconstitutional various elements of the New Deal legislative agenda.[127] Reversal comes in 1941 with *United States v. Darby*, an opinion that relies heavily on a vertical claim of fundamentalism.[128]

The change begins several years earlier, with *National Labor Relations Board v. Jones & Laughlin Steel*, which sustained the constitutionality of the National Labor Relations Act.[129] What is most impressive about this opinion is how little the doctrinal language shifts from the earlier cases, even as the outcome shifts dramatically. Characteristic of the earlier cases had been *Carter Coal*, which declared the Bituminous Coal Act unconstitutional.[130] That act had regulated both wages paid coal miners and the price of coal. It had done so in order to avoid labor unrest and to sustain an orderly market—the same goals at stake later in the National Labor Relations Act at issue in *Jones & Laughlin Steel*.

The earlier case struck down the coal act because it regulated production, not commerce. While recognizing that a strike in the coal fields would dramatically affect commerce, the opinion declared that effect "indirect" because not "proximate[]."[131] These were qualitative, not quantitative, distinctions. Accordingly, the opinion declared that if one man shoveling coal is not a matter of interstate commerce, then a million men shoveling coal is not a matter of interstate commerce. It finds support in the common-law doctrine that master-employee relationships are matters of domestic (as in family) law.[132] As a matter of law, a coal company's relationship to its workers was more like a familial relationship than a transaction in interstate commerce. To the Court, these doctrinal distinctions are all part of an erudite science of law. That the scientific explanation of phenomena is counterintuitive hardly counts as an argument against it.

Jones & Laughlin Steel attempts a cooptation and redirection of this erudite science of law—a shift so subtle that a reader might not notice it. The nineteenth-century science of political economy, which relied on qualitative distinctions, is nudged out of the way by the new, quantitative science of economics. The earlier cases had relied on a test of "direct effect" that followed the common-law tort conception of proximate causation. *Jones & Laughlin Steel* announces, as if it were uncontroversial, that it does not matter how the effect arises. Rather, what matters is the actual quantitative effect on the national economy. The doctrine of proximate causation is out; microeconomics is in. Absent this rereading of the doctrine in light of contemporary developments in the social sciences, what had looked like erudition would have appeared as a false science—as if the Court continued to insist on alchemy after the invention of chemistry. Such a claim of erudition will persuade no one at all.

The opinion manages this transition, in part, by emphasizing the corporate structure of Jones and Laughlin Steel. The company is an industrial behemoth that operates across state lines as it produces and sells steel. It is vertically integrated, owning the facilities for production, transportation, and sale. As a corporate entity, it has no single home; rather, it occupies the space of interstate commerce. Who, the Court asks, but the federal government could regulate this new corporate subject? This was exactly the sort of question the Court had rejected as irrelevant in *Carter Coal*.

Jones and Laughlin Steel, operating on a national scale, directly affects interstate commerce, but what else does? Is the opinion reinterpreting the rule that only states can regulate the conditions of production or is it establishing an exception? Is the opinion telling us only that there is an exception based on size and corporate organization? That idea is plausible, but why focus on size? A corporate organization is just one way of organizing economic activity: it brings "in-house" services and relationships that could otherwise be established by contract.[133] Why should the form of business organization affect Congress's power to regulate interstate commerce? The Court may not have perceived the underlying economic theory of the firm, but it did come to see the stakes for the national economy pretty quickly. This focus on size looks, in retrospect, as merely a transitional matter—helpful in generating a counterintuition to the older idea that production is not commerce.[134]

The remaining doctrinal work of reversal is done in *Darby*, which involved a small lumber mill in Georgia—quite the opposite of a vertically integrated, nationally organized, industrial behemoth. The owner was criminally prosecuted for failing to comply with the wage and hour requirements of the Fair Labor Standards Act. He too claimed that his workers were engaged in production not commerce, and moreover that only a portion of his production ever entered interstate commerce. The Court's response is to overrule *Hammer*.

The opinion does not simply announce a change in interpretation of the Commerce Clause. In fact, it does not purport to be acting, so much as reading. Interpretation is abandoned for the sake of just looking at the text. The critical passage reads as follows:

> *Hammer v. Dagenhart* has not been followed. The distinction on which the decision rested that Congressional power to prohibit interstate commerce is limited to articles which in themselves have some harmful or deleterious property—a distinction which was novel when made and *unsupported by any provision of the Constitution*—has long since been abandoned.[135]

"Unsupported by any provision" is another way of saying that "the text does not say this." Failing to find textual support, the opinion would have us believe that the entire doctrinal line never had much depth. It was judicial invention—mere opinion—without textual foundation. No matter how erudite the opinions may have been, they can be overruled because the authoritative text does not say this.

Darby shows us something else about legal fundamentalism: emphasizing the authoritative text, the opinion portrays the Court as if it were passive. Looking is the most passive of all cognitive acts: you cannot help but see if your eyes are open. Overruling a precedent is portrayed as if it were just a matter of looking at the text a bit more closely. The critical work of the Court is portrayed as if it were more like judicial housekeeping than substantive decision making.

> The conclusion is inescapable that *Hammer v. Dagenhart* was a departure from the principles which have prevailed in the interpretation of the commerce clause both before and since the decision and that such vitality, as a precedent, as it then had has long since been exhausted. It should be and now is overruled.[136]

The entirety of *Darby* pushes toward an ideal of passivity, signifying the marginalization of the Court to the emerging project of regulation of the national economy. Thus, just as the opinion concluded that *Hammer*'s distinction between production and commerce was unfounded in the constitutional text, so the Tenth Amendment disappears as a judicially enforceable norm limiting federal action out of respect for state sovereignty. *Darby* refers to the amendment as a "truism," but what it really means is that the text is only a tautology. A tautology cannot be the ground of decision, for it adds nothing to the law: "The amendment states but a truism that all is retained which has not been surrendered."[137]

Darby illustrates how quickly an erudite line of doctrine can collapse. Looking at the field of erudition that was the meaning of the Commerce Clause, the Court can no longer make any sense of it. It no longer sees a set of coherent distinctions granting and limiting federal power. Instead of a doctrine of rule and exceptions, it sees only arbitrary judgments—or false claims of knowledge supporting partisan political ideology. Thus, the opinion signals a return to the text itself: "The power of Congress over interstate commerce 'is complete in itself, may be exercised to its utmost extent, and acknowledges no limitations, other than are prescribed by the Constitution.'"[138] Instead of reading commerce authority as bound by the distinction of commerce from production, the opinion now sees the textual grant of authority to Congress as "complete in itself."

We see just how radical this rereading of the Commerce Clause is in the final case in this series of opinions, *Wickard v. Filburn*.[139] The opinion upholds federal regulations that control wheat production intended for home consumption. Congress's power now seems to reach even the family vegetable patch. The old erudite science of the law, with its distinctions between production and commerce, is derided as mere "nomenclature." The attempt to constrain power by distinguishing "direct" from "indirect" effects is described as "mechanical."[140] Regulation of commerce can be accomplished through intervention to control supply or demand. Could a modern economist possibly think otherwise?

The return to the text was used to dismantle an erudite reading of the Commerce Clause that had come to be seen as based on a false science. The result is to take the courts out of the business of enforcing limits on Congress's power under the Commerce Clause. In place of the courts, the new administrative agencies will become the point for expert management of the economy. They will not be using nineteenth-century concepts of political economy. No other result would have been plausible. This is not because a modern economy stands in need of substantial and continuing regulatory intervention. That may be true, but the point here is about judicial opinions, not economics. An opinion cannot require the deployment of what has come to be seen as a false science. It cannot do so because a text held to require such irrational behavior would persuade no one. It could not be seen as authored by the people. The people cannot understand themselves to have authorized governance to their own detriment. The text cannot say this.

There is, however, no last word. Fifty years after *Wickard*, doctrinal innovation begins again for the sake of protecting the states from federal authority. In a series of cases, federal statutes are struck down despite the fact that their regulatory reach would have an effect on interstate commerce.[141] They are stuck down now because the effect is too "indirect." New claims of erudition are developed as the opinions try to distinguish commerce from activities that are "truly local."[142] We learn that education and crime are local despite congressional findings, as well as common sense observation, that both are major factors in determining the growth and direction of the national economy. Legal categories no longer track the categories of economics or administration. There is a parallel recovery of the Tenth Amendment as a limit on federal power; no longer is it a mere "truism."[143] We are again moving out the horizontal axis.

To those who learned their constitutional law from reading the New Deal cases, this all appears as "déjà vu all over again."[144] The text is being interpreted in light of an erudite science of the law that has no relationship to modern economics. The dissenters persist, relying on their own version of plain-sight fundamentalism.[145] No doubt their wait will pay off, for the doctrinal cycle between fundamentalism and erudition, between the vertical and horizontal dimensions, will continue without end.

We cannot silence the radical, fundamentalist critique by pointing out that there is no noninterpretive, neutral position from which to read a text. This response fails because the legitimacy of every opinion depends on the structural distinction between an interpretation and the authoritative text. The text is necessarily represented as both external to and prior to the opinion, which is *only* an interpretation. A successful interpretation persuades us that it has hold of the meaning of the text, but it is not the text itself. An American court cannot easily say that the distinction between opinion and authoritative text has collapsed, for that is nothing other than a claim that it has the power to make law.

The distinction between interpretation and text keeps open the possibility of radical critique. As doctrine develops through the erudite drawing of analogies and distinctions, it becomes ever more possible to assert the fundamentalist critique. While erudite arguments can themselves support reversal—for example, *Lawrence*'s reversal of *Bowers*—those reversals will be cast as corrections of missteps along a broad path of progressive development. Fundamentalist arguments aim for reversals of entire lines of doctrinal development. Thus, *Darby* marks the end of an era. Vertical arguments are most powerful in this fundamentalist form. To the erudite interpretation, the fundamentalist responds "the text does not say that." When the opponent responds "Yes, but . . . ," she is already at a rhetorical disadvantage. She will be accused of "making" law.

Conclusion: The Life of Legal Doctrine

Fundamentalism serves as the prophetic sword of doctrine, promising a return to the truth revealed at the origins of a legal text. Erudition is the shield behind which doctrine ordinarily develops in response to the changing practices and beliefs of the society. Natality is the flash of the new that can appear as if from nowhere. It is the unpredictable turn in doctrine that may be necessary from a social or moral perspective, but it has no existing jurisprudential space to occupy. Together, these forms provide the overall shape of the development of doctrine through judicial opinions. Of course, they mark ideal models and any particular opinion may set forth elements of each of these approaches. As a rhetorical work, an opinion will draw opportunistically from the available arguments in its effort to persuade us.

Structurally—we might even say "ontologically"—every opinion must privilege text over interpretation. This privilege, however, does not mean that the return to text is the rhetorically strongest position to take in any particular case. The structural claim of textual privilege cannot resolve a competition among epistemic claims—that is, claims to know what the law is. One epistemic claim can only compete with another. We must be persuaded to read the text one way or another.

To the erudite practitioner, the claim to return to the text itself will always appear naive. If the text were enough, why would we need all those volumes of judicial opinions? Why, for that matter, would we need lawyers and law schools? Where we come out in this debate is likely to depend on whether we see the "science"—or even the common sense—in the science of the law. If erudition looks to us like "transcendental nonsense," then we may find ourselves proclaiming a need to return to the text itself.[146] If the claims of erudition are made to advance a project of self-government that we can see as our own, we are likely to see fundamentalist claims as naive and as themselves serving a partisan agenda.

There is nothing about the structure of interpretation that tells us what is the best way to read a text. Fundamentalists will claim that we need only to look plainly at the law. Their opponents will always respond that reading is not the same as looking. Meaning is always social and contextual. What, then, is the context within which we read a legal text? The text itself cannot answer that question.[147]

Context leads courts to choose among natal, progressive, and critical opinions. We cannot banish any of these options from the realm of possibility. They are built into the nature of interpretation. This is not a weakness of the law but its strength. For the unsettled nature of interpretation makes possible a rule of law that is both respectful of the legitimacy of authoritative texts and responsive to the changing conditions of our political, social, and economic life.

Law is not trying to work out a single theory of interpretation. It is not a project of theory but of practical self-governance. Courts and lawyers make use of these different conceptual tools in their attempts to construct persuasive arguments. We cannot know in advance what will persuade. All that we can confidently say is that the arguments offered will move on both the vertical and horizontal axes. The forms of that movement extend from natality, to progressive development, to critical destruction. That is the life of legal doctrine.

FACTS: STATING THE CASE

Lawyers know intuitively what law students must endlessly be told: there are no rules apart from facts, and no facts apart from rules. Legal rules do not have a meaning in the abstract; facts do not simply appear as if from nowhere. The proposition is so basic that it informs the very nature of legal education: the case method. One learns the law by studying the cases. To know something about a field of law is to be able to give an account of how the cases stand in relation to one another. Similarly, to understand a particular case is to be able to explain how the facts of this case stand in relation to the facts of other cases.

For this reason, one cannot know a single case alone. Every case is embedded in a larger context, for there is no law of the singular. The account of the facts of any single case always points beyond to other cases that we judge to be alike or different. That likeness or difference gives meaning to the legal norms at issue. One understands a law not from reading its text but by imagining how the law will be used to order a set of facts. The role of the opinion, in briefest form, is to make the case by linking facts to law through an account of likeness and difference. The case arises when there is controversy over how law and fact fit together; its resolution brings order by offering a narrative of how these facts stand within the larger order of law.[1]

Access to the Facts: Procedure

When lawyers speak of facts, they are usually not thinking of facts as they appear in appellate opinions. They are thinking of evidence. Their perspective is that of standing before a trial court or administrative body. They ask how to get information into, or kept out of, the record. Facts are not events in the world, which exist independently of legal procedures. Rather, facts are inferences from admissible evidence. One might know perfectly well what happened, but if the evidence is not sufficient to support an inference, that "fact" makes no appearance in the courtroom.

Facts in an appellate opinion are not all that different from facts at trial: both share the fundamental characteristic that they do not precede the law but are the consequences of legal judgments. We deal in both instances with something we might represent as fact-law. We can easily see fact-law operating at the trial court. When a defendant is held not guilty of a crime, for example, it hardly follows that he did not commit the act. The victim often does not need a trial to know who injured him. He is not going to change his mind if the defendant is not convicted. All that we can reliably say of such a defendant is that the state was not able to introduce evidence sufficient to support an inference of guilt beyond a reasonable doubt. "Not guilty" is not the same as factually or morally innocent. Even in a civil case, where the standard of proof is only a preponderance of the evidence, failure to meet the standard does not mean that the allegations are false as a matter of fact. Evidence may be lacking for all sorts of reasons—procedural and substantive—that have nothing to do with what actually took place.[2]

Of course, truth is not irrelevant to the ends of the judicial process. The work of the court should have some relationship to truth. Ideal justice requires that those who in fact did nothing wrong go free and that those who really did commit a criminal act be held accountable. Law's justice, however, inevitably falls far short of the ideal. There are evidentiary rules, burdens of proof, limits on investigative procedures, and statutes of limitation. There are also issues of controlling police behavior, recognizing pleas made and deals cut, and combating the unavoidable biases of the decision makers. For all these reasons, the end of a trial is not necessarily the end of the matter. This is not an invitation to private revenge but rather to the work of the historian and the journalist.

Legal procedure is not like a laboratory protocol: follow it and you are likely to reach the truth of the matter. Rather, it operates as a restraint on power: follow it and the state is less likely to abuse its immense power. Procedure is not about scientific method but about safeguarding a host of other values ranging from fairness to finality. Most of the time, a liberal state puts the worry about power ahead of the worry about truth.[3]

Procedure presents in the microcosm of the individual case the larger problem of the relationship of law to facts. A court never has direct access to the facts. No one, not even a Justice on the Supreme Court, can ask what the truth is, but only what he can legitimately claim to know—or more precisely, of what he can take cognizance, since it is a stretch to speak of knowledge here. In *Marbury*, Chief Justice Marshall knows perfectly well what happened with respect to the signing of Marbury's commission as well as to the failed effort to deliver the commission. He knows because he had been intimately involved in the events when he was secretary of state. Yet as a judge, he cannot draw on that knowledge. Instead, he writes of "[what] appears, from the affidavits."[4] Similarly, jurors are often told to disregard evidence; they are to act as if they don't know something about which they might otherwise have great confidence. Indeed, if a potential juror has independent knowledge of the facts of the case, he or she is likely to be excluded from the panel. That sort of knowledge would be a virtue in most settings, but not at trial.

Marbury was a case in the original, not the appellate, jurisdiction of the Supreme Court. The proceedings were, therefore, a trial similar to any other. Yet, the basic point that facts are the product of legal procedures is no less true for courts exercising an appellate function. Indeed, an appellate court may be even more constrained than a trial court, for it is bound by the conclusions of fact established in the record of the lower court. An appellate judge is not free to reject those conclusions even if she thinks that she would not have been convinced by the evidence offered at trial.[5] She cannot think that she "knows better," even when she does.

If we were to stop with this idea of the facts as matters of record, however, we would fail to reach the creative work of the appellate opinion. That work is, first of all, to imagine the facts as an expression of law, not simply to present facts as already established. As a work of persuasion, the opinion must convince us to see the world in a way that supports its legal conclusions; it must show us fact-law. The opinion asks us to see through the particular facts to the whole that is the legal order.

The opinion is not an inquiry in which a "neutral" statement of the facts is first written and then the question of the law is addressed. The reciprocal relationship between facts and law begins with the opinion's choice of a context within which to present the case, continues in the statement of the case itself, and then enters deep into the construction of analogies. Fact and law are inseparable at every stage of the opinion.

Setting the Context

A legal problem comes to a court when someone claims to have suffered or to be threatened with an injury. The facts of which he complains, however, do not come with a label, telling us where to look for the law. The facts become legally intelligible only as they are placed in a context that tells us what sort of a case we confront. In law school, the casebook tends to render this first and most important problem of fact invisible. The editor has already done the work of grouping relevant cases together. Much of the work of the lawyer, however, occurs in this initial decision of where to place the case. Until we know what sort of facts we confront, we cannot know what body of law to apply.

The burden on the lawyer is to persuade the court to frame a conflict one way rather than another. She tries to convince the court to set the controversy in a particular context, which means to see it against one horizon rather than another. She cannot do this in the abstract but must situate the facts of her case with respect to a range of other cases. Convince the court that it is a case about labor law and one outcome follows; convince the judges that it is a case about a public health law and another outcome follows. Thus, a New York statute limiting the hours of employment in bakeries was held unconstitutional in *Lochner* because the majority thought it a labor law;

the dissenters would have upheld it as a matter of public health.[6] In itself, it is not one thing or another. We learn the facts only as we learn the relevant law, but we learn the law only as we are persuaded to see the facts within one context rather than another.

How does the lawyer or the judge make the case for a context? In *Lochner*, the Justices argue about the appropriate horizon: some look to where the controverted law appears in the New York State Code; some consider the political origin of the law; some choose the context most favorable to upholding the constitutionality of the statute. Most of all, however, they rely on what they know as informed members of the national community. They have an intuitive sense of what this legislation is about. They engage in an imaginative act of authorship, asking themselves what their intent would have been had they voted for this law. Of course, they disagree on this as well: some think the legislation is nothing more than an attempt by employees to outflank the results of a competitive labor market;[7] some think it is a first step toward a general limit on working hours for the sake of public health.[8] One thing the court cannot do is appeal to law to answer this question of context, for only when we know the kind of case it is do we know which body of law is relevant.

The first task of an opinion is to convince us to see the facts against a particular horizon. Often the disagreement among the judges is over this question of context: they don't agree upon the characterization of the facts. Not agreeing on context, they look to different bodies of law in order to resolve the case. Where one person sees an issue of free speech, another may see an issue of corporate power; where one sees an issue of discrimination, another may see an exercise of free choice. For a dramatic example of disagreement consider the abortion controversy. Where some people see an act of infanticide, others see a choice regarding personal health. If we describe the facts as an act of murdering an innocent baby, have we not already decided the case? Conversely, if we describe the act as a medical procedure involving only the body of the woman, have we not also decided the case?

In these examples, we can see that there is no neutral way to characterize the facts. Before there can be a narrative of the facts, there must already be a decision with respect to context.[9] That choice can never be innocent; it takes a position on how and what we are to see. Just here, we begin to see why law students are advised that cases can be won and lost in the statement of the case. A legal argument does not begin only after the facts have been presented; it begins with the choice of how to present the facts.

Consider Marbury's problem and how one might describe the facts of his case.[10] Do we begin with President Adams's defeat in the election of 1800 and his effort to pack the courts through the midnight appointments? Do the facts include President Jefferson's subsequent decision to deny commissions to these appointees? Do we say Marbury was denied something that belonged to him—his property—or do we say that a government document is ordinarily available to the public? Do we care about the income Marbury would have had from the position? Do we include the reasons for the denial of the request for a copy of the commission? Can we characterize the facts as the termination of Marbury's employment rather than as the denial of a request for a copy of the commission? Or perhaps we describe it as a case in which he never assumed the position, so he cannot be fired. We need to know something about where we are going legally if we are to make decisions about where to begin factually.

Experienced lawyers generally agree on issues of context: they share an intuitive understanding of what to put together and what to separate. Sharing intuitions, they know where the argument lies. They are contesting the same issues, arguing about the proper interpretation of the same cases. Sometimes, however, the controversy arises because there is no shared intuition establishing a single horizon. Different lawyers see the world differently when they try to make sense of the facts. They have different understandings of what is going on and of the issues that need resolution. They read the facts through different bodies of law.

One of the most famous cases of modern constitutional jurisprudence illustrates the decisive importance of establishing context. *Youngstown Sheet & Tube Co. v. Sawyer* is the font of modern separation of powers doctrine.[11] The case arose out of President Harry Truman's

FACTS

decision to order the secretary of commerce to seize the steel mills and continue production just before the unions were scheduled to go on strike. The seizure came after months of administration efforts through various forms of regulatory intervention to bring the owners and the unions to agreement. When those efforts failed, the president acted. He justified the seizure by pointing first to the need for steel to supply munitions to the troops fighting in Korea and second to the need to prevent inflation in a wartime economy. He was not willing simply to allow the owners to increase the price of steel in response to the union demand for a wage increase. Immediately after ordering the seizure, he presented his reasons in a message to Congress in which he also affirmed that Congress was free to decide upon a different course of action. He was, he said, confident that he had the power to act as he did; no new legislation was needed. Nevertheless, members of Congress remained free to decide upon a different course of action. If they passed legislation prohibiting the seizure, he assured them he would comply with their directions.[12]

The political drama around the case is evident. It is probable that those political pressures, including the short time the Court had to produce a decision, account for the strange appearance of the case. This may be the only case in Supreme Court history in which every member of the majority also offers a concurrence, with Justice Felix Frankfurter even offering two. The actual opinion for the court has been largely ignored since the day it was announced. Instead, the most important opinions have been Justice Jackson's concurrence, followed by the longer of Justice Frankfurter's two opinions. We need to compare these two opinions to Chief Justice Fred Vinson's dissent. What divides the Justices is precisely the question of what kind of a case this is. Justices Jackson and Frankfurter view it as a labor case; Justice Vinson sees it as a case about national defense. This is the question of context, of establishing the horizon against which we understand what it is that the president has done. Until we answer this question, we don't even know what is the relevant body of law to which we must look. For the lawyers, to win this argument was to win the case.

Justice Jackson's opinion famously offers a three-part test for approaching cases that raise a separation of powers claim against the president.[13] The president, Jackson writes, can be acting pursuant to or in opposition to a congressional directive, or he can be operating in the absence of any congressional direction. The president is at his strongest when acting with the support of Congress, and at his weakest when acting contrary to its direction. In between, his power is indeterminate. The outcome in cases that belong in that in-between category, writes Jackson, will depend upon "contemporary imponderables."[14] A decision will be, in large part, a function of where the case lands on the tripartite scale. But cases don't simply land on the scale; they must be placed there.

Jackson portrays that initial act of placement as if it were uncontroversial. Congress's action establishes which of the three categories the controverted presidential action falls within. True, he speaks of "contemporary imponderables" in his second category, but those imponderables arise only when Congress has failed to act—that failure, at least, should be clear. The whole scheme, however, rests on a mistaken image: one in which the work of the opinion begins after the initial categorization has occurred. He writes, in other words, as if the Court need only check on what Congress has done. But Congress has always done many things. Sometimes we interpret even a failure to act as a decision about the law. How, for example, should we read Congress's failure to act in response to President Truman's message? Has it *decided* to acquiesce? Is this an expression of approval?[15]

The lawyer, on or off the bench, always starts from Justice Jackson's second category of contemporary imponderables. Her burden is to persuade us to see the entirety of the legal resources as permitting or prohibiting the president's act. There is no third category in between these two at the moment of decision. The second category, in other words, is not a stable point on a tripartite scale but the beginning point of every controversial case. No court can rest its decision on that second category, and none ever do. They do not cite "contemporary imponderables" as a ground of decision.

Youngstown shows us that the outcome of the case depends on the horizon against which we view the controversy. The disagreement between the majority and the dissent is not over how to read a particular legislative act but rather over which statutes are relevant to the decision. The majority sees the controversy as one involving intervention in a labor dispute; the dissent sees it as one involving national security. Jackson's scheme cannot help us to decide this issue. To decide, we cannot look to the law, because we do not know what law matters before the decision. But neither can we look to the facts, as if the president's act in itself carries the indicia of its character. We cannot ask the president whether he is intervening in a labor dispute or acting to defend national security. We must be persuaded to see the situation one way or the other, and persuasion is always a matter of fact and law together.

The Justices in the majority write as if it is clear that this case involves a labor dispute: the problem is presidential intervention in a labor dispute when the parties have not been able to come to an agreement.[16] Congress, in the majority's view, has not been quiet with respect to what the government can and cannot do in the face of such a dispute. Indeed, according to them, the president was acting within a dense network of legislation that defines his options in the face of a threatened strike, including strikes in defense industries. The president can invoke mediation; he can force a cooling-off period. He can even insist on continued production but only if he follows specified procedures, none of which were followed in this instance.[17]

Some of these avenues the president did indeed pursue. Nevertheless, when he ran out of options in the face of an imminent strike, he seized. That option, according to Jackson, had been precisely denied to the president: "Congress has not left seizure of private property an open field but has covered it by three statutory policies inconsistent with this seizure."[18] We are, in his view, squarely in category three. The conclusion follows quickly from that: the president has no power to disregard legislation that limits his options in the face of a labor dispute. His role is to execute, not to make, the law.

Justice Frankfurter writes a concurrence that covers much of the same ground.[19] He will, however, have nothing to do with Jackson's tripartite scheme; it is too broad for his taste. Nevertheless, he comes to an even stronger conclusion with respect to the context—it's a labor dispute—and with respect to what it is that Congress has done. "Congress has expressed its will to withhold this power from the President as though it had said so in so many words. . . . By the Labor Management Relations Act of 1947, Congress said to the President, 'You may not seize.' "[20] Strikingly, Frankfurter has gone from metaphor ("as though it had said") to directive ("You may not seize.") in less than a page. Of course, Congress did not say this expressly. Perhaps it did not say this at all. Arguably—at least according to the dissent—what it actually said was that the president can seize under certain circumstances.

Despite the extraordinary circumstances of the case, both Jackson and Frankfurter are working within entirely familiar legal territory. Having decided that they confront a controversy over the legality of an intervention in a labor dispute, they must interpret what it is that the law permits. Because federal legislation has authorized some seizures, a lawyer can argue by analogy or by distinction. Do we build an analogy from those instances of permissible seizure, arguing that this case is like those? Or, do we distinguish the permissible cases from the one at hand? Do we argue that Congress has no objection in principle to seizure and this case is *of the sort* that the legislation permits? Or, do we argue Congress excluded cases of this sort from the range of permissible seizures? Jackson and Frankfurter decide for distinction.

We do know that Congress did not actively object to *this* seizure. Congress took no action in response to the president's notification and his explicit acknowledgment that the legislature could choose to direct his actions through new legislation. Neither did Congress go to court to challenge the president. Of course, the owners of the steel mills did go to court. Their interest presumably is that of property owners: they want control of the disposition and use of their property. They also want compensation for the use of the property as long as the seizure continues. They would want these things regardless of whether the president was acting pursuant to a congressional directive. *Youngstown*, however, is not remembered as an opinion about property. It could have been, but property was not what most of the Justices saw when they looked at the case.[21] Instead, they saw a dispute between the president and Congress over executive power. The dissenters, however, did not see such a dispute at all. Rather, they saw a president carrying out the national security policies of Congress.

The dissent begins with an explicit appeal to context: "In passing upon the question of presidential powers in this case, we must first consider the context in which those powers were exercised."[22] That context is not that of an ordinary labor dispute of the sort Congress had in mind when it passed the Labor Management Relations Act of 1947. Rather, Chief Justice Vinson sees a nation at war, a nation confronting dire threats to its very existence as well as to its allies. "A world not yet recovered from the devastation of World War II has been forced to face the threat of another and more terrifying conflict."[23] Did Congress really say to the president, "You may not seize," in a situation in which failure to seize might lead to national defeat? Frankfurter and Jackson never quite reach that question: it is outside of the horizon they create.

If one were to agree with Vinson's characterization, then what exactly is the relevant legislation pursuant to which the president is acting? Vinson's gaze extends well beyond the labor laws that capture the attention of Jackson and Frankfurter. The dissent, accordingly, reviews national commitments, including ratification of the United Nations Charter, membership in NATO, and maintenance of a nuclear deterrent. The president is not intervening in a labor dispute, he is defending the free world. Congress has repeatedly directed the president to pursue these policies, enacting Defense Appropriations Acts, committing to the Truman and Marshall plans, and passing the Mutual Security Act of 1951.[24] Nowhere did it say "you may not seize" in pursuit of these policies. Indeed, against this horizon it is difficult to imagine that it would say such a thing.

Against the horizon of national security policy, seizure of the steel mills looks entirely different from the way it was portrayed by

Jackson and Frankfurter. The president is acting to carry out legislative policy; he is not acting against congressional directives. Why, the dissent asks, should we focus on the act of seizure as if it fell in a single, all-inclusive category of labor disputes, when Congress has frequently permitted seizures and the president has frequently acted to seize? Stop looking only to the employers and unions involved in this dispute, the dissent says. Turn your gaze to the soldiers who need ammunition and the national defense that relies upon airplanes and nuclear bombs. Evaluate the president's actions against this horizon, and you reach an entirely different conclusion as to what the law is.

We see here a perfect illustration of the importance of context. The argument is over the facts but not over the record. The opinions are trying to persuade us to put the dispute in one context rather than another. Until we do that, we don't know which law applies; we don't know how to construct analogies or make distinctions. We don't know whether the appropriate analogy is to other labor disputes or to other threats to national security. We can't answer the question of whether the president is acting to carry out congressional policy or in violation of such policy until we know what he is doing. The two sides in *Youngstown*, however, offer competing accounts of what the president is doing.

How we decide for one context or the other does touch upon the mystery of "contemporary imponderables" to which Jackson refers. Once we leave the domain of proof and enter that of persuasion, there is not a great deal that can be said in the abstract. What counts as persuasive depends on both the speakers and the listeners; it shifts over time and depends on the circumstances. It depends as well on the ability to present the case in a compelling manner. The court, like the rest of us, must be persuaded. About persuasion, there are no rules.

These imponderables point to what may be most surprising about the case from a contemporary perspective. Can we image a court today that would not have been persuaded by the dissent's invocation of national security? What would we make of the president's affidavit speaking of the grave national security dangers that would arise were production to stop?[25] Strikingly, there is no evidence offered to contest those claims. Sixty years on—even with authoritarianism a fading memory—we see differently. Indeed, we have been struggling with how to view presidential actions in the aftermath of 9/11. Is the proper context national security or criminal law?[26] Determining the horizon is, once again, likely to be outcome determinative. In virtually every recent case, in recent years, the opinions have adopted the national security horizon.[27]

In *Youngstown*, the entire weight of the argument is borne by this choice of context. The case is won and lost right there. Do we read the opinions and see a labor dispute or a national security crisis? Accepting one context or the other, we have effectively resolved the case. We see a more recent example of the importance of context in Chief Justice Roberts's opinion in *National Federation of Independent Business v. Sebelius*, which upheld the major healthcare reform initiative of the Obama administration.[28]

For most of the Court, including the dissenters, the context within which the Affordable Care Act was to be evaluated was that of the commerce in health care delivery: the buying and selling of health care services, including health insurance. That business amounts to about 20 percent of the national economy.[29] The most controversial provision of the act required all individuals to obtain insurance coverage—arguably a regulation of entry into the health insurance market. Seen from within this context of business regulation, the legality of the measure was to be evaluated under the Commerce Clause. The Chief Justice, however, offers an alternative context, arguing that the insurance mandate provision can also be seen as a tax. Where others saw a regulation of the health insurance industry, Roberts saw a tax.

Roberts joins four Justices to conclude that Congress has no power under the Commerce Clause to require people to enter the health insurance market. The case had already invoked vigorous argument over the reach of Congress's Commerce Clause power on the way to the Supreme Court. The opinions of the majority and the dissent go through these arguments again: they reach different conclusions but within a common horizon. Each side deploys analogies and makes distinctions building from familiar precedents in the field. Of particular concern is how to interpret *Wickard v. Filburn*, which had upheld a federal regulation limiting the amount of wheat farmers could plant, even when intended for home consumption.[30] The *Sebelius* majority thought the case was distinguishable because the farmer had chosen to enter the wheat market, while here the individual has not chosen to enter the market for health insurance. Regulating a market is different, they held, from compelling entry into a market. The dissenters could see no such distinction. After all, the wheat farmer who cannot grow his own wheat is compelled to enter a market to purchase that wheat.

This disagreement over the Commerce Clause was not, however, the end of the case. Even though Chief Justice Roberts joined the majority on this point, he went on to join the Commerce Clause dissenters to form a different majority upholding the act as a federal tax. The argument this majority put forth was that the only operative effect of the insurance mandate was to impose a tax on those who failed to meet the requirement. With that description of the facts, a different horizon of interpretation opens up. The relevant body of law is no longer Commerce Clause cases, but those involving federal taxation authority. The federal government often pursues its policy objectives of encouraging or discouraging forms of private behavior by imposing taxes. It could, the majority held, do the same in pursuit of its goal of extending health insurance coverage to the uninsured.

From the perspective of the arguments in *Youngstown*, Roberts's opinion for the Court in *Sebelius* is innovative. It is as if Justice Jackson or Frankfurter had said that the president's seizure of the mills was unconstitutional as a matter of labor law but constitutional as a matter of national security law. Why say the first if you believe the second? Believing the law to be constitutional, why did Roberts voice his views about the Commerce Clause at all? Doing so, he effectively offers an opinion that says, "It depends upon how you look at it."

That is certainly true, but that admission comes with an explicit claim that it is up to the individual Justices to decide what kind of law they think it is. In response, we are likely to count votes and speak of how easily the decision could have gone the other way.

The opinion is less, not more, persuasive because of Roberts's act of telling us what he thinks about issues that he did not have to reach. Transparency may be a virtue in many areas of government decision making but not necessarily in the judicial opinion where the end is to persuade readers to see the law as the product of our own self-authorship. To draw attention to the importance of the individual Justice's vote always works to undermine the belief that the narrative voice of the opinion is that of the people. Roberts, one suspects, was also counting votes and thinking of tactical and strategic reasons for acting as he did. The cost was an opinion that has persuaded very few. It also resulted in an assault on Roberts's own integrity by those who had otherwise been his political supporters.[31]

Together *Youngstown* and *Sebelius* show us that an opinion can be more or less successful at this task of establishing the context within which to understand the facts. The most spectacular modern failure is found in *Roe v. Wade*.[32] *Roe* has been endlessly criticized. Those arguments usually focus either on the opinion's derivation of a legal rule protecting freedom of choice from the existing case law or on its remedial order imposing a trimester regulatory regime. The failure I am concerned with occurs earlier—in the long account of the history of abortion practices with which the opinion begins. This too is a narrative of facts the point of which is to establish the context within which to evaluate the controverted state statutes prohibiting abortion.

The account begins with one of the strangest lines to be found in any judicial opinion: "The Ephesian, Soranos, often described as the greatest of the ancient gynecologists, appears to have been generally opposed to Rome's prevailing free abortion practices."[33] From there, it goes on to review the Hippocratic oath (dismissed as the position of only the Pythagoreans), English common law, English statutory law, American legal practices—both early and late—and finally the positions of a variety of professional associations including the AMA and the ABA. For the historian, these are issues that would require volumes, not paragraphs. For the lawyer, the issue is not the quality of the research but the contribution the account makes to the persuasiveness of the opinion. Does it persuade us to see the context for the decision one way rather than another?

We can frame the problem of context creation in *Roe* as follows. Abortion is an issue upon which people have dramatically conflicting views. Some people think that it is a moral offense on the order of infanticide; others think that only the woman has a cognizable interest in this decision concerning her own body. The former think that action is required to save innocent human life; the latter think that the issue involves only a medical procedure in which the state has no more interest than in any other medical procedure. Of course, there are lots of positions in between. Where there is disagreement about policy, we usually leave it to political institutions to decide. Some communities might decide to prohibit abortion; others might leave the choice to the mother. About some issues, however, we think minority views must be protected from the majority. With respect to such issues, we say individuals have rights. The question of context, accordingly, is to which category does the abortion decision belong: is it a matter of public policy or of individual rights? We must be persuaded to see the abortion decision as like other rights or as like other matters of policy.

No doubt, the opinion sets into this history of abortion practices to help us to see the choice for abortion as falling into the category of rights. At least that is the logic of the opinion. Unfortunately, the argument never gets there. Worse, in the end, the history seems to point in exactly the opposite direction. The narrative persuades us that approaches to abortion have varied dramatically over time, that different communities have held different beliefs on this issue, that American practices have not been consistent over time or across regions, and that the present moment is one in which practices and beliefs are rapidly changing. There is little in the history that suggests anything other than that communities have worked out these issues for themselves. Policies have changed, but not always in the same direction. Arguably, more recent changes have reflected a medicalization of the decision rather than a shift toward a claim of right. In short, there is nothing about this history that persuades us to see the issue against the horizon of individual rights.

The point is not that the holding of *Roe* is incorrect. The conclusion might be entirely persuasive for other reasons.[34] Many commentators, for example, argue that a stronger ground for the conclusion could have been found had the opinion relied on equal protection doctrine in place of substantive due process.[35] In that case, an entirely different account of the facts would have been called for—one that emphasized the place of women in the social, political, and economic order. Perhaps this could have been done. Still, the account that is offered fails to persuade. The opinion creates an appearance of historical erudition. We are surprised to learn that the Justices have been studying Soranos and the Pythagoreans. But this erudition is not marshaled to make a point one way or the other on the issue about which we need guidance.

In the end, we turn away from *Roe* quite uncertain. We may have learned a lot of facts, but they have not led us to one context rather than another. We don't know why the abortion decision is one of individual right rather than of community standards. The individual rights paradigm suggests that it is like the choice of a religious faith. The community standard paradigm suggests that it is like the criminalization of other morally disapproved activities, such as prohibitions on the use of drugs.[36] The narrative the opinion offers does not help us to make any progress on choosing between these different paradigms. Unless we can find other resources, we are unpersuaded, even if we are pleased with the outcome. As it turned out, many people were neither persuaded nor pleased. Absent a persuasive account of the relevant context, the opinion looked like an assertion of a power to make law, not an exercise of the judicial power to tell us what our law is.

FACTS

This Is the Way the World Is: Persuasive Facts

Reading the statement of the case in a well-crafted opinion, we may feel that we know what the decision must be even before we get to the discussion of the law. Reading the statement, we feel that there is only one reasonable way to resolve the controversy. We think that any other decision would simply make no sense, for it would be in substantial tension with what we know about the world. The burden of persuasion, in such a case, has been carried by the account of the facts. This experience is not unusual precisely because the law must be interpreted as a purposive intervention in the world. Creating a law, we are trying to do something that makes sense in light of our understanding of the way the world is. When an opinion persuades through its statement of the facts, we have already come to the conclusion that there is just one reasonable response to these facts.

Even in those cases—most of them—in which the statement of the case won't do all the work of persuasion, the opinion aims for an account of the facts that points to, or is supportive of, the legal conclusion. The opinion is trying to make sense of the situation, which is always a matter of fact-law. If facts and law do not connect, then we are left with an impression that the judges themselves have decided what should be done given these facts. Such an opinion is not a success, for we can only understand ourselves as authors of a law that makes sense given what we believe about the world.

This potentially persuasive character of the statement of the facts is well illustrated in one of the recent abortion decisions, *Gonzales v. Carhart*.[37] Here, the Court upheld a federal prohibition on "partial birth" abortion procedures. This opinion is at the extreme opposite end of the scale from *Roe*. While the account of the facts in *Roe* went nowhere, the account of the facts in *Carhart* overwhelms the reader's sensibilities.

Carhart may be the most difficult opinion to read in the entire judicial corpus. It is, I suspect, no easier to read for a supporter of the outcome than for an opponent. The difficulty lies in the detailed description of the medical procedure at issue. Unlike a medical text book that would describe the procedure in a technical language of instruments, measurements, and Latin terms, this description uses ordinary language. It speaks of crushing the skull, of vacuuming out the brain, of the dismemberment of arms and legs, of pulling the body apart. This use of ordinary language extends to those upon whom the procedure is performed: not the woman but the fetus, who appears at various points in the text as an "unborn child" or a "baby." The mother, when she does appear, is also cast as a victim: the opinion speculates on the psychological harm she will suffer when she realizes that she has allowed the dismemberment of her child.[38] The physician becomes not an obstetrician tending to her patient but an "abortion doctor." We have victims on one side and an aggressor on the other. What kind of person, we are left wondering, could perform such outrageous acts on a baby? That, at least, is what the statement attempts to persuade us to ask. If we do ask *that* question, the case is over.

The language of the opinion is quite literally the language of atrocity. We would expect to hear this sort of language offered in testimony at the trial of someone accused of gross violations of human rights or perhaps in a report from Human Rights Watch. Indeed, at various points, the opinion shifts into the testimonial mode, quoting passages from abortion opponents' statements that are in the legislative record. This is a language that cries out for a response. It can literally overwhelm us morally, which is just what it is designed to do. Once we allow this into our field of vision, it is hard to resist the outcome the opinion reaches. It performs the work of persuasion that *Roe* ignored.

The dissent objects to the language. It points to the "loaded" character of the descriptions of the procedure and of the doctors.[39] It seeks to displace attention to the medical professional, whose role is to advise the patient of the best procedure under the circumstances. The law, the dissent argues, should give this relationship a wide scope, which is exactly the meaning of the relevant precedents according to the dissent. All this may be true, but it suggests what the dissent fully knows: a decision to strike down the law must shift the focus from ordinary language to the technical language of law and medicine.

Failing to accomplish this shift, the dissent is left on extremely weak grounds when it quotes *Stenberg*—an earlier case involving a similar state restriction that was struck down—to the effect that ordinary, second-term abortions could be described in similar terms: "[T]he notion that either of these two equally gruesome procedures ... is more akin to infanticide than the other ... is simply irrational."[40] Anyone who has suffered the moral assault of the majority opinion may indeed question the distinction but not in the direction that the dissent would hope.

Carhart is an emotionally wrought illustration of a more general idea: sometimes to describe a set of facts is to decide the case. This is not because we are compelled by conscience but because the description leads us to believe that any other resolution would make no sense. Moral self-evidence is only one form of self-evidence. An opinion aims to create a belief that "this is the way the world is." An interpretation of the law must show it to be an expression of our reasonable selves.

Consider again *Wickard v. Filburn*, the much-disputed precedent central to the Commerce Clause arguments of *Sebelius*.[41] *Wickard* introduces what is an elementary principle of a modern introductory economics class: in a free market, supply and demand will have equal, reciprocal effects on price. Increase demand and the price goes up; increase supply and the price goes down. Once this observation is admitted into the legal field of knowledge, it is difficult to think that the Constitution could allow regulation of price but not of supply. That proposition makes no sense when "everyone knows" that supply, demand, and price are all linked in a single equation: they are each a function of the others. The choice to regulate through limiting supply or controlling price becomes a matter for experts designing a regulatory scheme to deal with particular markets. If supply, demand, and price are equivalent market factors, the distinction between them can involve no constitutional principle. To think that the Constitution insists that there is nevertheless a distinction to be made is like continuing to believe in alchemy in the face of modern chemistry. Why would we do that?

Interestingly, *Wickard* goes on to consider how grain markets are organized in the rest of the Western world.[42] After all, if markets obey the same rules everywhere, we may learn something if we were to discover that all of these markets adopt the same forms of regulation. As producers and sellers of grain, national differences are not relevant. The same is true of any science, and modern regulatory regimes put science to work in the formation of policy. All grain producers—and all regulators—are in the same position with respect to global markets, just as they are in the same position with respect to the use of fertilizer. The horizon has shifted from earlier Commerce Clause cases in which federal regulation was viewed against the background of state sovereignty, which had to be protected against federal "invasion."[43] That earlier language reflected the shadow of the Civil War. By the time of the Depression, markets are no longer sites for competition over jurisdiction, nor for the realization of individual freedom; rather, they are failed institutions in desperate need of expert, remedial intervention. Of course, this story never really ends, as we see in the return to *Wickard* in the recent *Sebelius* case.

In *Lawrence*, which reversed *Bowers*, we see something very similar to *Wickard*'s shifting of the horizon.[44] Just as the *Wickard* opinion considered foreign grain markets, *Lawrence* directs our attention to the manner of regulation of sexual relations in foreign states. It notes that the European Court of Human Rights, as well as some national authorities, have recognized a "right of homosexuals to engage in intimate consensual conduct."[45] This is followed, perhaps more surprisingly, by "There has been no showing that in this country the governmental interest in circumscribing personal choice is somehow more legitimate or urgent."[46] Just as in *Wickard* market regulation is a fact about the world, so human rights have become a fact about the world in *Lawrence*. The opinion persuades when it convinces us that this is the way the world is. The decision on the law follows from recognition of these facts.[47]

To the dissent, of course, the very fact that these are foreign practices is enough to ground a distinction.[48] The appropriate horizon, for the dissent, is constituted by American laws, practices, and beliefs. The distinction between us and them is assumed to be a background condition to every available narrative respecting constitutional law. If we are persuaded by this distinction, there is no lesson to be learned from foreign practices because by definition the analogy must fail.

The dissent's position in *Lawrence* has become for many readers not just a mistake about what the law must be but a mistake of fact, a failure to see a truth about the world. It is as if a judge were to say that as a matter of law "the world is flat." It makes no sense to claim that the law requires us to shut our eyes to the plainest facts about the world in which we live.[49] As our understanding of the world changes, so must our understanding of the law, for the law is our common project of doing something in and about the world. The *Lawrence* opinion, in freely looking abroad, suggests that just as there can be only one science in the modern age, there can be only one regime of human rights. Many people in our cosmopolitan era do believe this. They have come to see human rights as a natural fact about the world. As that view became more and more prevalent, *Bowers* came to seem more and more a case in which the Court had done the moral equivalent of declaring the world to be flat. Not surprisingly, when it is overruled, the Court claims not that the Justices have changed their minds but that *Bowers* was wrong when it was decided.[50] The world was never flat.

Consider one more example of a classic case from the New Deal era. In *Nebbia v. New York*, the Court abandoned its earlier, due-process-based resistance to state regulation of markets.[51] No longer did it see markets as sites of a constitutionally protected right to liberty of contract. *Nebbia* involved a criminal charge brought against a local grocer for selling half a gallon of milk below the state mandated price. The opinion persuades us to see the milk industry from the perspective of a state legislature creating a modern regulatory regime. It explains in great detail the nature of this industry in New York State. It does so not in ordinary language but in the language of modern economics. The legislative effort to base policy on new forms of expertise is described in detail, including legislative reports of hundreds of pages filled with charts and graphs and hearings in which experts testified on agro-economics. The point of this description is to convince us that a failure to uphold the law would be irrational. Were we to conclude that the Constitution prohibits this regulation, then the milk industry in the state would be doomed to suffer the effects of deep market failure. Can we imagine that the Constitution requires the ruin of farmers, the collapse of retailers, the failure of the milk supply, and the inevitable effects on child health? Why would we do such a thing to ourselves? If we accept the description of the facts, then we have already been persuaded of what the law must be.

The dissent must contest the horizon against which we view the facts. While questioning the economics of the state legislature, the real work of the dissent is to try to shift our focus from markets to bargains, from the relative abstraction of the overall situation of the industry to the particular transaction out of which the case arose. Thus, the dissent focuses on the individual exchange; a child wants to buy two quarts of milk and a loaf of bread from a grocer.[52] The grocer was willing to sell at a price lower than the regulation allowed. Some bureaucrats at headquarters decided to intervene in this transaction. How is preventing this child from getting milk any business of theirs? Our sympathy should be with the child and the grocer, not with the men at headquarters. Do we look at milk and see the family farm and young families or do we see agribusiness in need of a regulatory regime covering everything from production to consumption? This is the real contest of the opinions.[53]

Majority and dissent offer two competing accounts of the facts of the case. Neither is more true than the other. We might think that the dissent is deploying the image of the little girl to do the work of corporate interests that oppose regulation. But similarly, we might think that the majority's account of a regulatory regime working for the good of all ignores the problems of agency capture. We cannot turn to the law to tell us which set of facts presents the truth of the matter. We only know the facts, when we have been persuaded one way or the other.

If we ask why it is that the administrative vision of agricultural economics won, the answer would point to the entire trend of modernity to develop and deploy new forms of social science, including quantitative economics. If we ask why the dissenting vision was not without power, we would point to the romantic idea of the local farm and of an anti-centralization tradition that has been so much a part of the American imagination. Majority and dissent each capture an aspect of a deep conflict in our understanding of ourselves and our communities. As long as both ideas remain attractive, we should expect the case law to cycle between the two ideas as different contexts evoke one or the other more or less forcefully.[54] The persuasive burden of the statement of the case is to put us in mind of one or the other normative ideal.

If the *Nebbia* dissent appears now as little more than an expression of recalcitrant opposition to the inevitable movement of modernity, it is not because the romance of the local—the concern for the little grocer as against a centralized bureaucracy—has disappeared. That romance remains, but it is much harder for it to prevent the deployment of the tools of the modern, regulatory state. That state with its regulatory apparatus has become simply the way the world is. To the extent that the romantic image of the local continues to exist, it must find expression in different contexts. Today, that often turns out to be in the schools, where the struggle between a national and a local perspective is still very much with us and still contested in the opinions.[55]

Analogy One More Time

In chapter 4, I discussed analogy from the perspective of the development of legal doctrine. Here, I want to examine analogy from the perspective of facts. Earlier, the issue was how analogy is used to interpret the normative premise of the precedents; here it is how analogy persuades us to see the facts as appropriately characterized one way or another. That analogy is at work with respect to both law and fact emphasizes how tightly the two are bound together in every legal claim. A legal controversy can usually be equally well characterized as a dispute over the meaning of a norm or over the characterization of the facts. Think, for example, of a protestor's First Amendment claim. Are we arguing over the meaning of the norm that protects speech or over the characterization of his action as speech?[56]

To bring into focus the role of analogy with respect to facts, we can start again with *Bowers*. The norm that the Court identified in that opinion was that familial relations are constitutionally protected. To apply that norm requires us to decide whether a homosexual relationship can be described as constitutive of a familial relationship. Once we know this, we know whether we can make the following argument: family relations are a constitutionally protected liberty interest; a homosexual relationship is a family relationship; therefore, homosexual relationships are protected. But to "know" this, we must decide whether homosexuals are similar to heterosexual couples in the relationships they form. We don't answer this question by applying a principle or by "just looking" at the evidence. Rather, we must draw analogies and make distinctions. This is the work that the *Bowers* opinion completely ignored when it claimed that it was "evident" that a homosexual couple does not involve a family relationship.[57] That was not really the case even in 1986. By the time of *Lawrence*, what was evident had completely turned around.

It is in the very nature of analogical reasoning that the connection between the two sides of the analogy—are heterosexuals and homosexuals similarly situated with respect to family?—is a matter neither of definition nor of demonstration. When one rejects an analogy, one cannot be accused of contradicting oneself. Whether we see married couples as "like" unmarried couples—the move from *Griswold* to *Eisenstadt*—is not a matter of proof but of persuasion.[58] The same is true of the homosexual couple. Analogy is a mode of rhetorical address: I appeal to your sympathetic imagination when I ask you to put yourself in the place of another. Conversely, I might appeal to your antipathetic imagination when I ask you to see someone as entirely different from yourself. If analogy is a product of persuasion, we should expect views to change over time as we come to see things differently. Such changes are not arbitrary, but neither are they logically necessary. We have our reasons for seeing as we do, and successful arguments build from those reasons.

Bowers asserted that there is no analogy to be drawn between the gay couple and the heterosexual couple because we understand the latter through an imagined possibility of reproduction. Only against that possibility do decisions regarding sex gain their constitutional stature. One can respond that not all heterosexual relationships occur in a reproductive context: people can be infertile or simply determine not to have children. The precedents, after all, involve nonreproductive sex, protecting access to contraceptives and abortion. These are not problems at the margins of the legal rules but at their very center once the question of homosexual couples arises.[59] These are just the sort of arguments from analogy one would make to try to persuade someone to see heterosexual and homosexual couples as alike. If we find ourselves describing homosexual couples as facing decisions about children, we have probably already been persuaded that the analogy to heterosexuals holds.

We are not going to settle these matters by looking up definitions in dictionaries, nor by appeal to any sort of formal application of rules. The law is managing complex life situations and cannot somehow be made less complex than the situations to which it responds. It is not a game with rules but a way of working out together how we want to live. Thus, by the time of *Lawrence*, the analogy that a majority could not see earlier is easily accessible. There is indeed a connection between "family, marriage, or procreation" and "homosexual activity." So obvious is this connection now that we are likely to deny that analogy is involved: gay couples and heterosexual couples are simply *the same*. The case has become easy for many, if not most, people.

We don't learn how to place the gay couple in relation to the heterosexual couple by reading the legal sources more closely; we learn it by looking at ourselves and the other members of our communities. *Bowers* was on the wrong side of history. A court is no better than the rest of us at discerning the path of history. Nevertheless, a court cannot avoid the problem of judgment. Where and how we see similarities and difference are inevitably products of who we are. And we are bound to history. When the family next door is a gay couple, it is no longer plausible to argue about differences. Theory has been eclipsed by life. This is what Justice Holmes meant when he famously wrote that "the life of the law has not been logic; it has been experience."[60]

Caperton v. A. T. Massey Coal is a particularly good example from which to consider the role of analogical reasoning in determining the presentation of the facts because it deliberately takes up the question of the nature of legal judgment.[61] At issue was whether a judge on the West Virginia Supreme Court was constitutionally required to grant a motion seeking his removal from a case. He declined, explaining his reasons in detail. The United States Supreme Court reversed, concluding that his failure to recuse himself amounted to a denial of due process. All of the issues of fact that I have identified—context, statement of the case, and analogy—are at issue in the opinion, but I want to focus particularly on its use of analogy.

Judges in West Virginia are elected. Like candidates for other offices, they raise money and run campaigns. One of the parties to the Caperton controversy had spent about three million dollars to support the election of the judge whose failure to recuse was at issue. Supporting the judge's campaign violated no laws despite the fact that the party to the case made the contribution after a jury had reached a fifty-million-dollar judgment against him in a complex contract dispute—the underlying dispute in the present case. The candidate—now the judge—had challenged a sitting judge, defeating him by a margin of some 7 percent. In due time, the contract case arrived before the state Supreme Court; the recusal motion was filed and the new judge refused to remove himself. He joined two other justices, giving a three-to-two ruling reversing the judgment below. Did his sitting on the case violate the losing party's constitutional right to due process?

To appreciate the opinion, we need to be clear on what is not in the case. There are no allegations of secret deals, of quid pro quo arrangements, or of corruption. There is no claim that the matter was even discussed at any point by the relevant parties. Again, neither the judge/candidate nor the contributor violated any federal or state law in giving or receiving the contribution. We are not to assume that the challenged judge did anything other than make a good faith judgment on the merits of the case.

In addition, nothing was done in secret. The judge issued a detailed explanation of why he would not remove himself. He noted that no evidence of bias or wrongdoing had been offered, and he did not think he was biased. There were no allegations of bad faith on his part. Nor was there any dispute as to what the parties actually did in the course of the campaign, although there was a disagreement on how important the contributions were to the election result. Some argued that the losing judge, who had himself raised millions of dollars, lost because of a particular speech in which he showed himself to be unbalanced. It may also be relevant that all but one of the state newspapers endorsed the winner. Obviously, we cannot know why one party won and the other lost, for elections turn on many factors.

We might feel that something went wrong here, but what is it? Agreeing on the record does not mean that we agree on the characterization of the facts. For that, we need some direction. Is the problem that West Virginia elects its judges? Such elections can create the appearance of influence on the judge apart from the law and the evidence of a case. West Virginia, however, is hardly alone in this practice and the issue of the constitutionality of the practice was not before the Court. Can we have elected judges without elections and elections without contributions? Is the problem that of the economic inequality between the parties to the case? One party could afford to make a large contribution; the other could not. Surely, however, it is not news that the rich spend more on campaigns. Nor is it news that such contributions bring influence of one sort or another. People with an agenda make contributions, but why should public policy not be responsive to the interests of constituents who engage in the political process, whether through contributions or canvassing? What if instead of a businessman with a case it had been a pro-choice group contributing money to a judicial candidate? What if instead of a businessman concerned about mining operations it had been an environmental group concerned about those same mining operations? Is not citizen involvement the goal of elections? Can it matter what the interests or the group are?

Each time I pose the question "What if . . ." I am drawing attention to a different possible analogy. I am asking whether the facts here are like those in another case. Is a businessman like a public interest group? Is a judicial campaign like a campaign for any other office? In each case, I ask whether there is an analogy to be made or a distinction to be drawn. I draw the analogies, or make the distinctions, aiming to link the facts of this case to some other set of facts about which I am already confident I know the law. If I am sure that a public interest group must be free to participate in any political campaign, asking whether the business man is like such a group characterizes the facts and decides the case in the same move.

The opinion for the court considers two lines of precedents, asking whether the facts here are analogous to the facts in those earlier cases. In the first, judges have been disqualified because they have an actual financial interest in the outcome of the case before them. Not exactly the issue here, since the contribution was not contingent on the decision. But are the facts here analogous to those cases? It becomes like them if we think that what matters was the influence of money on judicial character—as the Court puts it, "interests that tempt adjudicators to disregard neutrality."[62] In place of our original distinction based on the absence of a quid pro quo, we now see sameness in the presence of temptation. The relevant facts have changed: no longer profit, but temptation.

The same thing happens with respect to the second line of precedents, which involved judges who were participants in the underlying dispute: for example, the judge was himself the one insulted in a contempt of court action on which he subsequently ruled. The West Virginia judge was not in such a position; he had no involvement in the trial court decision of the contract dispute. Again, however, the question is whether we can draw an analogy. Are the earlier cases better described as instances in which we had reason to believe that judicial judgment might be knocked off balance by some extraneous influence? That sounds more like the facts here. This is what the opinion concludes.

We learn the relevant facts only as we are persuaded by analogies and distinctions. As the opinion pursues different analogies, our understanding of the facts shifts. We come to understand the meaning of the precedents at the very moment that we say that the precedents are determining the outcome. The majority opinion tellingly collapses into a tautology: the precedents, it says, stand for the proposition that the court must ask in each case "whether there is an unconstitutional 'potential for bias.'"[63] Of course, we were looking to the precedents to answer the question of what kind of bias is unconstitutional. When the conclusion is said to follow directly from the rule, the argument is over. The Court has persuaded itself. Now, the only question is whether it has also persuaded the readers.

The dissenters fear that the majority is adopting a rule of "too much influence" or "unbalanced judgment," which is no rule at all. They argue that the holding will vastly increase the number of recusal motions filed, for without a limiting rule every possible influence will be pursued. Maybe they are right. Maybe it will become unmanageable. But we cannot know that until we see how future courts make use of this precedent in drawing analogies and making distinctions among different situations of fact.

We don't know how to characterize the facts until we know what it means to be alike or different with respect to some norm. But we don't learn that by simply looking at the norm. Rules don't come with directions on how they are to be applied.[64] We have to reason it out, which means that we draw analogies and make distinctions to test a proposition. Some persuade us; some don't. Sometimes we cannot reach a point of agreement. On a court, that is the point at which we count votes to see who won. The lawyer making the argument, however, does not have this option. She must argue one way or the other.

You might think this description of the creative work of analogy is true only in hard cases—those in which a court has to use its discretion because there is no clear answer to what the legal norm requires or how to characterize the facts. But judgment in easy cases is not different in kind simply because we are all persuaded by the same analogies. If we all agree that a painting is beautiful, that does not mean that the painting is beautiful as a fact of the matter. Legal judgment is no different.

In both art and law, judgments change over time. Easy cases regularly become hard cases, and vice versa. Affirmative action was an easy case immediately after the Civil War: remember forty acres and a mule? Even in the early years of court-mandated desegregation, most people still thought that a school board surely was free to adopt for itself a program of affirmative action. Bussing to achieve integration was a problem only when a court ordered it, not when a school board thought it a good idea as a matter of educational policy.[65] The fact that mattered was who decided: school board or court? At some point in the last generation, many people were persuaded to see the facts differently. Affirmative action had come to look like segregation: both were race-based decision making. What had been easy became hard as new analogies became compelling. We cannot judge which fact-situations are like each other by referring to the rule of equality, for what is at stake is what the rule means with respect to these facts.

Deciding a case, judges are not asked to disregard their beliefs about the world within which the law operates. Indeed, quite the opposite: the opinion is the space within which those beliefs operate. This does not mean that these beliefs are themselves impervious to argument, legal or otherwise. We do change our minds in the individual case as well as over time: we come to see things differently. The same is true of judges. Many people, for example, have shifted their views on affirmative action because the context against which they view the meaning of equal protection has shifted. What used to be seen in terms of group subordination—elimination of an underclass—has come to be seen in terms of an individual right to equal treatment.[66] That change of context was no doubt influenced by the cases themselves but also by everything else happening in our world. This sort of change was even more evident, perhaps because more rapid, with respect to claims for gay rights. What had been an easy case in one direction became an easy case in the other direction in less than a generation. The facts are not one thing or another independently of these judgments.

Law and Fact: The Relative Autonomy of the Law

Formally, an opinion has something of the same structure that informs trial-court procedure. The opinion is likely to begin with a statement of the case and then turn to the application of the law, just as a trial court will begin with submission of evidence and then turn to law in the judge's charge to the jury. The opinion's opening statement usually summarizes the findings below, but its focus inevitably broadens. This statement sets up—or should set up—the argument of the opinion. It describes the background conditions against which the law must be interpreted. Against that background, the particular facts of the case are read as a pattern more or less repeatable. If they are not representative of similar instances, we are not likely to be interested in the opinion. An opinion written so narrowly as to offer no resources for any future case would simply disappear, for it would effectively have nothing to say beyond affirm or reverse.

The opinion is not exactly broadening the characterization of the facts in order to be useful for future adjudications—although that need is likely to have a disciplining effect on the writing of the opinion. Primarily, the opinion is characterizing the facts in order to understand the law. Law, unlike contract, is not created for the single case; it is not addressed to the parties' particular problem but to the sort of problem that they have. The facts of the case, accordingly, take on a kind of anecdotal quality, in the same way that a particular example of a problem may function for a legislator in crafting a legal response.[67]

The event that triggers a legislative response is often beyond repair; it is over. The legislation aims to intervene with respect to the possibility of future events of that kind. The opinion is doing the same sort of thing in its effort to interpret the law. It takes the particular facts of the controversy—the event—as if it were an instance of a general kind to which the legal norm is a response. The opinion is, in some sense, reverse engineering the law. It must, accordingly, represent the parties' problem as of a certain sort, that is, as an instance of a more general problem. Thus, in *Caperton* we are not concerned about how much money was given to whom but about the significance of these facts as representative of a certain kind of problem to which the law is addressed. In *Roe*, we are not concerned with what happened to Jane Roe. As an unnamed woman, she literally comes to represent every possible woman. In *Bowers* and *Lawrence*, we are not concerned with what sort of relationship actually existed among the couples involved in the cases.

In this chapter, I have been exploring exactly how the opinion answers this question of characterization of the facts, starting from the most general response—context—and proceeding to the most specific—analogy. All of these efforts to characterize the facts begin from the belief that law is a purposive act. We cannot characterize the relevant facts without having some purpose in view, for absent some purpose they are not one thing or another. Nature may act for "no reason," but a free act is always one upon which we have decided for a reason.[68] If law is our collective free act, then the reasons must be ours as well. When we try to imagine cases in which law appears as a command to be obeyed without any knowledge of the purpose of that command, what we are usually imagining are cases in which there are multiple possible reasons for the command. When we think that we need not make a determination among those multiple possibilities to know what we must do, we think we are only obeying the command. When a controversy arises, however, we do indeed need to make such a determination.

H. L. A. Hart famously discussed the legal rule "No vehicles in the park."[69] We can think of aesthetic, safety, environmental, and traffic control reasons for such a law. We don't have to know what the actual purpose was in order to comply in the ordinary case of an automobile entering the park. But when the question arises of whether bicycles are included, we may have to settle on a purpose. If we ask whether bicycles are analogous to cars, we reply that it depends on the problem to which the statute was addressed. If we thought the statute was designed to encourage environmentally friendly forms of transportation in the park, then it would make no sense to say that bicycles too are prohibited. If we were to decide that bicycles are actually prohibited by the text of the act, then we would have to interpret the purpose of the act differently. If we were literally unable to do so, we would say the text contains a mistake in drafting.[70] Whether courts can correct such a mistake is a secondary matter, although the harder it is to correct, the more pressure there will be to read the rule in a way that makes sense as a purposive act.

We could decide that a bicycle is not a vehicle, distinguishing it from forms of motorized transport. Were we to do so, we could not quite answer the question of whether the issue turns on fact or law: have we interpreted the rule or characterized the facts? We have done both at once. Ultimately, all we can say is that we have been persuaded to imagine the world one way rather than another.

Seen from the perspective of scientific disciplines, law's rendering of fact will always be deficient. If we think of law as rules to be applied to facts, then this will be troubling. It is always easy to identify how much an opinion gets wrong, for the judges are not experts in any field other than the law. They don't know much economics, sociology, psychology, or even history. Factual errors can be a real problem, and not just when a court convicts the innocent. They are a problem when the courts insist on a vision of contractual freedom that has little relationship to the distribution of power in the workplace or on a vision of free speech that fails to recognize how power can undermine the goals of the democratic exchange of ideas. A court that refuses to consider the relevance of statistics in ruling on a claim that racial bias operates in the application of capital punishment is refusing to see the plainest facts of our world, for today it is uncontroversial that policy must be based on empirical evidence and evidence must satisfy standards of statistical accuracy.[71]

These are genuine problems, but still we might find some virtue in the interdependence of fact and law in the opinion. That interdependence means that law can never be more than a relatively autonomous discipline. The old dream of a science of law must fail once we understand that legal rules cannot, in and of themselves, generate any outcomes. Our law is not a science but a practice of self-government through persuasion.

Persuasion works with respect to the law and the facts—sometimes separately, sometimes together. The description of facts, no less than the conclusions of law, raises issues of character. How we see is a function of who we are: who the judges are and who we, the readers of their opinions, are. Ultimately, the character of the nation is at stake in its law and thus in what the opinions persuade us to believe. The Court, reflecting on the sources of its own legitimacy, has said just this:

> Like the character of an individual, the legitimacy of the Court must be earned over time. So, indeed, must be the character of a Nation of people who aspire to live according to the rule of law. Their belief in themselves as such a people is not readily separable from their understanding of the Court invested with the authority to decide their constitutional cases and speak before all others for their constitutional ideals. If the Court's legitimacy should be undermined, then, so would the country be in its very ability to see itself through its constitutional ideals.[72]

If empathy matters for judges, it matters here. A judge without empathy will fail to persuade his readers because the world he describes will not be their own. His readers, however, are citizens, and if he has not persuaded them to see themselves in his work, then he has undermined the legitimacy of the judicial role. He is asking for their trust but has failed to demonstrate a character that would deserve that trust.

An opinion can succeed only when the narrative it offers—a narrative of fact-law—makes sense alongside everything else we believe. If it doesn't make sense, we will not be persuaded. If you reply that persuasion does not matter as long as the state has the power to enforce, then you are no longer talking about the rule of law as a democratic project of self-government. Law can, of course, take an authoritarian form. But a law enforced by a policeman with a gun offers no puzzle as to its source or character. Reading opinions is not likely to be a very important aspect of the law in such a regime. Currying favor is. Of course, even under such a regime, a law that makes little sense is not likely to be a very effective device for organizing behavior. Why would anyone follow it when they could escape a penalty? The police cannot be everywhere at once.

A proposition that is viewed as irrational or even unreasonable cannot claim the protection of law in a democratic regime. Why, we will ask, would we think that the law requires that? We judge the reasonableness of the law based on what we already know to be the case about the world. If an opinion is to interpret the law as a product of our own authorship, it must convince us that we had good reasons to act as it describes. Once we understand those reasons, we will understand it as part of our common political project. That project always takes place in the world as we know it to be. That common world is not just a matter of fact but of moral norms as well. This was the point of my discussion of *Lawrence:* our contemporary world simply is one in which human rights norms are as much a feature as the environment or the law of supply and demand.

Just as human rights could no longer be ignored in *Lawrence* because they have become part of our world, so one might speculate that in the not too distant future climate change will be such a firmly established fact about the world that interpretations of law will have to make sense in light of this belief. A court that resists such a change of belief will find itself in the same sort of political crisis as that which occurred in the New Deal when the Court resisted Roosevelt's legislative response to the Depression. New forms of knowledge swept out nineteenth-century beliefs about the nature of political economy. The Court too had to enter the twentieth century, although it took it longer to get there than the elected branches.

Of course, we recognize that we don't all agree on what should be done, but the unity of political life and action is never a matter of unanimity. To have a common political project is not to reach unanimity but rather to recognize the need for cooperation even when we differ. It is not unreasonable for me to agree to act in common with other members of my community even when I disagree about the shape of a particular project. I must, however, recognize the project as one that my community could have reasonably adopted. Of that, the opinion must persuade me.

Thus, whether a proposition appears to us as unreasonable is not itself determined by law. Judges cannot rely on their commissions to assert propositions that we simply do not believe.[73] We bring all of our beliefs about ourselves, our communities, and the world to the law, including to our practice of reading opinions. We also bring our understandings of other institutions and other forms of expertise. The opinion must take account of all of these beliefs and practices.

To say that we bring all of our beliefs and practices to the law is not to suggest that we could set forth our beliefs in a list prior to reading the opinion. We find out what we think when we realize that we have been persuaded one way or the other. Often we don't know what we think until we reflect on the matter. We are open to persuasion because our beliefs and practices are indeterminate with respect to a controversy. That may be because those beliefs are not particularly strong or because they operate at a level of generality that permits more than one resolution of the particular controversy. When they are strong and specific, we may be in general agreement with other members of the community, in which case a controversy is unlikely to arise. When they are strong and specific, but we are nevertheless in disagreement, it is may be too much to think that any judicial opinion can bring us together. Some of us will support the majority opinion; others the dissent.

Over time, what had once been unimaginable becomes simply the way the world is. No one thinks seriously about that local grocer and little girl in *Nebbia* any longer. Instead, we think of competition in global markets and we understand that every economic transaction is related to the whole. Or so we think we believe until a new case comes along that asks whether someone can be compelled to purchase health insurance against his wishes. Now we are not so certain, just as an earlier generation was not so certain about that little girl. Over time that insurance resister may come to look as outdated as the local grocer. That will not be because of the law alone but because of changes across the full range of our beliefs and practices. Something similar is happening with respect to the regulation of intimate relations among persons of the same sex. We may shortly look back at a time not very long ago and wonder how it was that gay marriage did not seem *the same as* marriage between heterosexuals.[74]

It is only a postulate of faith to think that some rule is so clear that we can be compelled to follow it by reason alone. In truth, some rules are clear some of the time because we agree on how to apply them—not because they compel our behavior. As soon as a case arises of which we are uncertain, we turn to analogies and distinctions. We reason with facts; we don't apply rules to the facts. This is not a fault of the law but a virtue. It is the reason that we generally have the law that we deserve. If we think that we deserve better, then it is up to us to make the arguments. We must persuade each other. We cannot wait for the law to do this work for us.

CONCLUSION: MAKING THE CASE FOR A HUMANIST STUDY OF THE LAW

For more than a generation, the study of law has been divided between those who come from the humanities and those who come from the social sciences. There is, in principle, nothing wrong with this. Ours is a pluralistic age in which diverse forms of knowledge and inquiry can and should be welcome. This disciplinary divide becomes problematic only when diversity is displaced by competition, when each side thinks it has hold of the only truth that matters. The danger, then, is that each side will make claims about the whole of law. Those on the humanist side of the divide cannot afford such a competition, for we are very unlikely to be the winners in today's academy. Philosophy has long been displaced by economics as the dominant paradigm of inquiry in all fields that touch on the study of social practices.

The social scientist, typically an economist, brings a broadly utilitarian framework to the study of every area of law. The task of law, on this view, is instrumental; law is a means to an end or really to multiple ends. In a well-working polity, we can generally speak of the public good as the end of law. From the point of view of the economist, however, the public good is only the aggregation of individual goods. Only individuals can decide what has value because there is no measure of that value apart from how much an individual is willing to invest in its pursuit. I can argue that you should value something, but I cannot make you value it. Listening to the salesman, you may still decide not to make the purchase. Absent some sort of market failure, it makes no sense to say that something is worth more than anybody is willing to pay. You are certainly not willing to pay more than the market price because someone else has a theory about what the price should be.

For the economist, law must take these value judgments as given. In general, the law itself should be neutral with respect to the value of different ends. The values arise outside, or independently of, the legal rules. Law can respond to specific market failures, but it cannot claim to know what is good independently of people's own values. Any such claims would be mere rhetoric hiding the reality that some groups are advancing their ends at a cost to others. Accordingly, the normative question that this form of inquiry brings to the study of law is simply whether our laws are efficient. Are they maximizing aggregate, individual satisfaction? If not, they should be reformed. Inefficiencies can arise from many sources, but the deepest threat to law arises from the opportunities political institutions create for rent seeking and agency capture. Groups and individuals will always seek political power in order to create laws that will advance their interests by imposing costs on others. Politics appears, therefore, as a threat to the efficiency of law.

A utilitarian framework looks forward, not backward. To the social scientist, law is a matter of rules, and we can formulate useful rules only if we can make accurate predictions of the consequences of their application. This is why the science of statistics developed in lockstep with the regulatory state. Past events, on this view, are relevant only if they can be turned to a predictive use. To accomplish this, the social scientist must turn the record of the past into a statistical form—that is, into data that forms the basis for predictions. Paradoxically, data are deployed as evidence of that which has not yet happened. Short of becoming data, our evidence is merely "anecdotal"—a vaguely pejorative term that suggests we are likely to be misled if we rely upon our ordinary experience.

The humanist is not particularly interested in a utilitarian framework nor in evidence presented as data. His attention is drawn to the event—indeed, to the anecdotal. In place of statistical aggregation, he uses a method best described as "thick description."[1] He is less interested in outcomes than in the legal process itself. He approaches the legal imagination as the source of a way of understanding oneself and one's world that is fundamentally built around a collective subject's history. Law, he thinks, is not merely a means toward ends that arise apart from the law. Rather, it is its own normative practice. The legal imagination places the present in relation to a partic-

CONCLUSION

ular past and opens a particular horizon on the future. This is a thoroughly value-laden enterprise. For the humanist, the problem of understanding law is not that of deciding what the law should be but of explaining how we actually live with the law we have even as we argue with each other about what the law means.[2] The humanist study of law is an interpretive practice; it is about meaning, not efficiency.

The humanist, accordingly, tries to gain clarity on the world of meaning within which he finds himself. His methodology of thick description of practice and belief uses a language that is continuous with the terms of self-understanding used by the participants themselves. We are rightly suspicious of a humanist discourse that strays too far from ordinary language. The account should feel right in the same way that a work of history should feel right. Interpretation of law, I have argued throughout this book, makes use of the narratives that we deploy in our everyday life. This must be the case if we are to understand the law as something we do together.

The lawyer-economist, on the other hand, believes that science begins only when those ordinary categories are displaced by a technical discourse that allows aggregation and disaggregation of data. The data can then be used to discover causal connections. The more surprising, the better: for example, perhaps he can demonstrate that legalizing abortion caused a reduction in crime rates twenty years later.[3] The humanist is in no position to contest such a causal claim, but he does wonder how it will be received. At stake are notions of personal responsibility, family, crime, and welfare. These are all at work in our legal imaginations; they will all shape how we receive the conclusions from the data. Knowing the "facts" does not tell us what to make of them. Indeed, in chapter 5 I argued that we cannot even know the facts without some sense of what we are to make of them.

At the root of this difference in approaches is a deep disagreement. The social scientist, as a scientist, believes that human behavior follows laws of cause and effect. The observation about the relationship between abortions and crime rates illustrates this assumption.[4] In this example too, we see that the pattern of causality is not evident to ordinary perception. Past events must be modeled statistically to reveal the underlying causal connections. Laws intervene in a causally ordered world. They then become causes contributing to new effects. The social scientist believes that the consequences of these interventions should be the subject of measurement, not speculation. Short of that, we have no way of knowing whether any of our claims are true or false. The study of law for the lawyer-economist is one of constantly dispelling the illusions that arise when we make knowledge claims in the absence of data. Science is not for amateurs. Law school, on this view, should teach statistics and economics as the entry point for understanding the law as a malleable tool for reaching our ends.[5]

The humanist believes that action must be approached as free, not caused. Of course, people can be coerced, commanded, and threatened. The rule of law, however, is another matter. Law, the humanist believes, works through persuasion. We care about what the law means, not just what it does. We cannot separate the latter from the former, which means we cannot escape the need for interpretation. If our law is to appear to us as the product of our own self-government, then it cannot coerce but only persuade. Accordingly, we must study what is said and how it is received. We can understand persuasion only by listening, that is, by letting ourselves be persuaded.

To the social scientist's claim that we should ignore the rhetoric and just look at what happens, the humanist responds that what happens in and through law is not separate from the imaginative construction of a world of meaning. Law does not happen to us; rather, collectively we do it to and for ourselves. Absent this belief, we cannot imagine how the rule of law and the rule of the people can coincide. That coincidence, however, is just what we mean by freedom through law.

The humanist does not draw the line between fact and fiction in the same place as the social scientist. He admits that law is a sort of fiction: it is a set of practices that have no truth apart from our common beliefs. Those beliefs go to who we are, who we have been, and who we will become. About such beliefs, we are quite literally deadly serious. Law may be a fiction, but it is one for which people live and die. This experience will always be outside of the data, which can tell us mortality rates but not how it is that people understood the meaning of life and death.

The social scientist views evidence from the outside; the humanist, from the inside. The former believes that facts must be categorized in ways that make it possible to "run operations" on them. The humanist approaches law as an imagined world and asks how events, persons, and institutions appear in that world. This dispute over the nature of evidence is equally a dispute over the nature of rules. The social scientist believes that legal rules can be specified apart from their application. Only if this is so can statistics be relevant to the assessment of the effects of those rules. The humanist believes that the meaning of rules does not precede judgment but is rather a consequence of judgment. Prior to judgment, the rule opens a field for interpretive controversy. The judgment tells us which interpretations count for now. The process will, of course, continue with the new understanding of the rule.

The fundamental conflict between these two disciplinary themes is that between studying law as a cause of behavior and studying law as a free act. For the economist, one follows the law to one's benefit or detriment; for the humanist, we give the law to ourselves. This dualism between causation and freedom haunts the study of many domains, including psychology, history, morality, and metaphysics. The study of law is no better than these other fields at offering a unified theory. We must learn to live with the divide rather than seek its resolution, for the only resolution is to abandon one side or the other.[6] Both, however, have much to teach us. Legal pedagogy must accept both of these forms of inquiry.

Pedagogically, we might start by considering the ways in which the diverse institutions of law are accountable to different forms of knowledge. The courtroom is one thing, the legislative hearing another. The well-trained lawyer will know what to say in each forum. The humanist can no more ignore the place of the social scientist in the law than he can ignore the biological scientist in medicine. We want doctors who are sympathetic to the way in which the patient imagines her pain and who treat the patient as a free, moral agent

CONCLUSION

entitled to dignity and respect. We also want doctors to understand the causes of disease and the effects of various pharmaceuticals. No study of regulation or regulatory reform can do without the techniques and work of the social scientists. Equally, no study of the judicial opinion can do without the work of the humanist.

We can and should bring to bear interdisciplinary studies. Thus, we should also study opinions by examining the economic consequences of the doctrines they articulate. Equally important, we should study the rhetoric of administrators and the institutional imagination of the legislative committee. They too pursue persuasion among groups of speakers and listeners. Legal history should collect data, but it should also study shifts in the social imagination.[7] To identify the latter, the historian will have to engage in a close study of texts, including but not limited to judicial opinions. The study of law will be enriched if we move from competition to collaboration across these disciplinary approaches.

In this book I have pursued the idea that judicial opinions are rhetorical performances that take up the task of persuasion in a democratic community. To understand how the opinion does this work, we must use the tools of the humanities. Those tools include the study of narrative, voice, and argument. Arguments in law are rhetorical, and rhetoric always combines norms and facts. Neither appears without the other in the opinion. To understand the opinion is to understand what it means to speak in the language of those who must make and justify legal decisions. We learn what it is we must say to judges by learning what it is that they say to us. Learning to read the opinion is the only way in which one can learn how to speak the ordinary language of the law.

But will this inquiry convince the social scientists of the law? Have I persuaded them of the dual nature of legal pedagogy? Will they be persuaded by my presentation of a thick description of the poetics of the opinion and the nature of legal argument? Perhaps not. They may respond that I simply don't know what is really going on among the judges and in the courtroom. I don't know because I have no data. I am making generalizations based on anecdotal accounts. They will

CONCLUSION

be suspicious of conclusions based on the analysis of only a few opinions. Until I generate data, there is no way to know where the truth of the matter lies.

If the question is what it is that judges do and to what effect, the social scientist can see no reason for looking for evidence in what it is that judges say. We always have reason to be suspicious of the accounts people give of themselves. To rely on what judges say is like relying on people's self-reporting to determine the causes of their illnesses. That language may offer some evidence, but we need actual data to reveal the patterns of cause and effect. The social scientist believes, for example, that if we want to know when judges are influenced by factors outside of the strict parameters of a case—the issue raised by *Caperton* discussed in chapter 5—then we must perform empirical studies. We might create experiments that ask about judgment under different conditions. Or we might compare judicial performance in states that elect judges with judicial performance in states that do not. We would then be in a position to aggregate and compare the data. Until we know what is going on, we cannot know whether opinions are addressing a problem, creating one, or simply obfuscating.

It may well be the case that judicial behavior falls into statistically accessible patterns; it may be that a court's resolution of a case will have nonoptimal effects on future behavior. Not without reason have statistics been an essential tool in the creation of the modern regulatory state. Nevertheless, even if we were to turn to the social scientists to offer us the most efficient rule, that rule would still have to be applied. At the moment of application, we cannot turn to them again for help. Their insight at the moment of judgment is exhausted with the admonition "apply the rule." But between the rule and its application there is a free act. In that free act is an entire world of meaning. The judge must be persuaded, just as she will write an opinion to try to persuade us. At that moment, even the social scientist must turn to the humanist to understand the practices and beliefs at work in the language of the law.

NOTES

Preface

1. Decades ago, Karl Llewellyn made the same point speaking to new law students. "[Y]ou must learn to read. To read each word. To understand *each* word. You are outlanders in this country of the law. You do not know the speech. It must be learned. Like any other foreign tongue, it must be learned." Karl N. Llewellyn, The Bramble Bush 34 (1930). More recently, approaching legal education as the learning of a new language has been at the center of the work of James Boyd White. *See* James Boyd White, Justice as Translation xiii (1990) ("For me it is more valuable to think of law in a third way, as a culture—as a 'culture of argument'—or, what is much the same thing, as a language."); *see also* James Boyd White, *Reading Law and Reading Literature: Law as Language, in* Heracles' Bow: Essays on the Rhetoric and Poetics of the Law 77 (1985); James Boyd White, *The Judicial Opinion and the Poem: Ways of Reading, Ways of Life, in* Heracles' Bow: Essays on the Rhetoric and Poetics of the Law, *supra*, at 107.
2. Llewellyn, *supra* note 1.
3. Many opinions today deal with issues of statutory interpretation. For an application of the approach I describe in this book to issues of statutory interpretation, see Paul W. Kahn & Kiel R. Brennan-Marquez, *Statutes and Democratic Self-Authorship*, 56 Wm. & Mary L. Rev. (2014).
4. See the conclusion.
5. For a comprehensive statement of my approach to law, see Paul W. Kahn, The Reign of Law: *Marbury v. Madison* and the Construction of America (1997); and Paul W. Kahn, The Cultural Study of Law: Reconstructing Legal Scholarship (1999). James Boyd White takes a similar view of the opinion as performing a rhetorical task of constructing an ethical community of a certain sort. *See, e.g.*, White, *Justice as Translation*, *supra* note 1, at 101 (describing the opinion "as rhetorically constitutive: as an act of expression that constitutes a community . . ."). He does not, however, put self-government at the center of this ethos.
6. 134 S. Ct. 1434 (2014).

Chapter One. Why Read the Opinions?

1. *See* Alexander M. Bickel, The Least Dangerous Branch: The Supreme Court at the Bar of Politics 239 (2d ed. 1986).
2. *See* Robert A. Burt, The Constitution in Conflict (1992).
3. *See* J.L. Austin, How to Do Things with Words (J.O. Urmson & Marina Sbisà eds., 2d ed. 1975).
4. *See* Alec Stone Sweet, *Judicialization and the Construction of Governance*, 32 Comp. Pol. Stud. 147, 149 (1999) (arguing that triadic dispute resolution—two disputants and a dispute resolver—is "a universal . . . phenomenon" and "a primal technique of organizing social authority").
5. William D. Popkin, Evolution of the Judicial Opinion: Institutional and Individual Styles 60–85 (2007).
6. See Paul W. Kahn, The Reign of Law: *Marbury v. Madison* and the Construction of America 112–13 (2002).
7. Justice Thomas has rejected the idea of a dormant Commerce Clause, concurring alone in *United States v. Lopez*, 514 U.S. 549 (1995) and *United States v. Morrison*, 529 U.S. 598 (2000). He has rejected claims of constitutional rights for children, dissenting alone in *Brown v. Entertainment Merchants Association*, 131 S. Ct. 2729 (2011). On First Amendment free speech questions generally, Thomas has taken a solitary and absolutist line. *See generally* Steven B. Lichtman, *Black Like Me: The Free Speech Jurisprudence of Clarence Thomas*, 114 Penn. St. L. Rev. 415 (2009).
8. *See, e.g.*, J.G.A. Pocock, The Ancient Constitution and the Feudal Law: A Study of English Historical Thought in the Seventeenth Century 30–55 (2d ed. 1987) (discussing the seventeenth-century English view of the common law as immemorial, unchanging custom).
9. Justice Douglas, one of the most liberal justices of the twentieth century, held a similar view of the nature of judicial authority. *See, e.g.*, G. Edward White, *The Anti-Judge: William O. Douglas and the Ambiguities of Individuality*, 74 Va. L. Rev. 17, 18 (1988) who argues that "Douglas can be seen as an 'anti-judge' in that he rejected both of the principal twentieth-century devices designed to constrain subjective judicial lawmaking: fidelity to constitutional text or doctrine, and institutional deference." White argues that Douglas's background as a Legal Realist contributed to his judicial independence. *Id.* at 45–46.
10. Understanding outcomes as a function of individual preference will lead to a broadly economic approach to the study of law, for economics is the study of preference aggregation under conditions of scarcity—not all judges can win all the time. *See, e.g.*, Joshua B. Fischman, *Interpret-*

ing Circuit Court Voting Patterns: A Social Interactions Framework, 29 J.L., Econ. & Org. 1 (2013).

11. Legislative committees do issue reports and individual members of Congress may express their views in floor debate. These expressions of "opinion," however, rarely reach a wider public and are disfavored as sources for interpreting statutes.

12. *See, e.g.*, Amy Gutmann & Dennis Thompson, The Spirit of Compromise: Why Governing Demands It and Campaigning Undermines It (2012).

13. John Manning, for example, has argued that because congressional representatives and staff bargain "in complex and often unknowable ways over a statute's wording," interpretations that stray from the formal text can rework a balance struck by a particular coalition or representative body at one moment in time—a coalition that could be impossible to reproduce. Looking beyond text thus represents judicial tinkering with constituency building and bargaining. John F. Manning, *Justice Scalia and the Legislative Process*, 62 N.Y.U. Ann. Surv. Am. L. 33, 38 (2006); *see also* John Manning, *What Divides Textualists from Purposivists?*, 106 Colum. L. Rev. 70, 99, 102–03 (2006).

14. Stories of draft opinions failing to sustain a majority are legion. For a fascinating recent account of such a failure, see Patrick Weil, The Sovereign Citizen: Denaturalization and the Origins of the American Republic 145–65 (2013). Weil discusses three nationalization cases: *Nishikawa v. Dulles*, 356 U.S. 129 (1958), *Perez v. Brownell*, 356 U.S. 44 (1958), and *Trop v. Dulles*, 356 U.S. 86 (1958).

15. The importance of the opinion to the law is the theme of the criticism of the recent practice of some federal appellate courts issuing opinions that are not to be cited in the future. For recent criticisms of the practice of issuing such unpublished opinions, see, e.g., Scott E. Gant, *Missing the Forest for A Tree: Unpublished Opinions and New Federal Rule of Appellate Procedure 32.1*, 47 B.C. L. Rev. 705 (2006); Patrick J. Schiltz, *Much Ado About Little: Explaining the Sturm und Drang over the Citation of Unpublished Opinions*, 62 Wash. & Lee L. Rev. 1429 (2005); Jessie Allen, *Just Words? The Effects of No-Citation Rules in Federal Courts of Appeals*, 29 Vt. L. Rev. 555 (2005); Amy E. Sloan, *A Government of Laws and Not Men: Prohibiting Non-Precedential Opinions by Statute or Procedural Rule*, 79 Ind. L.J. 711, 732 (2004); and Richard B. Cappalli, *The Common Law's Case Against Non-Precedential Opinions*, 76 S. Cal. L. Rev. 755 (2003).

16. The phrase "national seminar" was introduced by Eugene V. Rostow, *The Democratic Character of Judicial Review*, 66 Harv. L. Rev 193, 208 (1952). Alexander Bickel developed the notion further. Bickel, *supra* note 1, at 25–26.
17. *See, e.g.*, Cass Sunstein, Republic.com 11 (2002). Sunstein poses the deliberative democracy model in contrast to the echo chambers created by online discussion sites.
18. The decision whether to review is also the consequence of a vote—usually without explanation. Because they are without explanation, we are to make nothing of the fact that review was declined—that is, it is not a decision on the merits of the case. In the 2012–2013 term, for example, the Supreme Court disposed of 7,616 cases, by granting review to 93; summarily deciding 86; and denying, dismissing, or withdrawing 7,437. *The Statistics*, 127 Harv. L. Rev. 408, 417 (2013).
19. *See* James Boyd White, Justice as Translation 91 (1990) ("The great contribution of the judicial mind is not the vote but the judicial opinion, which gives meaning to the vote.")
20. *See* Owen M. Fiss, *Against Settlement*, 93 Yale L.J. 1073 (1984).
21. The label comes from Bickel, *supra* note 1, at 16. For a discussion of the academic obsession with Bickel's idea, see Barry Friedman, *The Birth of an Academic Obsession: The History of the Countermajoritarian Difficulty, Part Five*, 112 Yale L.J. 153 (2002).
22. For a history of arguments for judicial election, see Jed Hendelsman Shugerman, The People's Courts: Pursuing Judicial Independence in America (2012).
23. For a view that it should be, see Joseph Goldstein, The Intelligible Constitution: The Supreme Court's Obligation to Maintain the Constitution as Something We the People Can Understand (1992).
24. Discussed in chap. 2, below.
25. National Federation of Independent Business v. Sebelius, 132 S. Ct. 2566 (2012). Discussed in chap. 4, below.
26. There are frequent exceptions to this general observation. A brief—particularly an amicus brief—might be used to get information before the court. Classically, the Brandeis brief was used to provide social science data relevant to a policy choice. On the use of the Brandeis brief, see, e.g., Owen M. Fiss, 8 History of the Supreme Court of the United States: Troubled Beginnings of the Modern State, 1888–1910, at 175 (1993).

27. *See* Abraham Lincoln, *The Perpetuation of Our Political Institutions: Address Before the Young Men's Lyceum of Springfield, Illinois, January 27, 1838*, *in* Abraham Lincoln: His Speeches and Writings 76 (Roy P. Basler ed., 1946).
28. A July 2014 Gallup poll found that the Supreme Court's approval rating was 47 percent. Rebecca Riffkin, *Americans' Approval of the Supreme Court Remains Divided*, Gallup (July 14, 2014), http://www.gallup.com/poll/172526/americans-approval-supreme-court-remains-divided.aspx. By comparison, Congress's approval rating in September 2014 was 14 percent, and President Obama's was 47 percent—about the same as the Supreme Court. Frank Newport, *Congress Approval Sits at 14% Two Months Before Elections*, Gallup (Sept. 8, 2014), http://www.gallup.com/poll/175676/congress-approval-sits-two-months-elections.aspx; Frank Newport, *Hispanics' Approval of Obama Down Since '12*, Gallup (Sept. 26, 2014), http://www.gallup.com/poll/177404/hispanics-approval-obama-down.aspx.
29. For data on the growing authorial role of clerks, see Jeffrey S. Rosenthal & Albert H. Yoon, *Judicial Ghostwriting: Authorship on the Supreme Court*, 96 Cornell L. Rev. 1307 (2011).
30. Opinions are actually citing law reviews less and less. *See, e.g.*, Brent E. Newton, *Law Review Scholarship in the Eyes of the Twenty-First Century Supreme Court Justices: An Empirical Analysis*, 4 Drexel L. Rev. 399 (2012). Chief Justice Roberts has not been shy about his disdain for law reviews. *See A Conversation with Chief Justice Roberts* (C-SPAN television broadcast June 25, 2011), *available at* http://www.c-span.org/video/?300203-1/conversation-chief-justice-Roberts ("There is a great disconnect between the academy and the profession. Pick up a copy of any law review that you see, and the first article is likely to be the influence of Immanuel Kant on 18th century Bulgaria.").
31. Such an opinion reminds one of the blackmailer's note composed from words cut out of magazines.
32. *See* James Boyd White, Heracles' Bow 58 (1985) (describing a case "as a deposit of the processes of the world, in which experience continually frustrates expectation, in which facts and arguments seem inexhaustible and inconclusive").
33. Karl Llewellyn's canonical phrase "situation-sense" was coined in The Common Law Tradition: Deciding Appeals (1960). For commentary on the concept, which provoked much controversy among Llewellyn's

contemporaries, see Patrick J. Rohan, *The Common Law Tradition: Situation Sense, Subjectivism, or Just-Result Jurisprudence?*, 32 Fordham L. Rev. 51 (1963).

Chapter Two. The Opinion and Narrative

1. On canonical opinions, compare Bruce Ackerman, 2 We the People: Transformations 359–77 (1998), who discusses "transformative opinions" of the New Deal era. In chapter 4, I take up the ordinary practice of reading precedents as a source for understanding an authoritative text. In such cases, the line between common-law reasoning and the interpretation of authoritative legal texts can become so thin as to disappear. *See* Karl Llewellyn, The Bramble Bush 78–81 (1930) (*id.* at 79: "The meaning of the statute in life, like the meaning of a case law rule, turns on the [judicial] answer. We must turn to prediction, then, of what the courts will do, if we would read the statute. We turn, if we can, to what the judges have already done, to make our prediction sound."); Edward H. Levi, An Introduction to Legal Reasoning 19–40 (1949) (discussing the application of statutes; see especially *id.* at 21, "reexamin[ing] whether there is any difference between case-law and statutory interpretation").
2. See chap. 4, below.
3. On unconscionability, see, e.g., *Williams v. Walker-Thomas Furniture Co.*, 350 F.2d 445, 449 (D.C. Cir. 1965) ("[W]here the element of unconscionability is present at the time a contract is made, the contract should not be enforced."); Uniform Commercial Code § 2–302 (allowing courts to refuse to enforce unconscionable contracts). On the unenforceability of certain property transfers, see, e.g., N.Y. Gen. Oblig. Law § 5–331 (McKinney 2014) ("Any promise, covenant or restriction in a contract, mortgage, lease, deed or conveyance or in any other agreement affecting real property, heretofore or hereafter made or entered into, which limits, restrains, prohibits or otherwise provides against the sale, grant, gift, transfer, assignment, conveyance, ownership, lease, rental, use or occupancy of real property to or by any person because of race, creed, color, national origin, or ancestry, is hereby declared to be void as against public policy, wholly unenforceable, and shall not constitute a defense in any action, suit or proceeding.").
4. United States v. Butler, 297 U.S. 1, 62 (1936).
5. For examples of the view that judicial objectivity is achieved by faithful adherence to the text, see Robert H. Bork, *Neutral Principles and Some*

First Amendment Problems, 47 Ind. L.J. 1, 3 (1971); Frank H. Easterbrook, *Method, Result and Authority: A Reply*, 98 Harv. L. Rev. 622, 629 (1985). For a survey of views on the relationship between history and judicial objectivity, see G. Edward White, *The Arrival of History in Constitutional Scholarship*, 88 Va. L. Rev. 485 (2002). For an example of the view that adherence to professional practices yields objectivity, see Owen M. Fiss, *Objectivity and Interpretation*, 34 Stan. L. Rev. 739, 745 (1982).

6. *See, e.g.*, Mark Tushnet, *Interdisciplinary Legal Scholarship: The Case of History in Law*, 71 Chi. Kent L. Rev. 909 (1996) (arguing that law-office history should not be evaluated according to the criteria of academic history generally); Alfred H. Kelly, *Clio and the Court: An Illicit Love Affair*, 1965 Sup. Ct. Rev. 119 (criticizing the Supreme Court's use of history).

7. *See* Paul W. Kahn, Finding Ourselves at the Movies: Philosophy for a New Generation (2013).

8. *See* Charles Taylor, Modern Social Imaginaries (2003); Benedict Anderson, Imagined Communities: Reflections on the Origin and Spread of Nationalism (1991).

9. Oliver Wendell Holmes, The Common Law 1 (1881).

10. On the importance of ethos to persuasion, see Eugene Garver, For the Sake of Argument: Practical Reasoning, Character, and the Ethics of Belief (2004).

11. This debate recently flared up during Justice Sotomayor's confirmation process. President Obama had announced that he would seek a nominee "who understands that justice isn't about some abstract legal theory . . . [i]t is also about how our laws affect the daily realities of people's lives." Press Release, The White House, The President's Remarks on Justice Souter (May 1, 2009), *available at* http://www.whitehouse.gov/blog/2009/05/01/presidents-remarks-justice-souter. "I view that quality of empathy," Obama continued, "of understanding and identifying with people's hopes and struggles as an essential ingredient for arriving at just decisions and outcomes." *Id.* The comment set off a firestorm of criticism. *See, e.g.*, Peter Slevin, *In Filling Supreme Court Vacancy, Obama Looks for a Jurist with Empathy*, Wash. Post, May 13, 2009, *available at* http://www.washingtonpost.com/wp-dyn/content/article/2009/05/12/AR2009051203515.html (reporting that Senator Mitch McConnell believed the remark demonstrated Obama would choose judges based on their "perceived sympathy for certain groups or individuals"). That debate grew more heated when then Judge Sotomayor's 2001 speech

at the University of California, Berkeley surfaced. She had declared that she "would hope that a wise Latina woman with the richness of her experiences would more often than not reach a better conclusion than a white male who hasn't lived that life." Charlie Savage, *A Judge's View of Judging Is on the Record*, N.Y. Times, May 14, 2009, *available at* http://www.nytimes.com/2009/05/15/us/15judge.html.
12. 131 S. Ct. 2729 (2011).
13. 131 S. Ct. at 2727 (citation omitted) (internal quotation marks omitted).
14. On the virtues of incompletely theorized opinions, see Cass R. Sunstein, *Incompletely Theorized Agreements in Constitutional Law*, 74 Soc. Res. 1 (2007).
15. This is symbolic of a larger shift in the culture toward privileging private over public spaces. To an earlier generation, the classroom had been the site of civic training in toleration. *See* W. Va. State Bd. of Educ. v. Barnett, 319 U.S. 624 (1943).
16. John Dewey, The Public and Its Problems 3 (1927).
17. 131 S. Ct. at 2751–59 (Thomas, J., dissenting).
18. 131 S. Ct. at 2741 (maj. op.).
19. 131 S. Ct. at 2735–38.
20. *See* Bd. of Educ. of Westside Cmty. Sch. v. Mergens, 496 U.S. 226 (1990); Tinker v. Des Moines Indep. Cmty. Sch. Dist., 393 U.S. 503 (1969).
21. Justice Scalia has led the effort of offering reasons for adopting an originalist approach. He argues that faithful adherence to the Framers' understanding of the law reduces the space for judicial bias. He believes this adherence to the Framers' original intent generates predictability and consistency in the law. Under the originalist theory of construction, "[t]he raw material for the general rule is readily apparent." Antonin Scalia, *The Rule of Law as a Law of Rules*, 56 U. Chi. L. Rev. 1175, 1184 (1989). He also argues that originalism is more compatible with democracy. Antonin Scalia, *Originalism: The Lesser Evil*, 57 U. Cin. L. Rev. 849 (1989). Of course, all of these are deeply contested claims.
22. *See* I. Bernard Cohen, Science and the Founding Fathers, chap. 5 (1995); Paul W. Kahn, Legitimacy and History, chap. 1 (1993).
23. *See* Planned Parenthood v. Casey, 505 U.S. 833, 861–63 (1992); *see also* Kahn, *supra* note 22, chap. 4.
24. 131 S. Ct. at 2768 (Breyer, J., dissenting).
25. 131 S. Ct. at 2769.
26. See chap. 5, below, on the relative autonomy of law.
27. See chap. 3, below, on voice.

28. *See* Duncan Kennedy, *Freedom and Constraint in Adjudication: A Critical Phenomenology*, 36 J. Legal Educ. 518 (1986).
29. 131 S. Ct. at 2742–51 (Alito, J., concurring in the judgment).
30. Jacobellis v. Ohio, 378 U.S. 184, 197 (1964) (Stewart, J., concurring).
31. *See* Guido Calabresi, A Common Law for the Age of Statutes 163–66 (1985) (on courts requiring a second look).
32. Joseph Raz argues that "the normal way to establish that a person has authority over another person involves showing that the alleged subject is likely better to comply with reasons which apply to him (other than the alleged authoritative directives) if he accepts the directives of the alleged authority as authoritatively binding and tries to follow them, rather than by trying to follow the reasons which apply to him directly." Joseph Raz, The Morality of Freedom 55 (1986). In other words, a patient is more likely to comply with the medical reasons for pursuing a particular course of treatment by following a doctor's advice than if the patient were to treat himself: the doctor's authority derives from this comparative expertise. The same argument can be made for judges and the law. See J.E. Penner, *Legal Reasoning and the Authority of the Law*, in Rights, Culture, and the Law: Themes from the Legal and Political Philosophy of Joseph Raz 71 (Lukas H. Meyer, Stanley L. Paulson & Thomas W. Pogge eds., 2003).
33. Consider Bickel's subtitle, The Least Dangerous Branch: The Supreme Court at the Bar of Politics (2d ed. 1986).
34. *See* Federalist No. 78 (Alexander Hamilton).
35. 60 U.S. 393 (1857).
36. *See, e.g.*, Panama Refining Co. v. Ryan, 293 U.S. 388 (1935) (finding unconstitutional section 9(c) of the National Industrial Recovery Act, which imposed various restrictions on the petroleum industry); A.L.A. Schechter Poultry Corp. v. United States, 295 U.S. 495 (1935) (rendering the entire National Industrial Recovery Act unconstitutional). *See* Ackerman, *supra* note 1, at 296–301, for President Roosevelt's response to the Court's decision in *Schechter Poultry*.
37. Citizens United v. Federal Election Commission, 558 U.S. 310 (2010); McCutcheon v. Federal Election Committee, 134 S. Ct. 1434 (2014).
38. Bickel, *supra* note 33, at 239.
39. See discussion of *Bowers* in chap. 4, below.
40. 531 U.S. 98 (2000).
41. A number of Florida ballots were so poorly designed that voters selected multiple presidential candidates, no presidential candidate, or the wrong

presidential candidate. The most infamous of these was the "butterfly ballot" used in Palm Beach County. Jeffrey Toobin, Too Close to Call 33 (2001). The names on these ballots were arranged in such a way that many voters unintentionally voted for Pat Buchanan rather than Al Gore. Even ignoring this problem of intention, the question of who garnered more votes in Florida in the 2000 election remains contested. In November 2001, the *New York Times* published the results of a "comprehensive review" of uncounted ballots in Florida. Ford Fesseden & John M. Broder, *Study of Disputed Florida Ballots Finds Justices Did Not Cast the Deciding Vote*, N.Y. Times, Nov. 12, 2001, *available at* http://www.nytimes.com/2001/11/12/politics/recount/12VOTE.html. The study revealed that "Mr. Bush would have retained a slender margin over Mr. Gore if the Florida court's order to recount more than 43,000 ballots had not been reversed by the United States Supreme Court." *Id.* However, the results of the study were later called into question for failing to count "overvotes," or ballots that registered a vote for two presidential candidates. If overvotes had been counted, Gore most likely would have prevailed. *Id.*

42. For subsequent efforts to make sense of the decision, see Bush v. Gore: The Question of Legitimacy (Bruce Ackerman ed., 2002).
43. The political character of the decision was emphasized in news reports that Justice Sandra Day O'Connor had expressed dismay on Election Night that Gore might prevail. "This is terrible," O'Connor reportedly exclaimed when CBS anchor Dan Rather called Florida for Gore. Michael Isikoff, *The Truth Behind the Pillars*, Newsweek, Dec. 25, 2000, *available at* http://www.newsweek.com/truth-behind-pillars-155985. O'Connor's husband then explained that she was upset because she wanted to retire from the bench but would be reluctant to step down if a Democrat were elected. Jess Bravin et al., *Supreme Interests: For Some Justices, the Bush-Gore Case Has a Personal Angle*, Wall St. J., Dec. 12, 2000, at A1.
44. 531 U.S. at 128–29 (Stevens, J., dissenting).
45. *Id.* at 123 (Stevens J., dissenting); *id.* at 144 (Breyer, J., dissenting).
46. *Id.* at 109 ("Our consideration is limited to present circumstances.").
47. *See* Llewellyn, *supra* note 1, at 39 ("Our legal theory does not admit of single decisions standing on their own.").
48. Predictably, the opinion's attempt at self-limitation did not work. Lawyers have used *Bush* in subsequent arguments and lower courts have cited the case in hundreds of opinions. *See, e.g.*, Hunter v. Hamilton Cnty.

Bd. of Elections, 635 F.3d 219, 231 (6th Cir. 2011); Lemons v. Bradbury, 538 F.3d 1098, 1105 (9th Cir. 2008); Romeu v. Cohen, 265 F.3d 118, 123 (2d Cir. 2001). The Supreme Court has even cited *Bush*. *See* Arizona v. Inter-Tribal Council of Ariz. Inc., 133 S. Ct. 2247, 2268 n.2 (2013). In this way, the ordinary processes of legal argument have tended to normalize *Bush*.

49. *See, e.g.*, Ackerman, *supra* note 42.
50. This argument is made in Jed Rubenfeld, "Not as Bad as *Plessy*. Worse," *in* Ackerman, *supra* note 42, at 20–38.
51. See chap. 1, above.
52. 3 U.S.C. § 19.
53. Bush v. Gore, 531 U.S. 98, 104 ("The State, of course, after granting the franchise in the special context of Article II, can take back the power to appoint electors.").
54. In dissent, Justice Breyer describes in some detail Congress's efforts to resolve the presidential election of 1876. *Id*. at 154–58 (Breyer, J., dissenting).
55. In 2013, Justice O'Connor told the *Chicago Tribune* that the Supreme Court may have erred in taking *Bush v. Gore*. She stated that the case had "stirred up the public" and "gave the Court a less-than perfect reputation." She wondered if "[m]aybe the court should have said, 'We're not going to take it, good-bye." Dahleen Glanton, *Retired Justice O'Connor: Bush v. Gore 'Stirred Up the Public,'* Chicago Tribune, Ap. 26, 2013, *available at* http://articles.chicagotribune.com/2013-04-26/news/chi-retired-justice-oconnor-bush-v-gore-stirred-up-the-public-20130426_1_bush-v-retired-justice-o-connor-high-court.

Chapter Three. Unity

1. *See* Jeffrey Toobin, Too Close to Call: The Thirty-Six-Day Battle to Decide the 2000 Election 252 (2001).
2. *See* Bush v. Gore, 531 U.S. 98, 128 (2000) (Stevens, J., dissenting) (the majority opinion "can only lend credence to the most cynical appraisal of the work of judges throughout the land.").
3. *See, e.g.*, Jack Bass, *Unlikely Heroes* (Univ. of Alabama Press 1990) (1981) (describing how federal judges in the South implemented the decision in *Brown v. Board of Education* despite intense popular resistance).
4. About some rules, however, we might think that their justice is not independent of their origin. *See* Robert Nozick, Anarchy, State, and Utopia (1974).

5. We can observe this relationship even more directly in the Latin roots of "author" and "authority": *auctor* and *auctoritas*, respectively. *Auctor*, defined most broadly, means "he that brings about the existence of any object, or promotes the increase or prosperity of it, whether he first originates it, or by his efforts gives greater permanence or continuance to it." Charlton T. Lewis & Charles Short, A Latin Dictionary (Clarendon Press 1987) (1879), s.v. "auctor." *Auctoritas* derives from the addition of the abstract quality suffix *-tas* onto the noun *auctor*. Like the English suffix -ity, the Latin suffix *-tas* expresses a state or condition. *See* Michèle Fruyt, *Word Formation in Classical Latin, in* A Companion to the Latin Language 157, 162 (James Clackson ed., 2011) (describing how the suffix functions). Just as, in English, popularity is the state of being popular, in Latin, *auctoritas* is the state of being an *auctor*. Thus *auctoritas* may be translated as "[a] view, opinion, judgment; Counsel, advice, persuasion, encouragement to something; Will, pleasure, decision, bidding, command, precept, decree; Liberty, ability, power, authority to do according to one's pleasure; Might, power, authority, reputation, dignity, influence, weight." Lewis & Short, *supra*, s.v. "auctoritas."
6. Of course, in chambers a judge may hold a clerk to be the author of a draft: the clerk will be held accountable for what is in the draft.
7. Because authorship is a social practice, copyright law is a contested normative field. Those contests are not answered by looking to the fact of who wrote what. Some modern copyright theorists describe authorship as a "fiction" because there are an indefinite number of causes that bear on the creation of a work. To say it is a fiction is just another way of saying it is a normative social practice. *See* Michel Foucault, *What Is an Author?, in* Language, Counter-Memory, and Practice: Selected Essays and Interviews 113 (Donald Bouchard ed., Donald Bouchard & Sherry Simon trans., Cornell Univ. Press 1977) (1969).
8. *See, e.g.*, Roland Barthes, *The Death of the Author, in* Image-Music-Text 142 (Stephen Heath trans., Noonday Press 1977) (1967) (providing the classic statement of the position that a text can be studied without attention to its author).
9. *See, e.g.*, Robert Alter, The Five Books of Moses: A Translation with Commentary, at x, xi (2004) (noting that "[s]cholarship for more than two centuries has agreed that the Five Books [of Moses] are drawn together from different literary sources, though there have been shifting debates about the particular identification of sources in the text and fierce difference of

10. Barthes, *supra* note 8, collapses the ideas of authors and scriptors, but maintaining the distinction is essential in the practice of reading religious—and legal—texts.
11. *See* Pauline Maier, American Scripture: Making the Declaration of Independence 99–154 (1997) (investigating Jefferson's intellectual influences and personal motivations as part of a history of the drafting of the Declaration).
12. The Declaration of Independence para. 5 (U.S. 1776).
13. *Id.*
14. *Id.*
15. Sanford Levinson, Constitutional Faith 180–94 (2d ed. 2011) (1988), discusses this experience of authorship in deciding to sign his name to the Constitution at a bicentennial exhibit that asked, "If you had been in Independence Hall on September 17, 1787, would you have endorsed the Constitution?" For Levinson, "adding one's signature would serve to transform the experience from a mere remembrance of times past to a renewed dedication to—a continuing ordination of, as it were—the Constitution as an ever-living presence encouraging the establishment of a more perfect Union committed above all to the realization of justice and the blessing of liberty." *Id.* at 180. In other words, to sign the document is to "join in affirming a 'constitutional faith.'" *Id.* at 181. Levinson signed the document in 1987, *id.* at 191–94, although in an afterword to the 2011 edition, he notes that he has subsequently lost his "constitutional faith," *id.* at 244–55.
16. Ludwig Wittgenstein famously attacked the idea of a private language in his *Philosophical Investigations* §§ 243–56 (P.H.S. Hacker & Joachim Schulte eds., G.E.M. Anscombe et al. trans., Wiley-Blackwell 3d ed. 2009) (1953).
17. The Declaration of Independence para. 2 (U.S. 1776).
18. *Id.*
19. U.S. Const. amend. XIV, § 1.
20. *Id.* preamble.
21. *See* Mistretta v. United States, 488 U.S. 361 (1989) (upholding the constitutionality of Congress's delegation of the task of crafting Federal Sentencing Guidelines to an independent expert body in the Judicial Branch).

22. This principle of democratic self-authorship plays an important role in statutory interpretation: a statute should be interpreted in such a way as to maintain the belief in popular authorship. *See* Paul W. Kahn & Kiel R. Brennan-Marquez, *Statutes and Democratic Self-Authorship*, 56 Wm. & Mary L. Rev. 115 (2014).
23. *See* Max Radin, *Statutory Interpretation*, 43 Harv. L. Rev. 863, 871 (1930) ("[I]n law, the specific individuals who make up the legislature are men to whom a specialized function has been temporarily assigned. That function is not to impose their will . . . on their fellow citizens, but to 'pass statutes," which is a fairly precise operation.").
24. *See* Fletcher v. Peck, 10 U.S. (6 Cranch) 87 (1810) (upholding a land sale carried out under the 1795 Yazoo Land Act, which Georgia legislators had been bribed to pass). As Chief Justice Marshall observed: "It may well be doubted how far the validity of a law depends upon the motives of its framers, and how far the particular inducements, operating on members of the supreme sovereign power of a state, to the formation of a contract by that power, are examinable in a court of justice. If the principle be conceded, that an act of the supreme sovereign power might be declared null by a court, in consequence of the means which procured it, still would there be much difficulty in saying to what extent those means must be applied to produce this effect. Must it be direct corruption, or would interest or undue influence of any kind be sufficient? Must the vitiating cause operate on a majority, or on what number of the members? Would the act be null, whatever might be the wish of the nation, or would its obligation or nullity depend upon the public sentiment?" *Id.* at 130.
25. See discussion of statutory interpretation below.
26. Roberto Unger captures this point when he says that we become "right wing Hegelians" when we read a statute: "The two dirty little secrets of contemporary jurisprudence—jurisprudence in the age of rationalizing legal analysis—are its reliance upon a rightwing Hegelian view of social and legal history and its discomfort with democracy: the worship of historical triumph and the fear of popular action. The rightwing Hegelianism finds expression in a daily practice emphasizing the cunning of history in developing a rational order . . . out of the uncompromising stuff of historical conflict and compromise." Roberto Mangabeira Unger, What Should Legal Analysis Become? 72 (1996).
27. For this reason, it is a rule of statutory construction that we read the texts in such a way as to avoid contradiction. *See, e.g.*, William N. Es-

kridge, Jr. & Philip P. Frickey, *The Supreme Court, 1993 Term—Foreword: Law as Equilibrium*, 108 Harv. L. Rev. 26, 98–100 (1994) (listing several canons of statutory interpretation to this effect: for example, "Avoid interpreting a provision in a way inconsistent with the policy of another provision," or "Assume that Congress does not create discontinuities in legal rights and obligations").

28. Of course, a representative may so abuse his position as to be acting outside the scope of the representation, in which case he may be violating the law or a professional norm. If his action is on its face *ultra vires*, it may not bind the principal.

29. *See* Jürgen Habermas, Between Facts and Norms: Contributions to a Discourse Theory of Law and Democracy 126–93 (William Rehg trans., MIT Press 1996) (1992) (discussing the formation of public opinion and its legitimating function); *see also* Robert C. Post, *Meiklejohn's Mistake: Individual Autonomy and the Reform of Public Discourse*, 64 U. Col. L. Rev. 1109 (1993).

30. Confronting the problem of the limited range of particular votes, Rousseau proposed periodic referenda on the question of whether the government should continue—an effort to eliminate the dead hand of the past. Jean-Jacques Rousseau, The Social Contract, book 3, chaps. 12–14, 18, *in* Rousseau: The Social Contract and Other Later Political Writings (Victor Gourevitch ed. & trans., Cambridge Univ. Press 1997) (1762). *See especially id.* at 119–20 ("The periodic assemblies . . . which have no other object than to maintain the social treaty, ought always to open with two motions which it should be impossible ever to omit, and which ought to be voted on separately: The first; *whether it please the Sovereign to retain the present form of Government*. The second; *whether it please the People to leave its administration to those who are currently charged with it*.").

31. On webs of significance, see Clifford Geertz, The Interpretation of Cultures: Selected Essays 5 (2000) (1973). ("The concept of culture I espouse . . . is essentially a semiotic one. Believing, with Max Weber, that man is an animal suspended in webs of significance he himself has spun, I take culture to be those webs, and the analysis of it to be therefore not an experimental science in search of law but an interpretive one in search of meaning.").

32. *See, e.g.*, Antonin Scalia, *Common-Law Courts in a Civil Law System: The Role of United States Federal Courts in Interpreting the Constitution and the Laws*, *in* A Matter of Interpretation: Federal Courts and the Law 3, 23

(1997) ("To be a textualist in good standing, one need not be too dull to perceive the broader social purposes that a statute is designed, or could be designed, to serve; or too hidebound to realize that new times require new laws. One need only hold the belief that judges have no authority to pursue those broader purposes or write those new laws.").

33. Ronald Dworkin, Law's Empire 178–84 (1986).
34. *See* Guido Calabresi, A Common Law for the Age of Statutes 2 (1982) (noting a pervasive "feeling that, because a statute is hard to revise once it is passed, laws are governing us that would not and could not be enacted today, and that *some* of these laws not only could not be reenacted but also do not fit, are in some sense inconsistent with, our whole legal landscape").
35. *Cf.* Dworkin, *supra* note 33 at 230–31 (assessing conceptions of law according to the two dimensions of "fit" (does this conception fit our legal practices as a whole?) and "justification" (does this conception justify our legal practices?)). These "represent different aspects of a single overall judgment of political morality." *Id.* at 235.
36. See discussion below on the limits of tolerable disagreement.
37. This is not to deny that participatory exclusion may in some circumstances undermine our capacity for seeing self-authorship.
38. Thomas Hobbes, Leviathan, part 2, chap. 17, at 121 (Richard Tuck ed., Cambridge Univ. Press 1996) (1651).
39. *Id.*, part 2, chap. 18, at 122.
40. *See* sources cited *supra* note 29.
41. State judges are often subject to various forms of electoral review or recall. Twenty-two states use elections to elect judges to their courts of last resort (eight are partisan, fourteen are nonpartisan), and all but twelve states have some form of retention election, partisan election, or nonpartisan election. *See Selection and Retention of Appellate Court Judges*, *in* Council of State Governments, The Book of the States 2014, at 250, 250–53 tbl. 5.6 (2014), *available at* http://knowledgecenter.csg.org/kc/system/files/5.6_2013.pdf. In Iowa in 2010, for example, voters removed three justices from the state supreme court, who had joined a ruling legalizing same-sex marriage. *See* A.G. Sulzberger, Jr., *In Iowa, Voters Oust Judges Over Marriage Issue*, N.Y. Times, Nov. 3, 2010, *available at* http://www.nytimes.com/2010/11/03/us/politics/03judges.html.
42. *See, e.g.*, Robert A. Dahl, Democracy and Its Critics 190 (1991) (1989) ("Jurists known to be sharply at odds with the basic outlook of the president or a majority of senators are not nominated by the president and

confirmed by the Senate. Thus the views of a majority of justices of the Supreme Court are never out of line for very long with the views prevailing among the lawmaking majorities of the country."); Barry Friedman, *Dialogue and Judicial Review*, 91 Mich. L. Rev. 577, 677–78 (1993) ("Just as the system will have cycles in which all waves are crossing the middle point, the system also works to ensure that no wave will get too far out of cycle. The process of election and judicial appointment works to keep the lines somewhat responsive to one another and within the rough bounds of public opinion. Of course, this process sometimes fails, leading to constitutional crises. *Dred Scott* may well represent a time when the waves were far out of sync; the period of judicial opposition to the New Deal may signal another. But such periods have been mercifully rare.").

43. *See, e.g.*, Or Bassok, *The Two Countermajoritarian Difficulties*, 31 St. Louis U. Pub. L. Rev. 333 (2012) (discussing the interaction between public opinion and the Court); Friedman, *supra* note 42, at 585 ("Courts . . . do not stand aloof from society and declare rights. Rather, they interact on a daily basis with society, taking part in an interpretive dialogue. Rights, by the same token, do not override majority will. Rather, 'the People' define and redefine their rights every day as the interpretive dialogue proceeds.").

44. Nat'l Fed'n of Indep. Bus. v. Sebelius, 132 S. Ct. 2566 (2012).

45. Learned Hand famously derided the idea that judges were qualified to be "Platonic Guardians." *See* Hand, The Bill of Rights 73 (1958) ("[I]t certainly does not accord with the underlying presuppositions of popular government to vest in a chamber, unaccountable to anyone but itself, the power to suppress social experiments which it does not approve. . . . Each one of us must in the end choose for himself how far he would like to leave our collective fate to the wayward vagaries of popular assemblies. . . . For myself it would be most irksome to be ruled by a bevy of Platonic Guardians, even if I knew how to choose them, which I assuredly do not.").

46. *See, e.g.*, Owen M. Fiss, *Objectivity and Interpretation*, 34 Stan. L. Rev. 739 (1982).

47. *See* Paul Kahn, *Legal Performance and the Imagination of Sovereignty*, 3 E-misférica (June 2006), *available at* http://hemisphericinstitute.org/journal/3.1/eng/en31_pg_kahn.html (issue devoted to performance and the law).

48. Indeed, in those states where judges do face the voters directly, we worry about the increasing politicalization of the courts. That is, we worry that

outcomes are being shaped with an eye to electoral success. While we might think that a virtue among other branches of government, it can lead to a crisis of legitimacy for the courts. *See infra* chap. 5 (discussing Caperton v. A.T. Massey Coal Co., Inc., 556 U.S. 898 (2009)).

49. As I explain below, judicial authorship is present in dissents and concurrences—explicitly so.
50. 5 U.S. (1 Cranch) 137 (1803).
51. The Twelfth Amendment was ratified in order to prevent this issue from arising again. *See, e.g.*, Akhil Reed Amar, America's Constitution: A Biography 341–47 (2005) (discussing the passage of the Twelfth Amendment and its ramifications).
52. *See* Paul W. Kahn, The Reign of Law: *Marbury v. Madison* and the Construction of America 11–17 (1997) (discussing *Marbury*'s political context); Cliff Sloan & David McKean, Jefferson, Adams, Marshall, and the Battle for the Supreme Court (2009) (providing further political and historical context for *Marbury*).
53. 5 U.S. at 178.
54. *Id.* at 171.
55. *Id.* at 162 ("Mr. Marbury, then, since his commission was signed by the President, and sealed by the secretary of state, was appointed; and as the law creating the office, gave the officer a right to hold for five years, independent of the executive, the appointment was not revocable; but vested in the officer legal rights, which are protected by the laws of this country. To withhold his commission, therefore, is an act deemed by the court not warranted by law, but violative of a vested legal right.").
56. Plato, The Republic, book 6, 509d–513e, *in* Complete Works (John M. Cooper, ed., trans. G.M.A. Grube & C.D.C. Reeve, Hackett 1997). Plato introduces the knowledge/opinion distinction earlier, *id.* at V.475e–488a, to distinguish true philosophers, who have knowledge, from lovers of sights and sounds, who have merely opinion.
57. Judicial authorship is a problematic idea even for the common law. Looking for an authoritative, external ground, courts will sometimes claim that the law is to reflect customary practices that precede the decision. Sometimes, they claim that they reflect past decisions that stretch back to "time immemorial." *See, e.g.*, J.G.A. Pocock, The Ancient Constitution and the Feudal Law: A Study of English Historical Thought in the Seventeenth Century 37 (2d ed. 1987) (1957) ("The common law was by definition immemorial custom. . . . Innumerable decisions were consequently on record as declaring that everything which

they contained, down to the most minute and complex technicality, had formed part of the custom of England from time out of mind."). Sometimes, they speak of a mythical "lost statute" at the origin. *See, e.g.,* Brace v. Shaw, 55 Ky. 43 (16 B. Mon.) 45 (1855) ("What portion of an ancestor's debts his heirs shall pay out of real estate, depends altogether upon legislation, or custom which is supposed to be founded on lost statutes."). *See also* Matthew Hale, History and Analysis of the Common Law 3–4 (London, J. Walthoe 1713) ("[D]oubtless, many of those Things that now obtain as Common Law, had their Original by Parliamentary Acts or Constitutions, made in Writing by the King, Lords and Commons; though those Acts are now either not extant, or if extant, were made before Time of Memory [July 6, 1189]; and the Evidence of the Truth hereof will easily appear, for that in many of those old Acts of Parliament that were made before Time of Memory, and are yet extant, we many find many of those Laws enacted which now obtain merely as Common Law, or the General Custom of the Realm."). The problematic character of these claims has supported a general turn to codification since the nineteenth century.

58. *See infra* chap. 5 on this dynamic of erudite commentary versus fundamentalism.
59. *See* Paul W. Kahn, Legitimacy and History: Self-Government in American Constitutional Theory (1992) (discussing changing understandings of the Constitution over the course of American history).
60. 5 U.S. at 178.
61. Thomas Jefferson, First Inaugural Address, *in* 1 Documents of American History 187 (Henry Steele Commager ed., 9th ed. 1973) (1801).
62. 5 U.S. at 176 (emphasis added).
63. *Id.*
64. In a moment of intense judicial self-reflection, for example, the Court returns to this ideal linking the legitimacy of the Court to national identity: "If the Court's legitimacy should be undermined, then, so would the country be in its very ability to see itself through its constitutional ideals." Planned Parenthood v. Casey, 505 U.S. 833, 868 (1992).
65. Bruce Ackerman uses this distinction between ordinary and constitutional politics in We the People: Foundations (1991).
66. State law that has its source apart from the federal Constitution poses other issues, most especially that of the locus of sovereign authority. A federal court is to defer to a state court's interpretation of its own law. *See* Erie R.R. Co. v. Tompkins, 304 U.S. 64 (1938).

67. Scalia and Garner, for example, in their treatise on statutory interpretation argue that judges should not "'make' law through judicial interpretation of democratically enacted statutes." Antonin Scalia & Bryan A. Garner, Reading Law: The Interpretation of Legal Texts 5 (2012).
68. One measure of a failure of judicial representation is when Congress responds to a judicial interpretation by amending the underlying statute. If Congress adopts a position that was already available as an interpretation of existing law—for example, the position taken by the dissenters in the case—we might think that the failure was not in the legislature that produced the original law, but in the court that interpreted it.
69. An exception might be *Kelo v. City of New London*, 545 U.S. 469 (2005), which allowed the city to use its eminent domain power to condemn several houses as part of a development plan. The Court's opinion notes that the city "intended the development plan to capitalize on the arrival of [a] Pfizer facility and the new commerce it was expected to attract." *Id.* at 474.
70. Compare the proposal for judicial biography by Jerome Frank in *Law and the Modern Mind* 148 (1930) ("All judges exercise discretion, individualize abstract rules, make law. Shall the process be concealed or disclosed? The fact is, and every lawyer knows it, that *those judges who are most lawless, or most swayed by the 'perverting influences of their emotional natures,' or most dishonest, are often the very judges who use most meticulously the language of compelling mechanical logic, who elaborately wrap about themselves the pretense of merely discovering and carrying out existing rules, who sedulously avoid any indications that they individualize cases.* If every judicial opinion contained a clear exposition of all the actual grounds of the decision, the tyrants, the bigots and the dishonest men on the bench would lose their disguises and become known for what they are."). This idea is based on a confusion of the meaning of authoring with that of drafting an opinion.
71. A written text will always invoke metaphors of both seeing and hearing, for reading is both.
72. S. Pac. Co. v. Jensen, 244 U.S. 205, 222 (1917) (Holmes, J., dissenting).
73. Consider, for example, the assumption against extraterritorial reach of statutes. *See* Kiobel v. Royal Dutch Petroleum, 133 S. Ct. 1659 (2013).
74. We find here part of the problem with taking the decisions of foreign courts as a source of law. *See* Paul W. Kahn, *The International Criminal Court: Why the United States Is So Opposed*, Crimes of War Project, The Magazine (Dec. 2003).

75. Consider *Holy Trinity Church v. United States*, 147 U.S. 457, 471 (1892), in which the Court described America as a "Christian nation." That claim can no longer serve as a useful precedent, even if it made sense at the time.
76. *Cf.* Calabresi, *supra* note 34, at 18 (observing that second-look doctrines can be used in statutory interpretation, "to induce the legislature to reconsider statutes that are out of date, out of phase, or ill adapted to the legal topography").
77. *See* Cass R. Sunstein, *Naked Preferences and the Constitution*, 84 Colum. L. Rev. 1689 (1984).
78. *See, e.g.*, Becke v. Smith (1836) 150 Eng. Rep. 724, 726 (Exch.) ("It is a very useful rule, in the construction of a statute, to adhere to the ordinary meaning of the words used, and to the grammatical construction, unless that is at variance with the intention of the legislature, to be collected from the statute itself, or leads to any manifest absurdity or repugnance, in which case the language may be varied or modified, so as to avoid such inconvenience, but no further.").
79. Known as the "whole act rule." *See* United Savings Ass'n of Texas v. Timbers of Inwood Forest Assocs., 484 U.S. 365, 371 (1988) ("Statutory construction . . . is a holistic endeavor."); Kokoszka v. Belford, 417 U.S. 642, 650 (1974); United States v. Fisher, 6 U.S. (2 Cranch) 358 366–70 (1805).
80. As of 2010, twenty-six states had codified the "presum[ption] that the legislature uses the same term consistently in different statutes." Jacob Scott, *Codified Canons and the Common Law of Interpretation*, 98 Geo. L.J. 341, 379 (2010). Similarly, as of 2010, fifteen states had codified a rule against implied repeals. *Id.* at 397. For example, in Minnesota, a statute provides that "[w]hen a general provision in a law is in conflict with a special provision in the same or another law, the two shall be construed, if possible, so that effect may be given to both. If the conflict between the two provisions be irreconcilable, the special provision shall prevail and shall be construed as an exception to the general provision, unless the general provision shall be enacted at a later session and it shall be the manifest intention of the legislature that such general provision shall prevail." Minn. Stat. §§ 645.26(1) (2014).
81. *See* James J. Brudney, *Confirmatory Legislative History*, 76 Brook. L. Rev. 901 (2011) (discussing Justice Scalia's distaste for this practice).
82. *See* William N. Eskridge, Jr., *Public Values in Statutory Interpretation*, 137 U. Pa. L. Rev. 1007 (1989) (discussing how substantive canons bring

to bear public values embodied in the Constitution, federal statutes, and common law).

83. Known as "the avoidance canon." *See* United States *ex rel.* Att'y Gen. v. Del. & Hudson Co., 213 U.S. 366, 408 (1909) ("[W]here a statute is susceptible of two constructions, by one of which grave and doubtful constitutional questions arise and by the other of which such questions are avoided, our duty is to adopt the latter.").

84. *See* Scalia & Garner, *supra* note 67 at 318–19 (Canon 52, "Presumption Against Change in Common Law. A statute will be construed to alter the common law only when that disposition is clear.").

85. *See* Gregory v. Ashcroft, 501 U.S. 452 (1991) (federalism or state sovereignty presumption); Dep't of Navy v. Egan, 484 U.S. 518, 527 (1988) (presidential power presumption); Demore v. Kim, 538 U.S. 510 (2003) (judicial review presumption).

86. Babbitt v. Sweet Home Chapter of Cmtys. for a Greater Or., 515 U.S. 687 (1995).

87. *Id.* at 697.

88. Another formal canon is at stake here: "A cardinal rule of statutory interpretation [is] that no provision should be construed to be entirely redundant." Kungys v. United States, 485 U.S. 759, 778 (1988).

89. Tenn. Valley Auth. v. Hill, 437 U.S. 153 (1978).

90. *Id.* at 180.

91. *See, e.g.,* Akhil Reed Amar, Marbury, *Section 13, and the Original Jurisdiction of the Supreme Court*, 56 U. Chi. L. Rev. 443 (1989) (arguing that the *Marbury* Court mistakenly interpreted section 13 of the Judiciary Act of 1789 as granting the Supreme Court original jurisdiction in mandamus cases); William W. Van Alstyne, *A Critical Guide to* Marbury v. Madison," 1969 Duke L.J. 1, 16–33 (discussing critically the *Marbury* Court's arguments for judicial review).

92. *See infra* chap. 4 on the significance of dissents.

93. The word "charisma" is derived from the Greek "χάρις" (charis), meaning "favor" or "grace." Oxford English Dictionary, s.v. "charisma," http://www.oed.com (last visited Dec. 6, 2014).

94. Max Weber, 1 Economy and Society: An Outline of Interpretive Sociology 241–45 (Guenther Roth & Claus Wittich eds., Ephraim Fischoff et al. trans., Univ. of California Press 1978) (1922) (on "Charismatic Authority"); *id.* at 246–54 (on the "Routinization of Charisma"). *See, e.g., id.* at 244 ("Since it is 'extra-ordinary,' charismatic authority is sharply opposed to rational, and particularly bureaucratic, authority,

and to traditional authority, whether in its patriarchal, patrimonial, or estate variants, all of which are everyday forms of domination; while the charismatic type is the direct antithesis of this. Bureaucratic authority is specifically rational in the sense of being bound to intellectually analysable rules; while charismatic authority is specifically irrational in the sense of being foreign to all rules. Traditional authority is bound to the precedents handed down from the past and to this extent is also oriented to rules. Within the sphere of its claims, charismatic authority repudiates the past, and is in this sense a specifically revolutionary force. It recognizes no appropriation of positions of power by virtue of the possession of property, either on the part of a chief or of socially privileged groups.").

95. For a psychoanalytic investigation of the idea of charisma similar to that I develop here, see Philip Rieff, Charisma: The Gift of Grace, and How It Has Been Taken Away from Us (2007).

96. *See* Marcel Mauss, The Gift: The Form and Reason for Exchange in Archaic Societies (W.D. Halls trans., Norton 1990) (1925).

97. *See* Simon Critchley, Infinitely Demanding: Ethics of Commitment, Politics of Resistance (2007) (on demand and acknowledgment in moral life). Also consider Saint Paul as an example in some tension with this claim. This is what puts Paul at the beginning of a tradition.

98. Abraham Lincoln, Address Before the Young Men's Lyceum of Springfield, Illinois (Jan. 27, 1838), *in* 1 The Collected Works of Abraham Lincoln 108, 115 (Roy P. Basler ed., 1953) ("The consequence was, that of those scenes, in the form of a husband, a father, a son or a brother, a *living history was* to be found in every family—a history bearing the indubitable testimonies of its own authenticity, in the limbs mangled, in the scars of wounds received, in the midst of the very scenes related—a history, too, that could be read and understood alike by all, the wise and the ignorant, the learned and the unlearned. But *those* histories are gone.").

99. *See* Max Weber, The Protestant Ethic and the Spirit of Capitalism 124 (Talcott Parsons trans., Routledge 2001) (1930). ("[T]he idea of duty in one's calling prowls about in our lives like the ghost of dead religious beliefs. Where the fulfilment of the calling cannot directly be related to the highest spiritual and cultural values, or when, on the other hand, it need not be felt simply as economic compulsion, the individual generally abandons the attempt to justify it at all.")

100. *Cf.* Rieff, Charisma, *supra* note 95, at 33 ("The weakest of all legal theories, bound to destroy the law as a codified expression of charisma, is

the rationalist one of people deliberately establishing such prohibitions or such regulations as suit their convenience at a particular time.... The lawyers' conception of law would make it derive, not from charismatic authority and embodied in charismatic institutions, but rather as a specification of popular opinion.").

101. Consider the spread of proportionality as the near-universal form of judicial reasoning. *See, e.g.*, Alec Stone Sweet & Jud Mathews, *Proportionality Balancing and Global Constitutionalism*, 47 Colum. J. Transnat'l L. 72, 74–75 (2008) ("Over the past fifty years, proportionality analysis (PA) has widely diffused. It is today an overarching principle of constitutional adjudication, the preferred procedure for managing disputes involving an alleged conflict between two rights claims, or between a rights provision and a legitimate state or public interest.... By the end of the 1990s, virtually every effective system of constitutional justice in the world, with the partial exception of the United States, had embraced the main tenets of PA.").

102. *See, e.g.*, Joseph A. Camilleri & Jim Falk, The End of Sovereignty?: The Politics of a Shrinking and Fragmenting World (1992); Stephen D. Krasner, Sovereignty: Organized Hypocrisy (1999); Yasemin Nuh u Soysal, Limits of Citizenship: Migrants and Postnational Membership in Europe (1994); Stephen D. Krasner, *Compromising Westphalia*, 20 Int'l Security 115 (1995); Susan Strange, *The Declining Authority of States, in* The Global Transformations Reader: An Introduction to the Globalization Debate 48 (David Held & Anthony McGrew eds., 2000).

103. *See* Paul W. Kahn, *American Exceptionalism, Popular Sovereignty, and the Rule of Law, in* American Exceptionalism and Human Rights 198 (Michael Ignatieff ed., 2005).

Chapter Four. Legal Doctrine

1. The claim to speak in the voice of We the People is by no means unique to the judiciary. President Obama's second inaugural address is structured around the repetitive use of the phrase "We, the people, still believe ... ," moving toward a more climactic "We, the people, declare today ..." Barack Obama, Inaugural Address by President Barack Obama (Jan. 21, 2013), *available at* http://www.whitehouse.gov/the-press-office/2013/01/21/inaugural-address-president-barack-obama.

2. Snyder v. Phelps, 131 S. Ct. 1207, 1220 (2011).

3. Judges in the United States generally refer to this as "balancing" competing interests. Outside of the United States, the epistemic expertise of judges is usually referred to as proportionality. To determine proportionality, a judge examines (1) whether the action is "appropriate for achieving the goal"; (2) whether there are "other means appropriate for achieving the goal that would undermine the principles that we want to protect (such as human rights) to a lesser degree"; and (3) whether the "harm to a protected value is too drastic in relation to the benefit of achieving the goal." Aharon Barak, *The Supreme Court 2001 Term: Foreword: A Judge on Judging: The Role of a Supreme Court in a Democracy*, 116 Harv. L. Rev. 16, 147–48 (2002); *see also* Barak, Proportionality: Constitutional Rights and Their Limitations (2012). Contrariwise, when Bickel spoke of an epistemic expertise of judges, he spoke of their responsibility for principled governance. *See* Alexander M. Bickel, The Least Dangerous Branch: The Supreme Court at the Bar of Politics (2d ed. 1986).
4. One way to think of American exceptionalism is in terms of these quite different attitudes toward the judicial voice. Even when American and foreign judges reach the same conclusion with respect to an issue, they are not saying the same thing. *See* Paul W. Kahn, *American Exceptionalism, Popular Sovereignty and the Rule of Law*, in American Exceptionalism and Human Rights 198 (2005).
5. *But see* Or Bassok & Yoav Dotan, *Solving the Countermajoritarian Difficulty?* 11 Int'l J. Const. L. 13 (2013) (on the importance of polling to the sociological legitimacy of judges).
6. *See* Robert M. Cover, Justice Accused: Antislavery and the Judicial Process (1975).
7. Abolitionist William Lloyd Garrison described the Constitution as a "'covenant with death, an agreement with Hell'—involving both parties in atrocious criminality; and should be immediately annulled." Garrison quoted in Ronald C. White, Jr., Lincoln's Greatest Speech: The Second Inaugural 91 (2002).
8. *See, e.g.*, Frederick Douglass, What to the Slave Is the Fourth of July? (July 5, 1852) *reprinted in* the Oxford Frederick Douglass Reader 108, 128 (William L. Andrews ed., Oxford Univ. Press 1996) ("[L]et me ask, if it be not somewhat singular that, if the Constitution were intended to be, by its framers and adopters, a slave-holding instrument, why neither *slavery, slaveholding*, nor *slave* can anywhere be found in it."). Lincoln's

view that the Framers had both protected slavery and put it on a path to extinction was a reading of the text that he hoped both sides could affirm as their own. This was the point of his House Divided speech: all citizens were to think of themselves as children of the same founding fathers; that is, as members of a single household. Abraham Lincoln, "A House Divided": Speech at Springfield, Illinois (June 16, 1858), *reprinted in* 2 The Collected Works of Abraham Lincoln 461 (Roy P. Basler ed., Rutgers Univ. Press 1953).

9. *See* Donald Braman, Dan M. Kahan & James Grimmelmann, *Modeling Facts, Culture and Cognition in the Gun Debate*, 18 Soc. Just. Res. 803 (2005).
10. 381 U.S. 479 (1965).
11. *Id.* at 485–86.
12. *See* Albert O. Hirschman, Exit, Voice, and Loyalty: Responses to Decline in Firms, Organizations, and States (1970).
13. Citizens United v. Fed. Election Comm'n, 558 U.S. 310 (2010). This point erupted into controversy in *Planned Parenthood v. Casey*, 505 U.S. 833, 867 (1992), when the majority spoke of its "interpretation of the Constitution call[ing] the contending sides of a national controversy to end their national division by accepting a common mandate rooted in the Constitution." Justice Scalia, in dissent, strenuously objected, calling this an "[i]mperial" view of the judiciary. *Id.* at 996 (Scalia, J., dissenting).
14. Justice Stevens recently extended this argument even to *Brown v. Board of Education:* "Unlike most admirers of the opinion, I have never been convinced that the benefits of unanimity outweighed what I regarded as two flaws in the Court's disposition of the cases." Justice John Paul Stevens, Five Chiefs: A Supreme Court Memoir 100 (2011). Stevens argued that the Court's directive that desegregation proceed with "all deliberate speed" was a "belated and somewhat tentative command" that "may have done more to encourage resistance to the clear message contained in Earl Warren's original opinion than would have a possible dissenting opinion joined by only one or two justices." *Id.* Moreover, a dissenting viewpoint may have actually strengthened the legitimacy of the opinion: "Even when a dissenting opinion makes convincing arguments on the losing party's behalf, responses by the majority may not only clarify and strengthen the Court's reasoning, but also demonstrate to the public that the dissenter's views were carefully considered before they were rejected." *Id.*

Justice Ginsburg has also extolled the benefits of a dissenting opinion. A dissent may "lead the author of the majority opinion to refine and clarify her initial circulation," and on occasion "a dissent will be so persuasive that it attracts the votes necessary to become the opinion of the Court." Ruth Bader Ginsburg, *The Role of Dissenting Opinions*, 95 Minn. L. Rev. 1, 3, 4 (2010).

15. *See generally* Guido Calabresi, A Common Law for the Age of Statutes (1985).
16. Jorge Luis Borges, *Pierre Menard, Author of the Quixote, in* Collected Fictions 88 (Andrew Hurley trans., Penguin 1998) (1939) (a fable about how differently a twentieth-century *Don Quixote* would appear to readers).
17. 133 S. Ct. 2612 (2013).
18. Tenn. Valley Auth. v. Hill, 437 U.S. 153 (1978).
19. 554 U.S. 570 (2008).
20. For an example in the opposite direction, consider the dormant Commerce Clause prohibition on intentional discrimination against commercial activity from another state—hardly a complicated rule, but one not located in the text of the Constitution itself. *See* City of Philadelphia v. New Jersey, 437 U.S. 617, 626–28 (1978). Richard Fallon emphasizes that such constitutional tests serve as directives to the lower courts, allowing the Court to manage the judiciary. *See* Richard H. Fallon, *The Supreme Court 1996 Term—Foreword: Implementing the Constitution*, 111 Harv. L. Rev. 54, 57 (1997) ("A crucial mission of the Court is to *implement* the Constitution successfully. In service of this mission, the Court often must craft doctrine that is driven by the Constitution, but does not reflect the Constitution's meaning precisely.").
21. U.S. Const. amend. XI.
22. *Compare* Alden v. Maine, 527 U.S. 706, 713 (1999) ("[T]he sovereign immunity of the States neither derives from, nor is limited by, the terms of the Eleventh Amendment. Rather, as the Constitution's structure, its history, and the authoritative interpretations by this Court make clear, the States' immunity from suit is a fundamental aspect of the sovereignty which the States enjoyed before the ratification of the Constitution, and which they retain today."), *with id.* at 793 n.29 (Souter, J., dissenting) ("The Court today may labor under the misapprehension that sovereign immunity can apply where the sovereign is not the font of law, but the Court adduces no evidence to suggest that the framers of the Eleventh Amendment held such a view.").

23. *See* Owen M. Fiss, *Groups and the Equal Protection Clause*, 5 Phil. & Pub. Aff. 107 (1976) (on mediating principles).
24. *See* Lawrence v. Texas, 539 U.S. 558, 576 (2003) ("The foundations of Bowers have sustained serious erosion from our recent decisions in *Casey* and *Romer*"). *Compare* Planned Parenthood v. Casey, 505 U.S. 833, 845–46 (1992) (plurality opinion) ("After considering the fundamental constitutional questions resolved by *Roe*, principles of institutional integrity, and the rule of *stare decisis*, we are led to conclude this: the essential holding of *Roe v. Wade* should be retained and once again reaffirmed.") *with id.* at 934 (Blackmun, J., concurring in part, concurring in the judgment in part, and dissenting in part) ("*Roe's* requirement of strict scrutiny as implemented through a trimester framework should not be disturbed. No other approach has gained a majority, and no other is more protective of the woman's fundamental right. Lastly, no other approach properly accommodates the woman's constitutional right with the State's legitimate interests."); *compare* Gonzales v. Carhart, 550 U.S. 124, 145 (2007) ("Whatever one's views concerning the *Casey* joint opinion, it is evident a premise central to its conclusion—that the government has a legitimate and substantial interest in preserving and promoting fetal life—would be repudiated were the Court now to affirm the judgments of the Courts of Appeals."), *with id.* at 163 ("This traditional rule is consistent with *Casey*, which confirms the State's interest in promoting respect for human life at all stages in the pregnancy."), *and id.* at 170 (Ginsburg, J., dissenting) ("Today's decision is alarming. It refuses to take *Casey* and *Stenberg* seriously."), *and id.* at 186 ("The Court's hostility to the right *Roe* and *Casey* secured is not concealed."). *See* Lawrence v. Texas, 539 U.S. 558, 576 (2003) ("The foundations of *Bowers* have sustained serious erosion from our recent decisions in *Casey* and *Romer*.").
25. Edward H. Levi makes a similar point referring to what he calls "satellite-like concepts," which are the product of what I have called erudition: "[N]o satellite concept, no matter how well developed, can prevent the court from shifting its course, not only by realigning cases ... but by going beyond realignment back to the ... category *written* into the document." Edward H. Levi, An Introduction to Legal Reasoning 7–8 (1949) (emphasis added).
26. Conversely, as a statute becomes older and more central to the legal order, it may come to have something like a constitutional function, in

which case it will be elaborated in many opinions moving out the horizontal axis. *See* discussion of super-statutes *infra* notes 30–31.
27. In response to the Court's decision in *Tennessee Valley Authority v. Hill*, 437 U.S. 153 (1978), Congress amended the Endangered Species Act to create a new Endangered Species Committee empowered to grant exemptions. The committee considers whether the costs of compliance with the ESA outweigh the benefits of the act; whether any reasonable alternatives to the exemption exist; and whether the action is in the public interest. Endangered Species Amendment of 1978, Pub. L. No. 95–632, § 3, 92 Stat. 3751, 3753–75 (codified as amended at 16 U.S.C. § 1536(2) (2006); *see also* Daniel A. Farber, *Statutory Interpretation and Legislative Supremacy*, 78 Geo. L.J. 281, 295 n.66 (1989) (discussing the history of the 1978 amendment to the ESA).
28. Marbury v. Madison, 5 U.S. (1 Cranch) 137, 174 ("It cannot be presumed that any clause in the Constitution is intended to be without effect. . . .").
29. Griggs v. Duke Power, 401 U.S. 424 (1971); *see also* Watson v. Fort Worth Bank & Trust, 487 U.S. 977 (1988) (refusing to find disparate impact analysis applicable only to objective selection criteria); United Steelworkers v. Weber, 443 U.S. 193 (1979) (permitting employers to rely on affirmative action plans in some circumstances); Albemarle Paper Co. v. Moody, 422 U.S. 405 (1975) (establishing a strong presumption that all members of plaintiffs' class are entitled to back pay).
30. William Eskridge, Jr., and John Ferejohn have dubbed these "super-statutes," defined as a law "that (1) seeks to establish a new normative or institutional framework for state policy and (2) . . . does 'stick' in the public culture such that (3) the super-statute and its institutional or normative principles have a broad effect on the law." William N. Eskridge & John Ferejohn, *Super-Statutes*, 50 Duke L.J. 1215, 1216 (2001). Super-statutes "tend to trump ordinary legislation when there are clashes or inconsistencies," and can even "reshape constitutional understanding." *Id.* For examples, see *id.* at 1231–43.
31. *See* Eskridge & Ferejohn, *supra* note 30, at 1231 ("The super-statute that emerges from Congress is not a completed product. It requires elaboration from administrators and judges, whose work is then subject to meaningful scrutiny and correction by the legislature or even the citizenry. This feedback loop is an essential feature of super-statutes, but its operation is variegated and impossible to predict. Each super-statute has a pre-enactment history and a post-enactment history that are

as important as—and usually more important than—its enactment history.").
32. Sometimes, the persistent dissenter is formally concurring in an outcome. *See, e.g.,* Town of Greece v. Galloway, 134 S. Ct. 1811, 1835 (2014) (Thomas, J., concurring in part and concurring in the judgment) (citation omitted) ("I write separately to reiterate my view that the Establishment Clause is 'best understood as a federalism provision.'"); United Haulers Ass'n Inc. v. Oneida-Herkimer Solid Waste Mgmt. Auth., 550 U.S. 330, 349 (2007) (Thomas, J., concurring in the judgment) ("As the debate between the majority and dissent shows, application of the negative Commerce Clause turns solely on policy considerations, not on the Constitution. Because this Court has no policy role in regulating interstate commerce, I would discard the Court's negative Commerce Clause jurisprudence.").
33. Roe v. Wade, 410 U.S. 113, 167–68 (1973) (Stewart, J., concurring) (footnotes omitted).
34. 554 U.S. 570 (2008).
35. *Id.* at 576 (quoting United States v. Sprague, 282 U.S. 716, 731 (1931)).
36. *Id.* at 652 (Stevens, J., dissenting). The dissent also argues against each of the originalist claims. Stevens argues that the Court misinterprets the phrase "to keep and bear arms," which the Framers intended to mean the right to "possess arms if needed for military purposes and to use them in conjunction with military activities." *Id.* at 46. Stevens also contends that the four non-textual sources upon which the majority relies—the seventeenth-century English Bill of Rights, Blackstone's *Commentaries on the Laws of England*, post-enactment commentary on the Second Amendment, and post–Civil War legislative history—"shed only indirect light on the question before us, and in any event offer little support for the Court's conclusion." *Id.* at 662 (footnote omitted). Stevens concludes that "the right the Court announces was not 'enshrined' in the Second Amendment by the Framers; it is the product of today's law-changing decision." *Id.* at 679.
37. *Id.* at 638 (footnote omitted).
38. *Id.* at 639 (footnote and citation omitted).
39. Dred Scott v. Sandford, 60 U.S. (19 How.) 393 (1856); see discussion in Paul W. Kahn, Legitimacy and History: Self-Government in American Constitutional Theory 46–53 (1992).
40. *See, e.g.,* Jaroslav Pelikan with Valerie R. Hotchkiss & David Price, The Reformation of the Bible: The Bible of the Reformation (1996). For a

similar development in Jewish law, see Moshe Halbertal, Maimonides: Life and Thought (Joel Linsider, trans., Princeton Univ. Press 2013) (2009).
41. *See* Robert C. Post & Reva B. Siegel, *Popular Constitutionalism, Departmentalism, and Judicial Supremacy*, 92 Cal. L. Rev. 1027 (2004).
42. *Cf.* Karl N. Llewellyn, The Bramble Bush: On Our Law and Its Study 67–69 (Oceana 1981) (1930) (on choice between strict and loose readings of a precedent).
43. Marbury v. Madison, 5 U.S. (1 Cranch) 137, 176 (1803).
44. *See* Owen M. Fiss, Comment, *Against Settlement*, 93 Yale L.J. 1073, 1089 (1984) (arguing that civil litigation should not be viewed in purely private terms, but rather as "an institutional arrangement for using state power to bring a recalcitrant reality closer to our chosen ideals").
45. The traditional view of arbitration is that because it is private, the arbitrator acts as an agent for the parties to the dispute, and the principals are free to select the law and procedures to be applied. Stone Sweet describes the rise of an alternative view that rejects the assumption that arbitrators look only to the particular dispute. Alec Stone Sweet, *Investor-State Arbitration: Proportionality's New Frontier*, 4 Law & Ethics Hum. Rts. 47, 55 (2010). Instead, he advocates for arbitrators to become involved in lawmaking that is general and prospective. *Id.* at 57. It is telling, Stone Sweet argues, that arbitrators' "insistence on giving reasons, the accretion of precedent, and calls for supervisory or appellate review, are justified in the name of 'justice.'" *Id.*
46. *See* Llewellyn, *supra* note 42, at 49 ("[N]o case can have a meaning by itself. Standing alone it gives you no guidance.").
47. Working from a common horizon is so important that there is a rule of professional responsibility requiring lawyers to inform the court of any controlling, adverse precedents that the court or opposing counsel may have failed to note. Model Rules of Prof'l Conduct r. 3.3(2) (2012) ("[A] lawyer shall not knowingly . . . fail to disclose to the tribunal legal authority in the controlling jurisdiction known to the lawyer to be directly adverse to the position of the client and not disclosed by opposing counsel.").
48. On the institutional Restatement project, see Benjamin N. Cardozo, *The Growth of the Law* 9 (1924) ("When, finally, [the Restatement] goes out under the name and with the sanction of the [American Law] Institute . . . it will be something less than a code and something more than a treatise. It will be invested with unique authority, not to command,

but to persuade. It will embody a composite thought and speak a composite voice."); *id.* at 19 ("If we were to state the law today as well as human minds can state it, new problems, arising almost overnight, would encumber the ground again. . . . [T]he changing combinations of events will beat upon the walls of ancient categories."); and Doug Rendleman, *Restating Restitution: The Restatement Process and Its Critics*, 65 Wash. & Lee L. Rev. 933, 934 (2008) ("The American Law Institute's *Restatements of the Law* are ambitious attempts to articulate the common law in disparate areas like torts, contracts, and restitution. Critics of the American Law Institute (ALI) process question both its legitimacy and its accuracy in undertaking to 'restate' common law.").

49. *See supra* chap. 3.
50. *See* Lon L. Fuller, The Morality of Law 157–58 (2d ed. 1969) (1964) ("The internal morality of the law demands that there be rules, that they be made known, and that they be observed in practice by those charged with their administration. . . . 'A lawless unlimited power' expressing itself solely in unpredictable and patternless interventions in human affairs could be said to be unjust only in the sense that it does not act by known rule. It would be hard to call it unjust in any more specific sense until one discovered what hidden principle, if any, guided its interventions.").
51. *See, e.g.*, United States v. Morrison, 529 U.S. 598 (2000) (holding law federalizing tort of sexual assault insufficiently related to interstate commerce); United States v. Lopez, 514 U.S. 549 (1995) (holding that a law banning weapons near schools was insufficiently related to interstate commerce).
52. *See, e.g.*, Seminole Tribe of Fla. v. Florida, 517 U.S. 44 (1996) (holding that the Eleventh Amendment prohibits not only action by a noncitizen against a foreign state but also by a citizen against his or her own state).
53. *See, e.g.*, Nat'l Fed'n of Indep. Bus.v. Sebelius, 132 S. Ct. 2566 (2012) (holding that the Affordable Care Act's expansion of Medicaid exceeded the federal government's powers of enactment under the Spending Clause).
54. *See, e.g.*, Printz v. United States, 521 U.S. 898 (1997) (holding that a law requiring state officials to conduct background checks violated anticommandeering principles); New York v. United States, 505 U.S. 144 (1992) (holding that the Tenth Amendment forbids the federal government from commandeering state legislatures).

55. *See, e.g.*, Shelby County v. Holder, 133 S. Ct. 2612 (2013) (holding unconstitutional § 4 of the Voting Rights Act, enacted to fulfill the Fifteenth Amendment's command that "[t]he right of citizens of the United States to vote shall not be denied or abridged by the United States or by any State on account of race, color, or previous condition of servitude.").
56. For discussion of the role of federalism principles in statutory interpretation, see William N. Eskridge, Jr., *The New Textualism*, 37 UCLA L. Rev. 621, 665–66 (1990); and Abbe R. Gluck, *Intersystemic Statutory Interpretation: Methodology As "Law" and the Erie Doctrine*, 120 Yale L.J. 1898 (2011).
57. United States v. Darby, 312 U.S. 100, 124 (1941) ("The [Tenth] [A]mendment states but a truism that all is retained which has not been surrendered.").
58. Ronald Dworkin, Law's Empire 228–38 (1986). Dworkin describes a chain novel as "an artificial genre of literature" in which "a group of novelists writes a novel *seriatim*; each novelist in the chain interprets the chapters he has been given in order to write a new chapter, which is then added to what the next novelist receives, and so on. Each has the job of writing his chapter so as to make the novel being constructed the best it can be, and the complexity of this task models the complexity of deciding a hard case under law as integrity." *Id.* at 229.
59. Robert Ferguson aptly describes this style: "[T]he monologic voice, the interrogative mode, and the declarative tone build together in what might be called a rhetoric of inevitability." Robert A. Ferguson, *The Judicial Opinion as Literary Genre*, 2 Yale J.L. & Human. 201, 213 (1990).
60. Edward Levi offered a broadly similar description of the three stages of doctrinal development: "creation of a legal concept" (characterized by fumbling), a period when the concept is "more or less fixed," and then the "breakdown of the concept." Levi, *supra* note 25, at 8–9.
61. Hannah Arendt, The Human Condition 247 (2d ed. 1998) (1958).
62. *Cf.* Ronald Dworkin, A Matter of Principle 119–45 (1985) (advancing a "right answer thesis"), Ronald Dworkin, Taking Rights Seriously 81 (1978) (1977) (same).
63. 381 U.S. 479 (1965).
64. Justice Black cites several of these cases in his dissent. *See id.* at 515 (Black, J., dissenting) (citing Lochner v. New York, 198 U.S. 45 (1905) (invalidating a New York law setting a maximum number of hours of work in bakeries); Coppage v. Kansas, 236 U.S. 1 (1915) (invalidating a Kansas state law prohibiting contracts that forbade employees from

joining unions); Jay Burns Baking Co. v. Bryan, 264 U.S. 504 (1924) (invalidating a Nebraska law standardizing the weight of loaves of bread); Adkins v. Children's Hosp., 261 U.S. 525 (1923) (invalidating a minimum wage law for women in the District of Columbia)).

65. The Supreme Court invalidated a series of major New Deal laws. *See* Carter v. Carter Coal Co., 298 U.S. 238 (1936) (invalidating the Bituminous Coal Conservation Act of 1935); Panama Refining Co. v. Ryan, 293 U.S. 388 (1935) (invalidating the petroleum code in the National Industrial Recovery Act); R.R. Ret. Bd. v. Alton R.R. Co., 295 U.S. 330 (1935) (invalidating a law that required common carriers to comply with a mandatory retirement age and pension plan); Schechter Poultry Co. v. United States, 295 U.S. 495 (1935) (invalidating the entire National Industrial Recovery Act). On President Roosevelt's response to this series of cases, see William E. Leuchtenburg, The Supreme Court Reborn: The Constitutional Revolution in the Age of Roosevelt 82–162 (1995).

66. *See* NLRB v. Jones & Laughlin Steel Corp., 301 U.S. 1 (1937) (upholding the constitutionality of the National Labor Relations Act of 1935); *West Coast Hotel Co. v. Parrish*, 300 U.S. 379 (1937) (upholding the constitutionality of a Washington state minimum wage law).

67. *Griswold*, 381 U.S. at 482; *see also id.* at 528 (Stewart, J., dissenting) ("We are told that the Due Process Clause of the Fourteenth Amendment is not, as such, the 'guide' in this case. With that much I agree. There is no claim that this law, duly enacted by the Connecticut Legislature, is unconstitutionally vague. There is no claim that the appellants were denied any of the elements of procedural due process at their trial, so as to make their convictions constitutionally invalid. And, as the Court says, the day has long passed since the Due Process Clause was regarded as a proper instrument for determining 'the wisdom, need, and propriety' of state laws.").

68. *Id.* at 484 ("[S]pecific guarantees in the Bill of Rights have penumbras, formed by emanations from those guarantees that help give them life and substance.").

69. *Cf. id.* at 508–09 (Black, J., dissenting) ("The Court talks about a constitutional 'right of privacy' as though there is some constitutional provision or provisions forbidding any law ever to be passed which might abridge the 'privacy' of individuals. But there is not. There are, of course, guarantees in certain specific constitutional provisions which are de-

signed in part to protect privacy at certain times and places with respect to certain activities.").
70. *Id.* at 485.
71. *Griswold*, 381 U.S. at 527 (Stewart, J., dissenting).
72. *See* Eric Foner, Free Soil, Free Labor, Free Men: The Ideology of the Republican Party Before the Civil War (1995) (1970).
73. *See* Paul W. Kahn, Putting Liberalism in Its Place 298–301 (2005).
74. On changes in American marriage practices from 1960 to 2000, see Andrew J. Cherlin, The Marriage-Go-Round: The State of Marriage and the Family in America Today 81–115 (2009). The divorce rate doubled from 1960 to 1980. *Id.* at 7.
75. *See* Herma Hill Kay, *Equality and Difference: A Perspective on No Fault Divorce and Its Aftermath*, 56 U. Cin. L. Rev. 1 (1987).
76. In his *Griswold* concurrence, Justice John Marshall Harlan relies upon his dissent in *Poe v. Ullman*, 367 U.S. 497 (1961), a case in which the Court had declined to reach the merits on a challenge to the same Connecticut statute at issue in *Griswold*. Harlan had argued that the Connecticut statute violated the Due Process Clause because it regulated martial relations: "Adultery, homosexuality and the like are sexual intimacies which the State forbids altogether, but the intimacy of husband and wife is necessarily an essential and accepted feature of the institution of marriage, an institution which the State not only must allow, but which always and in every age it has fostered and protected. It is one thing when the State exerts its power either to forbid extra-marital sexuality altogether, or to say who may marry, but it is quite another when, having acknowledged a marriage and the intimacies inherent in it, it undertakes to regulate by means of the criminal law the details of that intimacy." *Id.* at 553 (Harlan, J., dissenting). Harlan's misreading of the issue—relying on marriage rather than intimacy—demonstrates the openness of a natal opinion.
77. 405 U.S. 438 (1972).
78. *See* Roe v. Wade, 410 U.S. 113, 167–68 (1973) (Stewart, J., concurring) (footnotes omitted) ("[T]he Connecticut law did not violate any provision of the Bill of Rights, nor any other specific provision of the Constitution. So it was clear to me then, and it is equally clear to me now, that the *Griswold* decision can be rationally understood only as a holding that the Connecticut statute substantively invaded the 'liberty' that is protected by the Due Process Clause of the Fourteenth Amendment.

As so understood, *Griswold* stands as one in a long line of pre-*Skrupa* cases decided under the doctrine of substantive due process, and I now accept it as such.").
79. *Baird*, 405 U.S. 438.
80. *Roe*, 410 U.S. 113.
81. Bowers v. Hardwick, 478 U.S. 186 (1986) (5–4 decision).
82. Lawrence v. Texas, 539 U.S. 558 (2003).
83. During his Senate confirmation hearings, Robert Bork failed to recognize this. When asked about *Griswold*, Bork testified that "the right of privacy, as defined or undefined by Justice Douglas, [i]s a free-floating right that [i]s not derived in a principled fashion from constitutional materials." Nomination of Robert H. Bork to be Associate Justice of the Supreme Court of the United States: Hearings Before the S. Comm. on the Judiciary, 100th Cong. 116 (1987) (statement of Robert H. Bork). Senator Joseph Biden, Chairman of the Senate Committee on the Judiciary, asked: "As I hear you, you do not believe that there is a general right of privacy that is in the Constitution?" Bork responded: "Not one derived in *that* fashion." *Id.* at 117. Bork's criticism of *Griswold* was ill-received by the public, and his remarks likely contributed to the Senate's refusal to confirm him. *See* Michael J. Klarman, *Windsor and Brown: Marriage Equality and Racial Equality*, 127 Harv. L. Rev. 127, 160 (2013).
84. *Lawrence*, 539 U.S. at 578.
85. Some feminist thought sees intimacy too as a site of power, not liberty. *See, e.g.*, Andrea Dworkin, *Against the Male Flood: Censorship, Pornography, and Equality*, 8 Harv. Women's L.J. 1 (1985); Catharine A. MacKinnon, *Sexuality, Pornography, and Method: "Pleasure Under Patriarchy,"* 99 Ethics 314 (1989).
86. 347 U.S. 483 (1954).
87. *Id.* at 495.
88. It is not wrong to refer to natal opinions as "revolutionary," because revolutions too are known only after the fact. In both cases, the foundation depends upon the edifice that arises, not the other way around.
89. Brown v. Bd. of Educ. II, 349 U.S. 294, 301 (1955).
90. *See supra* note 14 on Justice Stevens's view.
91. The Court also tries to preempt resistance by offering a unanimous opinion, suggesting that there can be no reasonable disagreement. *See* Sanford Levinson, *Compromise and Constitutionalism*, 38 Pepp. L. Rev. 821, 838 (2011).

92. *See* Murray v. Pearson, 182 A.590 (Md. 1936); Missouri *ex rel.* Gaines v. Canada, 305 U.S. 337 (1938); Sweatt v. Painter, 339 U.S. 629 (1950).
93. *See Brown*, 347 U.S. at 491–92 (citations omitted) ("In more recent cases, all on the graduate school level, inequality was found in that specific benefits enjoyed by white students were denied to Negro students of the same educational qualifications.").
94. *Id.* at 429.
95. *Id.* at 490–91 (footnotes and citation omitted).
96. *Id.* at 494 (quoting Kansas trial court finding).
97. *Id.* at 494 n.11.
98. Precisely this point has been used against affirmative action programs in public schools. *See* Parents Involved in Cmty. Schs. v. Seattle Sch. Dist., 551 U.S. 701, 747 (2007) ("Before *Brown*, schoolchildren were told where they could and could not go to school based on the color of their skin. The school districts in these cases have not carried the heavy burden of demonstrating that we should allow this once again—even for very different reasons."). *Brown*, as a natal opinion, could not possibly speak to the range of issues that come up in the context of affirmative action and social remediation. That the dispute over these issues reaches back to *Brown* illustrates the role of the natal opinion.
99. *Brown*, 347 U.S. at 493.
100. *Id.*
101. *See, e.g.*, Turner v. City of Memphis, 369 U.S. 350 (1962) (restaurants); State Athletic Comm'n v. Dorsey, 359 U.S. 533 (1959) (athletic contests); New Orleans City Park Improvement Ass'n v. Detiege, 358 U.S. 54 (1958) (parks); Gayle v. Browder, 352 U.S. 903 (1956) (buses); Mayor of Baltimore v. Dawson, 350 U.S. 877 (1955) (beaches); Holmes v. Atlanta, 350 U.S. 879 (1955) (golf courses).
102. *See* Hannah Arendt, On Revolution (1965).
103. Both sides in *Parents Involved* laid claim to *Brown*. Chief Justice Roberts, writing for the Court, argued that Justice Breyer's dissent "is fundamentally at odds with our precedent, which makes clear that the Equal Protection Clause 'protect[s] *persons*, not *groups*.'" 551 U.S. at 743 (citation omitted). This "fundamental principle goes back, in this context, to *Brown* itself." Justice Stevens made the opposite claim, arguing it was the Court that betrayed *Brown*. "There is a cruel irony in the Chief Justice's reliance on our decision in *Brown*," wrote Stevens. *Id.* at 799 (Stevens, J., dissenting). While the Chief Justice noted that before *Brown*, schoolchildren were ordered where to attend school

based on the color of their skin, he "fail[ed] to note that it was only black school children who were so ordered; indeed, the history books do not tell stories of white children struggling to attend black schools." *Id.* (footnote omitted). And "in this and other ways, the Chief Justice rewrites the history of one of the Court's most importance decisions." *Id.* Justice Breyer echoed this view in his dissent: "To invalidate the plans under review is to threaten the promise of *Brown*. The plurality's position, I fear, would break that promise." *Id.* at 868 (Breyer, J., dissenting).

104. Bruce Ackerman analogizes the text of such canonical opinions to a constitutional amendment. *See* Bruce Ackerman, We the People: Foundations 140–59 (1991); *see also* Michael J. Klarman, *Constitutional Fact/Constitutional Fiction: A Critique of Bruce Ackerman's Theory of Constitutional Moments*, 44 Stan. L. Rev. 759, 763 (1992) (book review) (discussing Ackerman's conception of the "constitutional" role of certain opinions).

105. The judicial practice of expressing self-denial of power goes all the way back to *Marbury v. Madison*, 5 U.S. (1 Cranch) 137, 169–70 (1803).

106. This is true even of common-law judgments. A common-law judge does not simply "make up" the law. Rather, she interprets an existing body of doctrine that extends indefinitely into the past. For a discussion of the concept of time immemorial in the common law, see J.G.A. Pocock, The Ancient Constitution and Feudal Law: A Study of English Historical Thought in the Seventeenth Century 37 (1987) (1957).

107. 478 U.S. 186, 194 (1986).

108. Lawrence v. Texas, 539 U.S. 558 (2003).

109. Note the striking language in the Court's opinion: "*Bowers* was not correct when it was decided, and it is not correct today. It ought not to remain binding precedent. *Bowers v. Hardwick* should be and now is overruled." *Id.* at 578.

110. *See* Llewellyn, *supra* note 42, at 49 (describing the "case system game" as "a rough application of the logical method of comparison and difference").

111. U.S. Const. amend. XIV, § 1.

112. Adarand Constructors, Inc. v. Peña, 515 U.S. 200, 241 (1995) (Thomas, J., concurring in part and concurring in the judgment).

113. *Id.* at 245 (Stevens, J., dissenting).

114. Loving v. Virginia, 388 U.S. 1 (1967) (invalidating a Virginia law prohibiting interracial marriage); Skinner v. Oklahoma, *ex rel.* William-

son, 316 U.S. 535 (1942) (invalidating an Oklahoma law mandating the sterilization of felons convicted three times of a crime of moral turpitude); Pierce v. Society of the Sisters of the Holy Names of Jesus and Mary, 268 U.S. 510 (1925) (striking down an Oregon law requiring children to attend public schools); Meyers v. Nebraska, 262 U.S. 390 (1923) (invalidating a Nebraska law forbidding the teaching of foreign languages to young children).

115. Perhaps the *Bowers* majority is trying to taint the doctrine by association with these cases.
116. *Bowers*, 478 U.S. at 190–91.
117. In chap. 5, I discuss the dubious grounds for the construction of this minor premise as a matter of "fact."
118. *Bowers*, 478 U.S. at 191–92 (internal citations omitted).
119. Interestingly, this is the same argument that Justice Holmes used in his famous dissent in *Lochner*. A statute, he thought should be upheld, "unless it can be said that a rational and fair man necessarily would admit that the statute proposed would infringe fundamental principles as they have been understood by the traditions of our people and our law." Lochner v. New York 198 U.S. 45, 76 (1905) (Holmes, J., dissenting).
120. *Id.*
121. *Id.* at 57.
122. Dworkin, *supra* note 58, at 65–66.
123. *See* Justice Hugo Black, quoted in Edmond Cahn, *Justice Black and First Amendment Absolutes: A Public Interview*, 37 N.Y.U. L. Rev. 549, 553 (1962) (footnote omitted) ("The beginning of the First Amendment is that 'Congress shall make no law.' I understand that it is rather old-fashioned and shows a slight naivete to say that 'no law' means no law. . . . But what it *says* is 'Congress shall make no law respecting an establishment of religion,' and so on."); Hugo L. Black, *The Bill of Rights*, 35 N.Y.U. L. Rev. 865, 874 (1960) ("Neither as offered nor as adopted is the language of [the First] Amendment anything less than absolute.").
124. Cases upholding the constitutionality of the 1890 Sherman Act include *Northern Securities Co. v. United States*, 193 U.S. 197 (1904); *W.W. Montague & Co. v. Lowry*, 193 U.S. 38 (1904); *Addyston Pipe & Steel Co. v. United States*, 175 U.S. 211 (1899); *Hopkins v. United States*, 171 U.S. 578 (1898); and *United States v. Trans-Missouri Freight Ass'n*, 166 U.S. 290 (1897); *United States v. E. C. Knight Co.*, 156 U.S. 1 (1895). *See also*

Martin J. Sklar, *Sherman Antitrust Act Jurisprudence and Federal Policy-Making in the Formative Period, 1890–1914*, 35 N.Y.L. Sch. L. Rev. 791 (1990). For early cases upholding the constitutionality of the Interstate Commerce Act of 1887, see *Houston, East & West Texas Railway Co. v. United States (The Shreveport Rate Case)*, 234 U.S. 342 (1914); and *ICC v. Goodrich Transit Co.*, 224 U.S. 194 (1912).

125. 247 U.S. 251 (1918).
126. *See* Levi, *supra* note 25, at 84–90.
127. *See* cases cited *supra* note 65.
128. United States v. Darby, 312 U.S. 100 (1941).
129. 301 U.S. 1 (1937).
130. Carter v. Carter Coal, 298 U.S. 238 (1936).
131. *Id.* at 307–8.
132. *Id.* at 308.
133. *See* E. Oliver E. Williamson, Markets and Hierarchies: Analysis and Antitrust Implications (1975).
134. *Jones & Laughlin Steel* writes a narrative in which the company was trying to escape any regulation, and in which it must be held accountable for the destruction it is causing to the nation. This narrative accounts for the appearance in the opinion of a remarkable discussion of the "rights of the workers," which stand against the rights of the corporation. It is remarkable because it appears without citation to any authority. This discussion of rights is unanchored precisely because it lives only in the narrative of opposition to the corporate threat.
135. United States v. Darby, 312 U.S. 100, 116 (1941) (citations omitted) (emphasis added).
136. *Id.* at 116–17.
137. *Id.* at 124.
138. *Id.* at 114 (quoting Gibbons v. Ogden, 22 U.S. (9 Wheat.) 1, 196 (1824)).
139. 317 U.S. 111 (1942).
140. *Id.* at 123–24.
141. *See* cases cited *supra* note 51.
142. United States v. Lopez, 514 U.S. 549, 568 (1995).
143. In *National League of Cities v. Usery*, 26 U.S. 833, 836 (1976), the Court invalidated amendments of the Fair Labor Standards Act "extend[ing] the minimum wage and maximum hour provisions to almost all public employees employed by the States and by their various political subdivisions." Justice Rehnquist's opinion for the Court stated that "an express declaration" of the "limits upon the power of Congress to

override state sovereignty" can be "found in the Tenth Amendment." *Id.* at 842. Justice Brennan's dissent, citing *Darby*, states that the majority opinion's "reliance . . . upon the Tenth Amendment as 'an express declaration of [a state sovereignty] limitation' not only suggests that they overrule governing decisions of this Court that address this question but must astound scholars of the Constitution." *Id.* at 861–62 (Brennan, J., dissenting) (alteration in original). *National League of Cities* was subsequently overruled by *Garcia v. San Antonio Metropolitan Transit Authority*, 469 U.S. 528 (1985).

144. Justice Souter emphasizes this point in his dissent in *United States v. Morrison* 529 U.S. 598 (2000). He contends that the Violence Against Women Act "would have passed muster at any time between *Wickard* in 1942 and *Lopez* in 1995," 529 U.S. at 637, and that the majority's "attempt to distinguish between primary activities affecting commerce in terms of the relatively commercial or noncommercial character of the primary conduct proscribed comes with [a] pedigree of near tragedy," *id.* at 641. Souter goes on to cite the infamous string of cases from 1887 to 1937, including *Hammer*, *Schecter Poultry*, and *Carter Coal*. *Id.* at 642. He continues: "[O]ne might reasonably have doubted that Members of this Court would ever again toy with a return to the days before *NLRB v. Jones & Laughlin Steel Corp.*, which brought the earlier and nearly disastrous experiment to an end. And yet today's decision can only be seen as a step toward recapturing the prior mistakes." *Id.* at 642–43 (citation omitted).

145. *See, e.g.*, Printz v. United States, 521 U.S. 898, 941 (1997) (Stevens, J., dissenting) ("The text of the Constitution provides a sufficient basis for a correct disposition of these cases.").

146. The expression, although not the turn to fundamentalism, comes from Felix Cohen, *Transcendental Nonsense and the Functional Approach*, 35 Colum. L. Rev. 809 (1935).

147. *See* Stanley Fish, *Dennis Martinez and the Uses of Theory*, 96 Yale L.J. 1773 (1987).

Chapter Five. Facts

1. Controversies over facts alone—that is, over what happened—rarely raise issues for appellate review.
2. Because conviction is a technical, legal conclusion, it is usually a mistake to go to a courtroom to learn about history. A criminal trial will tell you whether someone is legally guilty, not what happened. Post-authoritarian

regimes often speak of the need for trials as a way of creating a record of the abuses of the previous regime. Justice and truth—the twin aims of a democratic transition—are not so easily brought together through a courtroom proceeding. *See* Martha Minow, Between Vengeance and Forgiveness: Facing History After Genocide and Mass Violence 9 (1998) ("Justice may call for truth but also demands accountability. And the institutions for securing accountability—notably, trial courts—may impede or ignore truth.").

3. The relative weights of these two concerns are very much at issue in our contemporary debate about government access to electronic communications. See, e.g., Daniel Byman & Benjamin Wittes, *Reforming the NSA: How to Spy After Snowden*, Foreign Affairs, May–June 2014, http://www.foreignaffairs.com/articles/141215/daniel-byman-and-benjamin-wittes/reforming-the-nsa ("The proposed reforms and Obama's less than full embrace of them reflect a fundamental clash when it comes to what the American public demands of its intelligence community. The real problem that Snowden's revelations brought to light was not a government agency run amok: the NSA never meaningfully exceeded the writ given to it by the White House, Congress, and the courts, at least not intentionally. Rather, those revelations highlighted a basic conflict between two things that U.S. citizens and their government demand from their intelligence agencies: a high, if not perfect, level of security, on the one hand, and strict privacy protections, accountability, and transparency, on the other. Those imperatives were never easy to reconcile and are even harder to resolve today.").

4. Marbury v. Madison, 5 U.S. (1 Cranch) 137, 155 (1803).

5. An appellate court can reject lower court findings of fact only if it determines the lower court findings were "clearly erroneous"—a very difficult standard to meet. *See* Fed. R. Civ. P. 52(a)(6) ("Findings of fact, whether based on oral or other evidence, must not be set aside unless clearly erroneous, and the reviewing court must give due regard to the trial court's opportunity to judge the witnesses' credibility."); Anderson v. City of Bessemer City, 470 U.S. 564, 573–74 (1985) ("This standard plainly does not entitle a reviewing court to reverse the finding of the trier of fact simply because it is convinced that it would have decided the case differently. . . . If the district court's account of the evidence is plausible in light of the record viewed in its entirety, the court of appeals may not reverse it even though convinced that had it been sitting as the trier of fact, it would have weighed the evidence differently. Where there are two

permissible views of the evidence, the factfinder's choice between them cannot be clearly erroneous.").
6. Lochner v. New York, 198 U.S. 45 (1905), discussed in chap. 4, above. Compare *id.* at 64 (maj. op.) ("It is manifest to us that . . . [the statute] has no such direct relation to, and no such substantial effect upon, the health of the employee, as to justify us in regarding the section as really a health law. It seems to us that the real object and purpose were simply to regulate the hours of labor between the master and his employees . . . in a private business.") with *id.* at 69 (Harlan, J., dissenting) ("It is plain that this statute was enacted in order to protect the physical well-being of those who work in bakery and confectionery establishments.").
7. *Id.* at 61–64 (maj. op.).
8. *Id.* at 71–72 (Harlan, J., dissenting).
9. On the centrality of decision to law, see Paul W. Kahn, Political Theology, chap. 2 (2011).
10. For a discussion of *Marbury*, see chap. 3, above.
11. 343 U.S. 579 (1952).
12. *Id.* at 582–84 (summarizing the facts of the case).
13. *Id.* at 635–38 (Jackson, J., concurring).
14. *Id.* at 637.
15. *See* Dames & Moore v. Regan, 453 U.S. 654, 686 (1981) ("Long-continued practice, known to and acquiesced in by Congress, would raise a presumption that the [action] had been [taken] in pursuance of its consent." (alteration in original) (quoting United States v. Midwest Oil Co., 236 U.S. 459, 474 (1915)) (internal quotation marks omitted)).
16. 343 U.S. at 645 (Jackson, J., concurring) ("I should indulge the widest latitude of interpretation to sustain his exclusive function to command the instruments of national force, at least when turned against the outside world for the security of our society. But, when it is turned inward not because of rebellion, but because of a lawful economic struggle between industry and labor, it should have no such indulgence.").
17. See *id.* at 662–63 (Clark, J., concurring in the judgment) ("Congress had prescribed methods to be followed by the President in meeting the emergency at hand. Three statutory procedures were available: those provided in the Defense Production Act of 1950, the Labor Management Relations Act, and the Selective Service Act of 1948." (citations omitted)); *id.* at 665–66 ("[N]either the Defense Production Act nor Taft-Hartley authorized the seizure challenged here, and the Government

made no effort to comply with the procedures established by the Selective Service Act of 1948.").
18. 343 U.S. at 639.
19. *Id.* at 593 (Frankfurter J., concurring).
20. *Id.* at 602–3.
21. Justice Douglas did see the case as one about the power to invoke eminent domain. See *id.* at 630–34 (Douglas J., concurring).
22. *Id.* at 667 (Vinson, J., dissenting).
23. *Id.* at 668.
24. *Id.* at 668–72.
25. Most likely, the majority did not believe this because they knew that President Truman had only to give in on allowing a price increase for steel to get the employers to agree to the union demands.
26. On conflict of paradigms—war or criminal law?—see Paul W. Kahn, *Imagining Warfare*, 24 Eur. J. Int. Law 199 (2013).
27. Consider, for example, the series of cases addressing the rights of detainees, several of which begin by invoking the events of September 11, 2001. See Hamdan v. Rumsfeld, 548 U.S. 557, 567–68 (2006) ("On September 11, 2001, agents of the al Qaeda terrorist organization hijacked commercial airplanes and attacked the World Trade Center in New York City and the national headquarters of the Department of Defense in Arlington, Virginia. Americans will never forget the devastation wrought by these acts. Nearly 3,000 civilians were killed."); Hamdi v. Rumsfeld, 542 U.S. 507, 510 (2004); Rasul v. Bush, 542 U.S. 466, 470 (2004).
28. 132 S. Ct. 2566 (2012).
29. *See, e.g.*, Eduardo Porter, *Acceleration Is Forecast for Spending on Health*, N.Y. Times, Apr. 22, 2014, http://www.nytimes.com/2014/04/23/business/economy/forecasting-the-scale-of-health-spendings-climb.html ("[H]ealth care ... consumes nearly 18 percent of the nation's gross domestic product.").
30. 317 U.S. 111 (1947). Discussed in chap. 4, above.
31. *See, e.g.*, Andrew C. McCarthy, *Obamacare's Unconstitutional Origins*, Nat'l Rev. Online, Oct. 5, 2013, http://www.nationalreview.com/article/360460/obamacares-unconstitutional-origins-andrew-c-mccarthy ("To sustain this monstrosity, Chief Justice John Roberts had to shed his robes and put on his legislator cap. He rewrote Obamacare as a tax—the thing the president most indignantly promised Americans that Obamacare was not.").

32. 410 U.S. 113 (1973).
33. *Id.* at 130.
34. *See* What Roe v. Wade Should Have Said: The Nation's Top Legal Experts Rewrite America's Most Controversial Decision (Jack M. Balkin ed., 2005).
35. Jack M. Balkin, Reva B. Siegel, and Robin West made this argument. See *id.* at 31 (Balkin), *id.* at 63 (Siegel), *id.* at 121 (West). *See also, e.g.*, Ruth Bader Ginsburg, *Speaking in a Judicial Voice*, 67 N.Y.U. L. Rev. 1185, 1199–200 (1992); Cass R. Sunstein, *Neutrality in Constitutional Law (With Special Reference to Pornography, Abortion, and Surrogacy)*, 92 Colum. L. Rev. 1, 31–44 (1992); Catharine A. MacKinnon, *Reflections on Sex Equality Under Law*, 100 Yale L.J. 1281, 1319–23 (1991).
36. The most explosive analogy is to the criminalization of infanticide. There is one faction in the debate that thinks the right frame is not community policy versus the rights of the woman, but rather the rights of the unborn child versus the interests of the mother.
37. 550 U.S. 124 (2007).
38. *Id.* at 159–60 ("While we find no reliable data to measure the phenomenon, it seems unexceptionable to conclude some women come to regret their choice to abort the infant life they once created and sustained. . . . The State has an interest in ensuring so grave a choice is well informed. It is self-evident that a mother who comes to regret her choice to abort must struggle with grief more anguished and sorrow more profound when she learns, only after the event, what she once did not know: that she allowed a doctor to pierce the skull and vacuum the fast-developing brain of her unborn child, a child assuming the human form.").
39. *Id.* at 186–87 (Ginsburg, J., dissenting) ("The Court's hostility to the right *Roe* and *Casey* secured is not concealed. Throughout, the opinion refers to obstetrician-gynecologists and surgeons who perform abortions not by the titles of their medical specialties, but by the pejorative label 'abortion doctor.' A fetus is described as an 'unborn child,' and as a 'baby;' second-trimester, previability abortions are referred to as 'late-term'; and the reasoned medical judgments of highly trained doctors are dismissed as 'preferences' motivated by 'mere convenience.'" (citations omitted)).
40. Stenberg v. Carhart, 530 U.S. 914, 946–47 (2000) (Stevens, J., concurring).
41. 317 U.S. 111 (1942).
42. 317 U.S. at 125–26.

43. *See* Hammer v. Dagenhart, 247 U.S. 251, 276 (1918).
44. Lawrence v. Texas, 539 U.S. 558 (2003); Bowers v. Hardwick, 478 U.S. 186 (1986).
45. 539 U.S. at 576–77.
46. *Id.* at 577.
47. The opportunistic character of legal argument is clear from the contrast of *Lawrence* with *Carhart*. At no point does *Carhart* look abroad to see what abortion procedures are used by medical professionals.
48. 539 U.S. at 598 (Scalia, J., dissenting).
49. The discourse of open and shut eyes has a long history in judicial opinions, starting with *Marbury*. See *Marbury*, 5 U.S. (1 Cranch) 137, 178 (1803) ("Those then who controvert the principle that the constitution is to be considered, in court, as a paramount law, are reduced to the necessity of maintaining that courts must close their eyes on the constitution, and see only the law."), 179 ("[O]ught the judges to close their eyes on the constitution, and only see the law"); *see also* Lochner v. New York, 198 U.S. 45, 64 (1905) ("It is impossible for us to shut our eyes to the fact that many of the laws of this character, while passed under what is claimed to be the police power for the purpose of protecting the public health or welfare, are, in reality, passed from other motives."); NLRB v. Jones & Laughlin Steel Corp., 301 U.S. 1 (1937) ("We are asked to shut our eyes to the plainest facts of our national life and to deal with the question of direct and indirect effects in an intellectual vacuum.").
50. 539 U.S. at 578.
51. *Id.* at 557–58 (McReynolds, J., dissenting).
52. 291 U.S. at 424.
53. That the dissent adopts this narrative of the familial is itself a shift from the dominant narrative at the turn of the century, when regulation was rejected against a horizon in which the family breadwinner was exercising his liberty to contract for his labor. In *Lochner*, for example, the market is the site of free negotiation between *sui juris*, autonomous adults. That is how we will think of markets if our horizon is slavery, which maintained a distinction between those who could freely contract for their labor and those who could not. By the time of *Nebbia*, this horizon of free labor has been displaced by that of family responsibility.
54. On subsequent cycles of national versus local, see, e.g., *National League of Cities v. Usery*, 426 U.S. 833, 851 (1976) ("If Congress may withdraw from the States the authority to make those fundamental employment decisions upon which their systems for performance of these functions

must rest, we think there would be little left of the States' separate and independent existence." (internal quotation marks omitted) (citation omitted)); *Garcia v. San Antonio Metropolitan Transit Authority*, 469 U.S. 528, 550–51 (1985) ("[W]e have no license to employ freestanding conceptions of state sovereignty when measuring congressional authority under the Commerce Clause."); *New York v. United States*, 505 U.S. 144, 188 (1992) ("States are not mere political subdivisions of the United States. State governments are neither regional offices nor administrative agencies of the Federal Government. . . . The Constitution instead leaves to the several States a residuary and inviolable sovereignty reserved explicitly to the States by the Tenth Amendment." (internal quotation marks omitted) (citation omitted)); *Gonzales v. Raich*, 545 U.S. 1, 17 ("Our case law firmly establishes Congress' power to regulate purely local activities that are part of an economic class of activities that have a substantial effect on interstate commerce. . . . We have never required Congress to legislate with scientific exactitude. When Congress decides that the total incidence of a practice poses a threat to a national market, it may regulate the entire class." (internal quotation marks omitted) (citations omitted)); *Shelby County v. Holder*, 133 S. Ct. 2612, 2623 (2013) ("Not only do States retain sovereignty under the Constitution, there is also a fundamental principle of equal sovereignty among the States." (internal quotation marks omitted) (citation omitted)).

55. *See, e.g.*, United States v. Lopez, 514 U.S. 549 (1995) (holding that the Gun-Free School Zones Act exceeded Congress's authority under the Commerce Clause).

56. *See, e.g.*, Moore v. Frederick, 551 U.S. 393 (2007) (holding that a high school principal did not violate a student's free speech right when she confiscated the student's fourteen-foot banner reading "BONG HITS 4 JESUS" [*sic*], and suspended the student).

57. 478 U.S. at 190–91.

58. Griswold v. Connecticut, 381 U.S. 479 (1965); Eisenstadt v. Baird, 405 U.S. 438 (1972).

59. *See, e.g.*, In re Marriage Cases, 183 P.3d 384, 430–33 (Cal. 2008) (rejecting the argument that because only a heterosexual couple can biologically produce children with one another, only heterosexual couples have the constitutional right to marry, in part on the grounds that the Supreme Court has repeatedly upheld a married couple's right to prevent procreation with contraceptives).

60. Oliver Wendell Holmes, The Common Law 1 (1881).

61. 556 U.S. 868 (2007).
62. *Id.* at 878.
63. *Id.* at 881 (quoting Mayberry v. Pennsylvania, 400 U.S. 455, 465–66 (1971)).
64. *See* Stanley Fish, *Fish v. Fiss*, 36 Stanford L. Rev. 1325 (1984) ("[R]ules *are* texts. They are in need of interpretation and cannot themselves serve as constraints on interpretation.").
65. Swann v. Charlotte-Mecklenburg Bd. of Ed., 402 U.S. 1, 16 (1971) (pursuing "a prescribed ratio of Negro to white students . . . as an educational policy is within the broad discretionary powers of school authorities").
66. For an early iteration of the debate, compare Owen Fiss, *Groups and the Equal Protection Clause*, 5 Phil. & Pub. Affairs 107 (1976) with Paul Brest, *The Supreme Court 1975 Term—Foreword: In Defense of the Antidiscrimination Principle*, 90 Harv. L. Rev. 1 (1976).
67. Legislatures can pass private bills, however, which "relat[e] to a matter of personal or local interest only." *Black's Law Dictionary* 196 (10th ed. 2014). *See, e.g.*, Faith Karimi, *Obama Signs Bill to Grant Nigerian Student U.S. Permanent Residency*, CNN (Dec. 29, 2012, 7:38 a.m.), http://www.cnn.com/2012/12/29/world/africa/us-nigerian-obama-law ("A Nigerian immigrant's dream came true when President Barack Obama signed into law a rare private bill granting him permanent residency in the United States. . . . Private bills—which only apply to one person and mostly focus on immigration—are rarely approved. His is the only one to pass in Congress in two years.").
68. *See* G.E.M. Anscombe, Intention (2d ed. 1963); Paul W. Kahn, Finding Ourselves at the Movies: Philosophy for a New Generation 31–38, 45 (2013) (on causes versus reasons).
69. H.L.A. Hart, *Positivism as the Separation of Law and Morals*, 71 Harv. L. Rev. 593 (1958).
70. On mistakes in statutory drafting and the absurdity doctrine, see John F. Manning, *The Absurdity Doctrine*, 116 Harv. L. Rev. 2387 (2003). Manning explains the traditional procedure: "If a given statutory application sharply contradicts commonly held social values, then the Supreme Court presumes that this absurd result reflects imprecise drafting that Congress could and would have corrected had the issue come up during the enactment process. Accordingly, standard interpretive doctrine (perhaps tautologically) defines an 'absurd result' as an outcome so contrary to perceived social values that Congress could not have 'intended'

it. So understood, the absurdity doctrine is merely a version of strong intentionalism, which permits a court to adjust a clear statute in the rare case in which the court finds that the statutory text diverges from the legislature's true intent, as derived from sources such as the legislative history or the purpose of the statute as a whole." *Id.* at 2389–90.
71. *See* McCleskey v. Kemp, 481 U.S. 279 (1987); *see also* Bruce Ackerman, Reconstructing American Law (1984).
72. Planned Parenthood v. Casey, 505 U.S. 833, 868 (1992).
73. Consider torture. Today, a court cannot proclaim torture to be permissible government policy and cite a precedent on national security for support. *See* Paul W. Kahn, Sacred Violence: Torture, Terror and Sovereignty 83–85 (2008) (discussing proposed torture warrants).
74. As this book went to press, the Court announced its decision upholding a constitutional right to same-sex marriage. *Obergefell v. Hodges*, 135 S.Ct. 2584 (2015).

Conclusion

1. *See* Clifford Geertz, The Interpretation of Cultures, chap. 1 (1973).
2. *See* Ronald Dworkin, Law's Empire (1986) (on law as interpretive practice).
3. John Donahue III & Steven D. Levitt, *The Impact of Legalized Abortion on Crimes*, 116 Q. J. of Econ. 379 (2001).
4. The scientist may not have a causal explanation; he may only observe a correlation. But absent the assumption of a causal connection, we would have no reason to think the correlation has any continuing significance.
5. Since Justice Holmes spoke of the future lawyer as "the man of statistics and the master of economics," the emphasis of modernization has been on importing social science into legal education. *See* O.W. Holmes, *The Path of the Law*, 10 Harv. L. Rev. 457, 469 (1897); *see also* Bruce Ackerman, Reconstructing American Law (1984).
6. The idea of "living with the divide" goes back to Kant's dual approach to the scientific knowledge of causes and the morality of free action.
7. For a model of such an approach, see William Sewell, Logics of History: Social Theory and Social Transformation (2005).

INDEX

abolitionism, 90
abortion, 90, 112, 139, 160; crime rates and, 175; "partial birth," 152–54; *Roe v. Wade* and, 92, 99, 101, 121, 122, 149–51, 153, 167
accommodation, 99
accountability, 7, 8, 50, 54, 56, 59
Adams, John, 64, 65–66, 140
administrative law, 33, 56, 88
affirmative action, 19, 119–21, 165
Affordable Care Act (2010), 8, 63, 147
agency capture, 157, 174
Alden v. Maine (1999), 207n22
Alien and Sedition Acts (1798), 66
Alito, Samuel, 35
antimiscegenation laws, 122
antitrust law, 100, 104, 126
appointments, judicial, 10, 13, 62–64, 65
arbitrariness, 59, 80
arbitration, 5, 6, 16, 104
Arendt, Hannah, 107, 117
association, freedom of, 109
authorization, 60
authorship: collective, 53, 78; legitimacy and, 48–51, 54, 59, 60; in political practice, 51–62; self-, 48, 58–61, 73, 75, 77, 80, 83, 88, 90, 91

Babbitt v. Sweet Home (1995), 81–83

bargaining, 104
Bible, 52, 69, 98, 103
Bickel, Alexander, 39
Bituminous Coal Act (1935), 127
Black, Hugo, 110, 121, 126, 214–15n69, 219n123
black letter law, 48
Bork, Robert, 216n83
Bowers v. Hardwick (1986), 159–60, 167; lessons of, 121–25; overruling of, 99, 118, 120, 132, 155, 156
Bramble Bush (Llewellyn), xiii
Brennan, William, 220–21n143
Breyer, Stephen, 24–25, 30–33, 217–18n103
briefs, 9
Brown v. Board of Education (1954), 8, 112–17, 119
Brown v. Entertainment Merchants Association (2011), 23–36, 38
burdens of proof, 136
bureaucracy, 84
Burr, Aaron, 64
Bush, George W., 7, 44, 72
Bush v. Gore (2000), 39–46, 47, 48, 63
bussing, 165

Calabresi, Guido, 196n34
California, 23–36, 38, 111
campaign finance, 39

INDEX

canons of construction, xii–xiii, 80–81
Caperton v. A. T. Massey Coal (2009), 161–64, 167, 179
capital punishment, 99, 168
Cardozo, Benjamin, xiii, 211–12n48
Carter v. Carter Coal Co. (1936), 127–28
case method, 135
causation, 128, 175–76, 177
certiorari jurisdiction, 40
charisma, 84–87
"checkerboard statute," 59
child labor, 122, 126
children, 25, 27, 28, 29, 33–34, 121–22
Christianity, 52, 84, 102–3
Circuit Courts Act (1801), 66
Citizens United v. Federal Election Commission (2010), 92
civil cases, 136
civil-law systems, 93
Civil Rights Act (1964), 100
civil servants, 62
Civil War, 155
Clark, Tom, 223–24n17
clerks, judicial, 11, 50–51
climate change, 31, 170
coal mining, 127
coherence, 78, 80–81, 105–6, 107
collective authorship, 53, 78
Commerce Clause, 95; Affordable Care Act and, 147–48, 154; dormant, 182n7, 207n20; federalism and, 106; during New Deal, 109, 126–27, 129–31, 155
committee reports, 4, 59
common law, 65, 78, 80, 81

comparative constitutionalism, 55
compelling state interest, 24, 29, 122
Concept of Law (Hart), xiii
concurrences, 9, 11–12, 23
confirmation, of judicial appointees, 64, 85
Constitution: equal protection stipulated in, 19, 41, 55, 97, 116, 119, 151, 165; legislation vs., 57, 76–77; *Marbury* as image of, 71; state legislatures and, 41
Constitutional amendments, 30; First, 24, 29, 61, 88–89, 109, 159; Second, 97, 101; Third, 109; Fourth, 90, 100–101, 104, 109; Fifth, 109; Ninth, 109; Tenth, 106, 130, 132; Eleventh, 98, 106; Twelfth, 198n51; Fourteenth, 97, 101, 114, 116, 124; Fifteenth, 96, 106
contraceptives, 90, 108–10, 122, 160
contract, xii, 1, 20; freedom of, 109, 110, 124, 156, 168; law vs., 166
corruption, 47, 56, 60
counsel, right to, 99
counter-majoritarianism, 6
court packing, 109
criminal law, 99, 136, 147, 168

Dahl, Robert A., 196–97n42
death penalty, 99, 168
Declaration of Independence, 52–55
delegation, of legislative authority, 56
demonstrable proof, 93
Depression, 110, 155, 170

INDEX

desegregation, 165
Dewey, John, 27
dictum, xiv
discrimination, 119–21
discursive democracy, 5
dispute resolution, 47, 88, 104
dissents, 9, 11–12, 17, 23, 83, 118; as democratic method, 93; persistent, 94, 100, 126
District of Columbia v. Heller (2008), 96–97, 101–2
divorce, 111
doctor-patient relationship, 110
doctrine, 34–37, 41, 58, 93–95, 104–34
dormant Commerce Clause, 182n7, 207n20
Douglas, William O., 182n9
Douglass, Frederick, 205–6n8
drafting, 50–57, 228–29n70
Dred Scott v. Sandford (1857), 39, 45, 102
drug laws, 151
due process, 80, 81, 112, 161; substantive, 101, 109, 111, 121, 151
Dworkin, Ronald, xiii, 59, 106, 125

economics, xiv, 128, 154, 156–58, 173–79
efficiency, 174
Eisenstadt v. Baird (1972), 111, 122, 159
elections, 7, 42–43, 61; as element of justice, 60; judicial, 161, 179; legitimacy grounded in, 62; women's participation in, 39
Electoral College, 42, 43
Eleventh Amendment, 98, 106

employment contracts, 124–25, 127–28
Endangered Species Act (1973), 81–82
endorsement, 99
equality, 81
equal protection, 19, 41, 55; affirmative action and, 119, 165; levels of scrutiny and, 97; *Roe v. Wade* and, 151; segregation incompatible with, 116
erudition, 96, 115, 117, 118, 121, 123, 125, 151; in Commerce Clause jurisprudence, 126–34; of horizontal arguments, 97; religious fundamentalism vs., 102–3; as technique of persuasion, 98
Eskridge, William, Jr., 209–10nn31,32
evidence, 135–36; statistical, 168, 174, 176, 177, 179; suppression of, 99
evolution, 31
exceptions, 96, 97, 99–100, 105, 124–25
expertise, 31–32, 37–38, 88, 168

fact-finding, 14–15
fact-law, 136, 138, 169
Fair Labor Standards Act (1938), 129, 220–21n143
Fallon, Richard, 207n20
federalism, 42, 43–44, 81, 106
Federalist Party, 64–66, 71
Ferejohn, John, 209–10nn31,32
Ferguson, Robert, 213n59
Fifteenth Amendment, 96, 106
Fifth Amendment, 109

233

INDEX

finality, 6
First Amendment, 24, 29, 61, 88–89, 109, 159
floor statements, 4, 59
Florida, 39, 42–44, 48
footnotes, 11
foreign law, 48, 49, 55, 86, 104, 155–56
Fourteenth Amendment, 97, 101, 114, 116, 124
Fourth Amendment, 90, 100–101, 104, 109
Frank, Jerome, 200*n*70
Frankfurter, Felix, 141, 144, 145–46, 148
freedom of association, 109
freedom of contract, 109, 110, 124, 156, 168
freedom of speech, 36, 110, 116, 126, 139; antigay protests and, 88–89; facts vs. norms and, 159; naive views of, 168; penumbra of, 109; technological innovation and, 26; video game regulation vs., 24, 29, 32
Friedman, Barry, 196–97*n*42, 197*n*43
Fuller, Lon, 212*n*50
fundamentalism: legal, 126–34; religious, 103
fundamental rights, 42

Garrison, William Lloyd, 205*n*7
gay rights, 166, 172; *Bowers v. Hardwick* and, 99, 118, 120, 121–25, 132, 155, 156, 159–60, 167; *Lawrence v. Texas* and, 99, 112, 118, 132, 155–56, 159, 160, 167, 170

Geertz, Clifford, 195*n*31
Ginsburg, Ruth Bader, 206–7*n*14, 225*n*39
globalization, 171
Gonzales v. Carhart (2007), 99, 152–55
Gore, Al, 45, 46
Great Britain, 104
Griggs v. Duke Power Co. (1971), 100
Griswold v. Connecticut (1965), 90, 100–101, 108–13, 117, 119, 121–22, 159
gun control, 90, 96–97, 101–2

Habermas, Jürgen, 61
Hale, Matthew, 198–99*n*57
Hamlet, 95
Hammer v. Dagenhart (1918), 126–27, 129–30
Hand, Learned, 197*n*45
Harlan, John Marshall, 215*n*76, 223*n*6
Hart, H. L. A., xiii, 167
hermeneutics, 19
Hobbes, Thomas, 60–61
Holmes, Oliver Wendell, xiii, 23, 78, 161, 219*n*119
humanism, 173–79
human rights, 153, 155, 156, 170
hypotheticals, 120–21

impeachment, 66
implied repeal, 80
intentional infliction of emotional distress, 88
interest groups, 4, 59, 73, 75–76
interstate commerce, 126–29, 131

INDEX

Introduction to Legal Reasoning (Levi), xiii
Islam, 52

Jackson, Robert, 141–44, 145–46, 148, 223n16
Jefferson, Thomas, 2, 52–53, 64–67, 70–72, 140
judicial activism, 74
judicial appointments, 10, 13, 62–64, 65
judicial clerks, 11, 50–51
judicial elections, 161, 179
judicial ethos, 23, 36
judicial independence, 85
judicial review, 64, 83
Judiciary Act (1789), 83
juries, 5, 63, 93, 137
jurisdiction, 40, 82, 83

Kelo v. City of New London (2005), 200n69

Labor Management Relations Act (1947), 144, 145
law clerks, 11, 50–51
Lawrence v. Texas (2003), 99, 112, 118, 132, 155–56, 159, 160, 167, 170
law reviews, 11
Law's Empire (Dworkin), xiii
legislation, xv; authorship of, 56–58; Constitution vs., 57, 76–77; interpretation of, 73–83, 99–100, 106; judicial opinions vs., 1, 4; prospectivity of, 166
legislative history, 5, 56–57, 80, 83
legislative intent, 80

legitimacy, 37, 42, 62, 73–74, 88; authorship and, 48–51, 54, 59, 60; justice and, 89–94
Levi, Edward, xiii
Levinson, Sanford, 193n15
libertarianism, 26, 36
liberty of contract, 109, 110, 124, 156, 168
life tenure, 85
Lincoln, Abraham, 10, 39, 85, 205–6n8
literary criticism, 51–52, 95, 98
Llewellyn, Karl, xii, xiii, 181n1, 186n1
Lochner v. New York (1905), 109, 121, 124–25, 138–39, 219n119
Loving v. Virginia (1967), 121

Madison, James, 66
Manning, John, 183n13, 228–29n70
Marbury, William, 65, 66, 67–68, 137, 140
Marbury v. Madison (1803), xiii, 73, 103, 140; authorship of, 71–72; background of, 64–65; invisible drafter in, 70; language of permanence in, 94–95; normative vs. descriptive in, 68–69; original jurisdiction and, 82, 99–100, 137; persuasiveness of, 84, 87; politics absent from, 66–67; weaknesses of, 83
marriage, 91, 108, 111–12, 121, 172
Marshall, John, 65, 67, 70–72, 87, 137, 194n24
Marshall Plan, 145
McConnell, Mitch, 187n11

235

INDEX

McCutcheon v. Federal Election Commission (2014), xv
mediation, 104
Meyers v. Nebraska (1923), 121
"midnight" appointments, 65, 67
military officers, 62
monopoly, 126
Muhammad, 52
Mutual Security Act (1951), 145

natality, 107, 108–17, 118, 133
National Federation of Independent Business v. Sebelius (2012), 63, 147–49, 154–55
National Labor Relations Board v. Jones & Laughlin Steel (1937), 127–28
National League of Cities v. Usery (1976), 220–21n43, 226–27n54
National Rifle Association, 90
national security, 15, 143, 145–48
Nature of the Judicial Process (Cardozo), xiii
Nebbia v. New York (1934), 156–58, 171
New Deal, 31, 39, 106, 109, 126, 132, 156, 170
9/11 attacks, 147
Ninth Amendment, 109
North Atlantic Treaty Organization (NATO), 145

Obama, Barack, 8, 147, 204n1
objectivity, 3, 21, 186–87n5, 188n21
O'Connor, Sandra Day, 190n43, 191n55

original jurisdiction, 82, 99–100, 137

Palsgraf v. Long Island Rail Road (1928), xiii
parental authority, 25, 27, 28–30, 33
Path of the Law (Holmes), xiii
penumbral rights, 109, 111–12
performative speech acts, 1
Pierce v. Society of the Sisters of the Holy Names of Jesus and Mary (1925), 121–22
plagiarism, 50–51
plain meaning, 80
Planned Parenthood, 108, 110
Planned Parenthood v. Casey (1992), 99
Plato, 68–69
Plessy v. Ferguson (1896), 115
Pocock, J. G. A., 198–99n57
pornography, 35
Post, Robert, 61
postmodernism, 51–52
precedent, x, xii–xiii, 18–19, 22, 37, 40, 70, 97, 98, 99; absence of, 108; grouping of, 119, 125; *stare decisis* and, 94; Weber's view of, 84
preclearance, 96
preponderance-of-the-evidence standard, 136
Presidential Succession Act (1947), 43
privacy, 90, 97, 100–101, 108–10, 118, 121
private law, 20
probable cause, 90
procedure, 135–38

236

INDEX

progress, 22, 24–26, 28, 30–31, 33, 34, 36
property, 20, 47, 144–45
proportionality, 89, 204n101
Protestant Reformation, 102–3
proximate causation, 128
public law, 20
public opinion, 63, 90
public purpose, 59, 60, 73, 75, 77, 80
public schools, 113–15, 165; local control of, 158

Qur'an, 52

ratification, 55
rational-basis review, 99
rationality, 78, 80, 170
Raz, Joseph, 189n32
reasonable doubt, 136
recounts, 44–45
recusal, 161–64
referendum, 58
Reformation, 102–3
Rehnquist, William, 220–21n143
religious texts, 52, 69, 98, 103
rent seeking, 174
representation, 53, 56–58, 61, 74
Republican Party (Jeffersonian), 64–66, 71
restatements, 105
restraint of trade, 100
Rieff, Philip, 202–3n100
right to counsel, 99
Roberts, John G., 35, 88–89, 147–49, 217–18n103
Roberts, Owen, 20–21
Roe v. Wade (1973), 92, 99, 101, 121, 122, 149–51, 153, 167

Romer v. Evans (1996), 99
Roosevelt, Franklin D., 39, 109, 170
Rousseau, Jean-Jacques, 195n30

Scalia, Antonin, 188n21, 200n67, 206n13
schools, 113–15, 122, 158, 165
scrutiny, levels of, 97, 99
search warrants, 90
Second Amendment, 97, 101
segregation, 113–16, 165
self-authorship, 48, 58–61, 73, 75, 77, 80, 83, 88, 90, 91
separate-but-equal doctrine, 113, 114–16
separation of powers, 81, 140–42
seriatim practice, 2
Shelby County v. Holder (2013), 96
Sherman Antitrust Act (1890), 100
situation sense, 16
Skinner v. Oklahoma (1942), 121
slavery, 53, 90, 102, 110
snail darter, 82, 96, 99
social contract, 60–61
Socratic method, xiv
sodomy, 112, 118, 121, 122
Sotomayor, Sonia, 187–88n11
Souter, David, 207n22, 221n144
speech, freedom of, 36, 110, 116, 126, 139; antigay protests and, 88–89; facts vs. norms and, 159; naive views of, 168; penumbra of, 109; technological innovation and, 26; video game regulation vs., 24, 29, 32
speech acts, 1, 48
standards of proof, 136
stare decisis, 94

237

INDEX

state legislatures, 41
statistics, 168, 174, 176, 177, 179
statutes, xv; authorship of, 56–58; Constitution vs., 57, 76–77; interpretation of, 73–83, 99–100, 106; judicial opinions vs., 1, 4; prospectivity of, 166
statutes of limitation, 136
Stenberg v. Carhart (2000), 154
Stevens, John Paul, 206–7n14, 210n26, 217–18n103
Stewart, Potter, 100–101, 110, 214n67, 215–16n78
strict scrutiny, 99
substantial effect, 99
substantive due process, 101, 109, 111, 121, 151
"super statutes," 100
suppression of evidence, 99
Supreme Court: authorship on, 11; *Bush v. Gore* bungled by, 39–46, 47, 48, 72; durability of, 38; as explicator, 5; inscrutable opinions of, 7–8, 40; legitimacy of, 38–39, 169; liberals vs. conservatives on, 3; original jurisdiction of, 82, 99–100, 137; selectiveness of, 6; seriatim practice in, 2
surplusage, 82, 100
syllogism, xi, 14, 18

taxes, 49, 59, 147, 148
Tenth Amendment, 106, 130, 132
textualism, 58–59, 70, 79
Third Amendment, 109
Thomas, Clarence, 2–3, 28–30, 33, 35
Title VII, 100

torts, 20, 128
treaties, 1
Truman, Harry, 140–41, 146–47
trusts, 126
TVA v. Hill (1978), 82, 96
Twelfth Amendment, 198n51

unconscionability, 20
unconstitutional vagueness, 35
undue burden, 99
Unger, Roberto, xiii, 194n26
United Nations, 145
United States v. Darby (1941), 127, 129–30, 132
United States v. Miller (1939), 101

vagueness, 35
video games, 24, 27, 28, 29, 31, 35–36
Vinson, Fred, 141, 145
voting, 7, 42–43, 61; as element of justice, 60; for judges, 161, 179; legitimacy grounded in, 62; by women, 39
Voting Rights Act (1965), 96

warrantless searches, 90
Weber, Max, 84
What Should Legal Analysis Become? (Unger), xiii
White, James Boyd, 181n1, 181n5
Wickard v. Filburn (1942), 131, 148, 154–55
woman suffrage, 30
writing ability, 11–13

Youngstown Sheet & Tube Co. v. Sawyer (1952), 140–47, 149